COBALT BLUE

To the Arizona Redhead for making it happen.
To the other redhead for getting me through it.

Fiction by
Budd Davisson

Cobalt Blue
The Stonewall File
(available fall, 2000)

Non-fiction
The World of Sport Aviation
Pitts Specials

Cobalt Blue
by
Budd Davisson

All rights reserved
Copyright © 2000 by Budd Davisson
This book may not be reproduced in whole or in part
by mimeograph or by any other means, without permission.
For information address the publisher:
Sonora Publishing
3536 E. Shangri-La Rd.
Phoenix, AZ 85028

Visit our website: www.airbum.com

ISBN 0-9702485-0-4
Manufactured in the United States of America

**Autographed first editions are available through
www.airbum.com**

Cover design, art and type composition by
Davisson, LTD, Phoenix, AZ

SONORA
Publishing
phoenix, arizona

3536 E. Shangri-La Rd.
Phoenix, AZ 85028
602.971.3991 • Fax 602.971.3896
e-mail: sonorapublishing@home.com

COBALT BLUE
Budd Davisson

SONORA
Publishing
phoenix, arizona

"Go West young man...is still pretty good advice."

PROLOGUE

Lights burned late on the second floor of the base administration building and a slow, cool rain pelted the multi-paned windows. A very nervous Lt. Colonel Ralph Johnson, U.S. Army Air Force, paced the length of his office. Periodically, he'd stop and scowl out at the dark. A short, balding, lump of a man, he felt twenty years older than he actually was. He bitched as he paced.

"Dammit! I just wish the whole goddamn thing would go away." He stopped and spun around. A young lieutenant stood at fear-stricken attention on the other side of his paper-strewn desk.

"Are you sure? I mean damn sure, the press doesn't know where those crates are?" Johnson barked.

"N-No, sir. I mean, yessir," the lieutenant stammered. "The plane is parked in with other ships in the depot area. We pulled the guard detail so there is nothing to draw attention to it."

The young lieutenant nervously licked his lips and said, "As soon as the weather lifts, the plane will leave. At the press conference tomorrow morning we'll announce everything is on the way to Eighth Air Force H.Q. in Fort Worth."

The news was welcome but gave Colonel Johnson little immediate relief.

The lieutenant sprinted out of the office and the colonel stared out the rain-streaked window. His stomach twitched and the sour taste of bile backed up into his throat.

He couldn't see a lone figure struggling across the dark ramp on the other side of the distant hangars.

Major John Williams, United States Army Air Force, was surprised at how heavy the wooden case was for its size. It wasn't large. Only slightly bigger than a fat suitcase. The blonde, hardwood exterior, birch he guessed, was heavily lacquered, like a piece of furniture. The brass hinges and latch gave off stray reflections as he struggled across the rain-swept ramp with it on his shoulder. The circular pattern of yellow triangles on its cover glowed each time lights hit it.

The box seemed to get heavier with every step and the line of airplanes didn't appear to be getting any closer. Goddamn government vehicles! If the stolen staff car hadn't decided to die half way across New Mexico, he would have made it to the Mexican border easy. That's where the money waited. He looked forward to becoming Mexico's newest and richest citizen.

Thank God the highway went right past an Air Force Base and the gate guard hadn't checked the car's trunk. Williams doubted if Los Alamos would discover their nuclear toy was missing until the next morning. When they did, they weren't going to be very happy. It wasn't a bomb, but it was close enough.

Williams glanced around as he shuffled across the glistening asphalt. Nothing had changed since he'd last been on base. When had that been? Three years? The fall of 1944 was when he had last seen this concrete spider web in the desert. At the time he was transitioning into B-29's.

The first two airplanes he came to, C-45's, small twin engine transports, had sealed, canvas cocoons over the engines and nose. They reminded him of sleeping falcons. The third one looked ready for flight. Williams ducked under the left wing and manhandled the box through the hatch. A quick preflight inspection and he scrambled up the boarding ladder and headed for the cockpit.

The field's rotating beacon periodically flashed through the small cabin's side windows. It had been stripped of all but the two front seats. The vacant space where the other seats had been was taken up by two long, newly made, wooden packing crates. The sweet smell of fresh lumber filled the tight confines. It looked as if the coffin-like crates had just been loaded for transport.

Williams didn't give a thought to the crates' contents. The crates were simply going to be delivered to an unscheduled destination. He doubted if their loss would affect national security. He smirked. His box, however, would definitely have an effect on national security. He smiled again. He didn't care about that either.

Williams dropped into the pilot's seat and his hands danced over the controls, familiar even in the dark. He had taken much of his multi-engine training in the C-45. It fit like a well worn pair of boots.

The maps in his lap were hard to read in the dull, red cockpit lights. He estimated one hour due south at ten thousand feet to clear the mountains, drop down to five thousand feet for another hour and he'd be rich. And independent for the rest of his life. Fuck the military. Fuck the government. Fuck the U.S. of A. Even as the thoughts flickered through his mind, the second engine coughed into life and he lined up on the huge, deserted ramp. He wouldn't bother with the runway.

The two 450 horsepower Pratt and Whitney engines lifted the airplane off the ground in little more than ten seconds. Moist, gray rooster tails hung in the dark air behind. Williams and his cargo were in the clouds before the lights at the far end of the empty ramp flashed under him. He was on his way to a new life.

As he reset the directional gyro to match the compass, he thought it strange he had to turn so much further right than he thought he would. Compasses, however, almost never lie. The operative word was "...almost." This one was staring through its single glass eye at John Williams and telling him a fatal untruth.

Williams couldn't feel the magnetic forces flowing out of the cargo behind him. He couldn't feel them, but the compass did. Those forces had made an absolute liar out of it. He was headed northwest, not south.

He would never know the mistake had been made.

"What the goddamn hell do you mean the plane is gone?"

Vivid red veins converted Lt. Colonel Ralph Johnson's sagging, pudgy face into a road map of his emotions. The lieutenant went two shades paler as he delivered the news.

Johnson barged through the open door of his quarters into the hallway still stuffing shirttails into his pants. The slightly-built lieutenant scampered after him.

"Sir, I don't know what happened to the aircraft. Security is looking into that. But what...," the lieutenant stopped speaking to catch his breath as he trotted behind the Colonel. "Sir, what do I tell the press? The press conference is in less than an hour."

The Colonel unexpectedly stopped, his hand on the doorknob. The lieutenant nearly rear-ended him in his haste.

"Lieutenant, I don't care what you tell them, but don't tell them we lost the damned airplane and everything in it. Tell them...tell them the whole fucking thing was a mistake. Shit, I don't know! You're the P.I.O. here. Use your goddamn imagination! You can tell them it was a goddamn balloon, for all I care."

Major Williams tugged at his necktie. Sweat glistened on his forehead even though a frigid blast thundered through the open side window. Eyes flickered nervously from the instrument panel to the black void outside. Earlier he had been sleepy. No longer. The uncertainty of not knowing where he was had taken care of that.

He scanned the darkness in all directions. There was nothing! Absolutely nothing! Even his headset was silent. The Satillo low freq beacon should have been showering his ears with dots and dashes. The lights of Chihuahua should be clearly visible. But, there was nothing. His altimeter was steady at five thousand feet.

Then he saw it. A light broke the void ahead. It was small, but at least it was something. To a tired Air Force Major desperate to get oriented, it looked to be a light many miles away. He couldn't guess the distance. Or the size.

Charley Yee huddled closer to his campfire. Although only fourteen years old, he stood on the verge of Apache manhood and his eyes danced wildly from image to image. None of the images were real. Peyote made them seem real, however. He rocked gently back and forth as wonderful sights raced through his mind. Peyote was not the Apache way. This he knew. But perhaps it would show him the things he needed to know. A low moanful chant worked its way from deep inside his heart and floated out over the edge of the cliff a few feet away.

He shivered. Even the powerful spell of ground peyote buttons couldn't convince his teen-aged body it was warm. At that altitude, well over a mile high, the darkness pressing around him was only slightly above freezing.

His fire was perched on the very tip of a small, rocky finger projecting off Arizona's steep Mogollon Rim which stretched for hundreds of miles in either direction.

Charley Yee was totally unaware of his spectacular surroundings. After four days of fasting, chanting and peyote, he was aware only of the spiritual vacuum within his soul. He was confused by the new ways surrounding his people. He couldn't follow the traditional ways of the warrior. The path was no longer clear. He desperately needed a vision to guide him to his future.

For a fraction of a second, a surprised Major John Williams clearly saw Charley Yee outlined in front of his campfire. The light which he had judged to be many miles distant suddenly grew and flashed beneath him. In that last instant, he realized the light was a small fire and he was only a few yards above it.

His muscles were still receiving commands to pull when the C-45's wing tips touched both walls of the narrow, tapering canyon directly behind Charley Yee. The canyon instantly ripped away both outer wing panels. The trajectory of the carcass carrying Williams and his precious cargo wasn't altered a degree.

In the darkness, John Williams never saw the mouth of the shallow cave coming. He wasn't aware of parts being shorn from both sides of the fuselage by the rocks. The process converted the airplane into a projectile and robbed it of its energy, gradually slowing it down.

Major Williams would have survived, if it hadn't been for a single, ancient stalactite. It flashed out of the darkness, as the remains of the fuselage slowly ground to a halt on the cavern floor. William's mind was still trying to cope with the chaos around him, when the stone structure slammed through the windshield. It compressed his brain into a tiny space against the rear cockpit bulkhead.

He didn't hear the wing tanks explode at the mouth of the cavern behind him. Nor did he hear the thunder of the avalanche the explosions touched off. The silence which descended upon his lifeless body was as complete as the blackness of the sealed cavern which had become his tomb.

Charley Yee was speechless. His vision had been so strong! So dramatic! It had roared at him out of the darkness. Its breath had blown on him so hard it had threatened to extinguish his camp fire. Its voice had been so strong as to force his hands to his ears. And it had drawn his eyes to follow it where it had hidden itself in the mountain.

Those were his gods. Of that Charley Yee would always be certain. His life had just been revealed and forever changed.

His mind still numb and singing the song of the peyote, he turned and stumbled after his gods. He would have to worship at the shrine. And this would be his secret holy place forever.

One

Marilyn Tipton had always been a stunner. Her husband smiled as he tucked the newspaper under his arm and leaned against the door jam. Sam Tipton enjoyed watching his wife zoom around the brightly lit, colonial-style kitchen. Even with rollers in her hair and fat, fuzzy frog slippers scurrying around beneath her ragged housecoat, he loved studying her every detail. She was a tall, long legged, well-built stunner with flowing auburn hair. And he loved her. Madly!

He grimaced as he very quietly laid the paper on the counter. The headline loudly proclaimed that President Bush was about to make another power play overseas. Not his strong suit, Tipton thought. As it whimpered to an end, the eighties had turned out to be a disappointing decade, he decided. He turned his thoughts to more pleasant matters.

He sneaked up and flicked his arm around his wife's middle. His aim was unerring. A hand flashed inside the robe and her reaction was immediate.

"Well, Mr. Tipton, we're feeling a little frisky this morning aren't we?" She spun around and drew him close.

"Whatsamatter, cowboy? Didn't get enough last night?" Her voice was a husky, overly-theatrical growl.

"Ain't no such thing as e-nuff, ma'am," Sam Tipton replied in a deep, equally theatrical drawl. As he smothered her lips with his own, she responded by worming even closer.

Without warning, a flying object hurled itself against Sam. It attached itself permanently by tightly wrapping its tentacles around his leg.

"Oh, daddy," a tiny voice squealed, "You and mom are so silly!"

Scooping the straw-haired bundle off the floor, Tipton wrapped his arms around both his women. Everyone in the tight little huddle giggled. Each for their own reasons.

"Well, Mr. Tipton, are you ready for breakfast?" As she returned to the duties of mother and wife, Marilyn Tipton's smile took on an impish quality that drove Sam crazy.

Three-year-old Melissa Tipton, however, burrowed even

deeper, widening the opening to Sam's heart which her mother had started. Tipton's reaction was immediate.

"Mommy, mommy, daddy's biting me again!" The squealing went on unending as Sam Tipton turned her end for end, finding every bit of exposed skin with his teeth.

"Sam, stop that!" Marilyn laughed. "We can't send her to day-school covered with hickeys!"

Reluctantly, Sam Tipton deposited his precious bundle on the floor. She scurried around the natural oak table and up onto her chair. As she did, a red ball of fur skittered across the polished tile floor to become a Pomeranian puppy when it slowed down to leap up into her lap.

"Melissa, what did I tell you about letting Foxy at the table?" Mom tried to be stern but her tone lacked conviction.

As Marilyn Tipton turned, her daughter sneaked the puppy a piece of toast then put a warning finger to her lips. It was a secret between puppy and mistress. Neither would tell. Her back to them, Melissa's mother smiled. Mothers always know.

Sam Tipton swung his leg over the back of a chair and dropped down at the table. He stuffed his tie into his light blue, pin-striped shirt, second button down and muttered quietly, "I don't know what idiot invented these damn things or why!"

Working at the stove, Marilyn Tipton didn't bother to answer. Sam knew what she was thinking. She had told him she wouldn't say a word until he stopped bitching each time he put on a tie. Then she'd begin worrying. Then they'd both know it was time to change jobs and escape the east coast before the Washington, D.C. suburbs ground them down any further.

"Tough one today, honey?" she asked.

Sam replied, "Yeah, I have to go up on The Hill and try to explain techno-thievery to some politicians who probably don't give a damn. I'm doing it as a favor to the Bureau. Man, I hate that intelligence stuff. I'm no damn spook. I'm an engineer!"

Marilyn Tipton again didn't respond. Sam hated his job and she knew it. Everyone knew it. He loved having the latest in computers and machine shops at his finger tips but he hated all the political trash surrounding the work.

Mostly he hated not being back home in Arizona. Being forced to flee D.C. each night for the Virginia suburbs was not his idea of living.

"Oh, hey, I almost forgot. How do these look?" As Marilyn

spoke, she held up a pair of freshly shined cowboy boots. The brown leather had a deep, lustrous glow.

"They look great, Babe! Thanks." Sam Tipton approved. "Keep them out and I'll wear them this weekend. All right!"

He stood and straightened his tie in the hall mirror. He tried to brush his brown hair out of his eyes, but it returned the second he dropped his hand. Sam Tipton had never been described as tidy. Or well kept. In fact, the face in the mirror looked out of place perched above the shirt and tie. Green-brown eyes were buried in a bone and muscle sculpture. There was no extraneous tissue and his leather-brown skin had seen too much wind and sun. Wrinkles at the corners of his eyes doubled as crow's-feet and laugh lines. They came from too much squinting and a life time of laughing. He stood an even six feet, but his body language added at least two more inches. He frowned at his reflection. Even to him it was the face of a westerner and sadly out of place. He gave up on the tie.

Marilyn Tipton padded down the driveway, housecoat, frog feet and all. She stretched to kiss her husband through the open window of his sparkling new 1989 Blazer, knowing full well half of their picket-fence neighborhood was watching. She gloried in their jealousy.

"Think you'll make it home for supper tonight?" She knew when he went into town, she stood at least a fifty-fifty chance of eating alone with Melissa.

"I doubt it. The way Daniel Guy sounded when he set up this meeting, it may run over to tomorrow morning. I'll call later and let you know, if I'm staying in town." Another part of the job he hated.

Sam Tipton kissed his wife hard on the mouth and shifted mental gears to do battle with beltway traffic.

Two

"**Daniel! What the hell do you want?**" Sam Tipton stood in the open hotel room door oblivious to the fact he was clad only in his skivvies. He brought his hand up and squinted at his watch. "Jesus! It's two o'clock in the morning!"

Daniel Guy, FBI Agent and Tipton's close friend since Vietnam, had never liked Washington. Tonight he hated it. It was forcing Guy to do the toughest thing he'd ever had to do.

"Sam, sit down, we need to talk." His tone was softly solemn.

"What the hell are you talking about?" Sam Tipton's sleep-blurred mind was struggling to come on-line. "I don't want to sit down. What's going on?"

"Sam," Daniel Guy's voice choked. He put his hand on his friend's shoulder and looked him in the face. "There's been an accident at home. A bad one..."

Tipton didn't let him finish. "Oh, Jesus, God...!" He had the agent by both shoulders. "Marilyn? Melissa?"

Daniel Guy dropped his head and nodded.

Sam Tipton, technical-intelligence consultant and engineer, ex-Marine fighter pilot, husband and father, never said a word. He walked silently to his suitcase and began getting dressed. The only sound in the room was a quiet whisper from Daniel Guy.

"Oh Jesus, I'm sorry. So, goddamn sorry!"

Sam didn't remember any of the eulogy. Or the funeral procession. One moment he was in his hotel room trying to wake up and the next he was standing in a cold, gray mist surrounded by friends while he stared at two coffins. One smaller than the other.

The several days separating the hotel room from the graveyard, were just a blur of places and friends. Many soft words and warm hugs. Every other word seemed to be "...sorry..."

Afterwards friends would remark how stoic he had been. He hadn't shed a tear and seemed to genuinely appreciate their efforts to carry part of his grief.

As Sam stared at the polished coffins, his mind saw inside them. He saw his Marilyn sleeping peacefully. Because of the bullets, they hadn't let him see her. That thought caused him to remember other times, other bullets. He tried to stop it, but the haunting image returned again. As it often did. The jungle parted and a young woman stared out at him. At first he saw only the hard smile. The gleaming white teeth. The smooth skin. She was beautiful. Her weapon was already spitting flame before he saw the black pajamas and AK-47. His instincts had saved his life, but the image of his own bullets turning the young face into a blood-gray mass sometimes returned. He squeezed his eyes tight. The image went away, replaced by another. Marilyn's face flashed across his mind. He wouldn't let the images mix. He couldn't.

His mind's eye saw Marilyn under the rain-painted metal. In his mind, she was wearing the white turtleneck that set off her long hair and olive skin so beautifully. Well-worn jeans hugged her hips and she wore her favorite rough-out boots. She smiled sweetly, as if having a wonderful dream in which she and Sam, were once again curled up together.

He tried not to think of the bullets.

In the smaller coffin his mind saw a squirming bundle in fuzzy Doctor Denton's waiting for daddy to tuck her in and tell her a story. Or tickle her. Or bite her. And she would fall asleep with her tiny hand curled around his finger while he stroked her soft, straw-colored hair.

Sam sensed there was a crowd around him at graveside, but he saw none of them. He was alone in the middle of a personal desert with nothing in sight but two coffins. With nothing but the long walk away from the coffins to a horizon he would never reach. No matter how long he walked, he knew he would turn and find the two coffins only a few feet away. Never out of sight. Never out of mind.

He felt strong arms around him and looked up to find the sad eyes of his father on one side and Daniel Guy on the other.

"Come on son, it's time to go. We're going over to Daniel's for a while. Come on." His father's voice was slow and deep, filled with the emotion born of a father's love for his only son. Although a man who had seen death in many forms, that was years earlier, as a warrior for his country. This was different. This was death out of place. Out of time. Although, as a rancher he'd faced desert fires and hard droughts and he'd been tempered by the West, that didn't stop the tears. That didn't stop him from being a father. A wrinkled, rough hand tightened around the trembling hand of his grown son.

Sam resisted momentarily. He reached out to each coffin. They were cold and damp to his touch. He leaned over and whispered, "I'll come to take you home. I promise. I love you."

As he walked away with friend and father, he fought the urge to look back.

Sam Tipton rode in the lead car with his father, while Daniel Guy climbed into his Bureau sedan with his long time partner, Fred Webster. Guy wiped a tear from the corner of his eye. The Tiptons had been family. Marilyn a sister. Sam a brother.

"Jesus, mother of God, I hope I never have to go through anything like this again." Suddenly Agent Guy turned to his partner, "What was Tipton working on for us other than the industrial espionage thing?"

"Nothing. That was it," Webster replied

"I don't get it," Guy said. "What the hell is this about?"

"I don't know," Webster replied. "My police contacts say it looks to be a drive-by shooting. The Tiptons just happened to be in the wrong place at the wrong time. Other houses were hit at the same time. Theirs just got hit harder."

"Bullshit!" Guy blurted. "The other houses took maybe a half dozen rounds and they claim they heard some shouting in Spanish. That's it!" He pulled their car up behind the Tiptons. "Tipton's house took a hundred .308 rounds through the bedrooms alone. Give me a goddamned break! Drive-by, my ass!"

"I don't know, man," Webster sounded skeptical. "The cops are writing it off as the first drive-by in a white-collar neighborhood. Mostly, they're afraid it may be the start of a trend. Maybe some sort of poor-versus-rich thing."

"Bull shit!" was all Daniel Guy had time to say before he merged with traffic. It was going to be a long drive home.

The house was dark, as Sam Tipton pulled into his driveway. He sat for a long time and watched the street lights play off the yellow police crime scene tape stretched across his front porch. His front porch! He didn't want to believe it.

Shattered glass in the windows caught the light. The reflections were incomplete and fractured. There hadn't been time to board them up. It didn't matter. It wouldn't matter. Not in the long run.

He stepped through the back door into the kitchen where he

had breakfast with his family only a few days earlier. The street light played with the shadows as he moved through the dark house. Glass crunched under foot. As his eyes probed the dark, he couldn't sort out his feelings. His thoughts and emotions were dulled to the reality of the situation.

He recognized what had happened, but couldn't bring himself to think past it. Past this life into another life. A life without Marilyn. Without Melissa.

As their names crossed his mind, he wandered towards their rooms. They said Melissa had been found in bed with Marilyn. He found it somehow comforting that they should die with their arms around each other.

Melissa's room was first and the buzz of flies caught his attention. A faint odor reached out to him. The street light touched a small, motionless mound of red fur in the middle of Melissa's disheveled bed. Foxy!

Even the goddamn dog!

That's when the tears began. That's when the lump which had been lodged in his throat from the moment Daniel Guy stepped through the hotel room door, broke free and released the tears. No one saw Sam Tipton as he slumped down in the doorway of his little girl's room. His sobs echoed throughout the dark, deadly-quiet house.

His body gave itself over to the pain. The sobs rolled over one another, barely allowing space to breathe. Only the night and the empty house heard what had been held back for so long.

Sam Tipton neither knew, nor cared, how long he had been sitting in the doorway. The tears stopped because there were no more. There was nothing left of Sam Tipton to give.

It took more strength than he thought possible to push himself numbly to his feet and walk through the dark kitchen to the garage. He grabbed a bottle of Jack Daniel's on the way. A shovel was in the other hand when he returned to carry the inert puppy to the backyard.

As he dug, he drank. As he drank, he talked.

"Dear God, I commend to your care, the tiny soul of Foxy Tipton. Please, God, please make sure he's with my Melissa."

He slumped to the ground beside yet another grave. This time bottle in hand.

Several hours later Sam Tipton walked unsteadily through

the dark house with a red can in his hand. First it was Melissa's room. Then he staggered down the hall and sloshed the liquid around the room in which he had spent the happiest moments of his life. The bed got an especially liberal soaking.

He stared at the ragged bullet holes in the walls and the jungle image returned to his mind. This time the face above the black pajamas was Marilyn's. The bullets started and he rushed the bottle to his lips. He didn't remove it until the image went away.

As he stepped into the kitchen looking for matches, the light reflected off a pair of newly-shined boots on the kitchen table. At the sight, he wanted the tears to start again, but they wouldn't. There were no more.

He tucked the boots under his arm and threw a match into Melissa's room. Yellow-blue flames leaped across the floor, over the bed and up the walls. In seconds the same scene repeated itself in the master bedroom. The flames made a hungry, dull roaring sound as they devoured the physical traces of what had been his life. He thought about climbing into bed and pulling the blankets over his head. But he couldn't bring himself to look at the bed. At the place where his life had died.

As the flames built, Mr. Daniel's liquid legacy whispered softly in his ear and he ambled slowly down the hall.

Daniel Guy coughed slightly as the smell of Sam Tipton's smoldering house found its way into his lungs. Gaunt, blackened bones of the structure appeared angry and naked in the early morning light. Water was everywhere. He shivered and it wasn't from the damp coolness.

"Agent Guy, my name is Lieutenant Shraeder." As the fireman spoke, he removed his yellow hard hat and wiped a smoke-smudged brow. "My guys were the first on the scene and I was right behind them. There wasn't much we could do. The house was already totally involved. We were damned lucky to get your friend out."

"My friend?" Guy asked.

"Yeah. He was sitting on the couch in the living room which was engulfed. He had a bottle in one hand and the TV remote in the other and was channel surfing as if nothing was wrong. He didn't want to leave and we damned near had to cold-cock him to get him out. Two of the guys tossed him on the front lawn. He was drunker'n a skunk."

"Where is he now?" Daniel Guy was looking around his friend's property. Sam Tipton was nowhere to be seen.

"We don't know," the fireman answered. "We got busy fighting the fire and didn't see him after that."

A new voice piped up from behind them, "I saw him." The speaker was a graying gnome of an old lady. A Hummel figurine in a tightly clutched housecoat. She was standing next to the white picket fence separating her neat front yard from what used to be Sam Tipton's neat front yard.

"For a while, while they were fighting the fire," she said, "he just sat in the water on his front yard. He was wearing a dark suit. But, he wasn't wearing any shoes and had his arms wrapped around a pair of cowboy boots."

She leaned forward, looked both ways and whispered, "I think he was drinking. He had a bottle with him."

"Where'd he go?" Guy asked.

"Go?" The gnome replied.

"Yes, where is he now?" Guy asked.

"Oh, I don't know. But, he was a nice man, you know." She smiled.

"Didn't you see which way he went?" Guy was getting impatient.

"Oh, yes, I did," she nodded as her mind went in another direction, "Well, let me see. I last saw him walking up Elm Street. Did I tell you he had no shoes?" Her voice lowered again, "And he was drinking."

She looked back at the water pooling in Tipton's front yard. Ashes and scorched reminders of the Tiptons' life floated in shallow pools. She shook her head and frowned.

She looked at Agent Daniel Guy and said, "You know, it really is a shame how some people can't seem to handle stress."

Grover's, one of Georgetown's long established meet and greet bars, hadn't changed much in the two years since the Tipton shooting. It still smelled of polished brass, oiled leather and old money. A slightly balding, middle-aged gentleman in a dark suit at the bar looked as if he hadn't changed much either. He was closely scrutinizing a half-empty glass of Scotch and didn't look up when a tall, thin, graying individual sat down next to him. Senator Foster Ward ignored the Scotch drinker as he settled on the stool and reached for a bowl of midget pretzels on the bar.

Only the occasional eye had followed Ward in. Senators weren't that unusual in Grover's. He popped a pretzel into his mouth then stared intently at a second pretzel as he quietly said, "So what's the latest on Tipton?"

"Nothing," came the answer. "He has evaporated. It's been over two years and we don't have a thing on him."

The speaker had his head down quietly addressing his Scotch and Ward had to strain to hear over the background noise. "He simply dropped off the face of the Earth. Our best guys figure he tried to commit suicide when the house burned and he probably succeeded somewhere else. Eventually his body will wash up somewhere. We're not worried about it."

"Not good, not good." Ward's words were quiet and worried. The pretzel disappeared into his mouth. "We would prefer a much more definitive end to this thing. Don't forget, I flew with that sonuvabitch in 'Nam and believe me, Sam Tipton's not to be underestimated. Given another two weeks on that technical thievery project and he would have nailed us on the memory-chip sale. If he's alive, he's still damn dangerous. The last thing I need is him re-surfacing after I get the cabinet appointment."

"Yes sir, we understand," the man again addressed his Scotch, " but either he's dead, or he's crawled in a hole somewhere. We haven't found a single person who even saw him after the fire."

"Okay, we'll drop it off the priority list," Senator Foster Ward said, "but don't even think about closing the case. Keep an ear to the ground in case he shows up someplace. It's essential we find him before the good guys do."

"So we're agreed?" Pale hazel eyes left the glass of Scotch and swiveled over to connect with Ward as the senator spoke. "The Sam Tipton case is inactive, but not closed."

Message delivered, Ward threw back another pretzel and disappeared into the crowd.

Three

Crazy Charley Yee, a rail-thin, elderly Apache, sat on the edge of the mesa watching the sunset. He had done so every night for over half a century and even as the new millennium arrived, he would continue doing so until his gods returned for him. They had come once, roaring down on him with silver wings. They would surely come again. His box seat for the natural light show in progress was a flat rock behind his ramshackle Navajo-style hogan. It sat next to the dusty road into what was left of the near-ghost town of Pitacho, Arizona.

Studying each sunset was required ritual for Charley Yee. The old Apache stared hard at the western horizon. He didn't turn his head at the raucous sounds rolling down the road from Roberta's. As best he could, he ignored that oasis of drunken civilization. During the weekdays that wasn't difficult. On Saturday, however, the old stone building forced its noisy personality upon the desert night.

Roberta's was tightly wedged between the broken and bleached remains of what had been Ogden's Hardware and an unnamed, long-defunct funeral home. The saloon was a magnet that drew every recluse, miner, would-be-miner, rancher and bum out of the surrounding hills and desert. Roberta's was one of the few buildings in town still serving any purpose. The rest were being slowly reclaimed by the high desert.

Roberta's survival was based on the simple fact that she had the only booze and neon within thirty miles. Most considered weekly injections of both as essential for survival in the high desert. Booze made them forget where they were. Neon made them think they liked where they were.

Charley Yee avoided Roberta's. He wasn't welcome. He made people nervous and people didn't like to be nervous when their immediate goal in life was to get shit-face drunk.

Charley made people nervous because he just sat and stared.

The closest Charley Yee came to Roberta's was the high curb outside. On Saturday night he would be sitting with his back against one of the weathered gray posts holding up the splintered wooden awning. A million people could walk past him. Bottles could come flying out of the open door or through the often-replaced front glass and he wouldn't blink. Charley Yee's thoughts were always someplace out past the sunset.

It wasn't by accident the locals knew him as Crazy Charley.

The deep, flat sound of a Harley echoed off the high dirt bank across the rutted road from Charley's hogan. Saturday night was about to begin in earnest. The bikers usually didn't blast into town until the sun was well down. They were early.

"Heeey, Crazy Charley," The voice was that of a young woman. The shrill, obnoxious tone cut through the near darkness to where the meditating Indian sat. He ignored her.

The voice faded in the distance, as the Harley disappeared in a dust plume headed for Roberta's.

"Yo, Charley, you crazy fuckin' Injun," another voice picked up where the woman had left off. Then another. And another. A dozen Harleys rounded the curve. Each rider had his, or her, own salutation. None of them would have pleased Emily Post.

Charley Yee moved to his hogan and ignored them as he ignored the rest of the town.

The candles flickered, their light eagerly sucked up by the dark interior of the hogan. Charley Yee pushed through the dusty, desert-worn blankets and rugs draped over a rope which separated the back of the octagonal dwelling from the front.

He knelt down and rocked back and forth as he stared at his shrine. His eyes were seeing into a dark void a half century old. A void that had produced his vision and guided his life.

As he rocked, his eyes never left his box-like shrine. Its finely finished surface showed the dulling effects of age and tiny cracks spider-webbed through the heavy lacquer. The wood had aged to a mellow gold since it had last ridden across a dark air base ramp on the shoulder of a fleeing Air Force Major. The brass fittings shone brightly despite their age. Charley Yee would never let his shrine tarnish. His gods had placed it in his protection during his vision quest. He would protect it forever.

Charley Yee blew out the candles. It was Saturday night and Charley Yee prepared to go forth and ignore an entire town. As he walked up the dark, dusty road towards the halo of neon that was Roberta's, his fingers traced endless triangles on the silver amulet hanging around his neck. His gods would always protect him.

Four

"**Goddammit, where'd** you put my goddamn car keys?" Frank Frederick was irritated. Not an unusual state.

"Dammit, woman, I had them right here on the goddamn engine cover."

Magazine stacks were knocked over, dirty clothes were jerked off the small counter top and thrown back in disgust.

"What the goddamn hell did you do with them?"

If the small motor home had been any larger, Frederick would have been able to stomp and pace. Its size, however, limited him to slamming a few cabinet doors and an occasional kick against the cheap baseboard.

Turning to stare at his wife, a faded, heavily painted blonde on the near side of seventy years, he again kicked the base of the cabinets. Dust rose each time he kicked.

He coughed.

"I'm getting pissed! Now where are the goddamn keys? I want to get out of this hell hole and go find another one just like it!" He stopped talking as a cough rose up in his throat. Then another. And another. In seconds his medium height, rotund frame was leaning against the bathroom door, his hands on his knees. Coughs racked his body.

Getting a respite from the coughs, Frederick scavenged his throat with a deep rasping sound and threw open the door. He spewed the results into the dry dust outside. A lizard scurried under a dead cholla barely avoiding getting hit.

"Jesus, I thought this goddamn state was supposed to be good for guys like me." He flopped down into the passenger's chair which was rotated around to face the interior. He muttered under his breath, the sarcasm as obvious as the foam coming through the chair's upholstery, "I just love goddamn retirement. Just goddamn love it! Now, where are the goddamn keys?"

May Frederick lay on the faded, torn cushions on the bench across the back of the motor home. She ignored him. She moved the woman's magazine she was reading for the seventeenth time closer to the open window to get some fresh air. The motor home had begun smelling like a wet dog right after the last hard rain.

She let her husband of forty-nine years stew. Letting him get all worked up over nothing was her only entertainment. She glanced the short length of the motor home. Forty-nine years, she was thinking. Forty-nine goddamn years in every backwater small city big enough to have an FBI office and this is it. This is life. This is the American dream. A leaking shit box on wheels, underwear over three years old, and just enough government pension to keep gas in the tank and Spam in that little goddamn icebox that only worked about half the time.

"I've still got my gun. Now where are my goddamn keys?" He was nearly whining, he was so frustrated.

May Frederick couldn't resist. It was too good this time and she cut him off with a finger to her smirking, ruby lips.

"Why sweety," she cooed, "Why didn't you ask me for the keys in the first place."

The coo came out as a throaty croak. Several thousand cartons of Camels had left their mark.

"I believe they are right where you left them." She hesitated, knowing the pause would send her husband into spasms again. And it did. He turned and slammed his hand against a cabinet door, rocking the motor home in the process.

Before he could open his mouth, May Frederick pointed forward with the ruby red false nail perched on the end of a gnarled, age-spotted finger. The years had not been good to May Frederick. Frank Frederick, retired FBI agent, turned to follow her pointing finger.

The sunlight glistened off the keys hanging in the old Dodge motor home's ignition.

He slammed the cabinet again and lunged for the front seat. His swearing nearly, but not quite, drowned out May Frederick's laughter.

The motor home's ailing V-8 breathed hard as it worked its way up the steep dirt road and the yellowed headlights strained to pick out the shallowest ruts. Frank Frederick wrestled the wheel with both hands. The road wasn't that rough, but the front end of the old RV was so loose, every rut or rock made it dart one way or the other. With each bump the no-name RV body creaked one step closer to total disintegration.

"Goddamn, I knew I should have turned left." He immediately regretted having said that.

His wife seized the opportunity and started again. "You are such a klutz! Have you made one goddamn right decision in your life? I remember the time you..."

Frederick didn't hear the rest. He didn't have to. He could recite what his wife would say word for word. She would start with cases and agency offices as far back as the Los Alamos thing and work right up to present day.

As the road leveled out, his lights flashed across a leaning Indian hogan and a faded sign. All he caught was something about Charley Yee's something or other.

In the near distance the neon glow of civilization in the form of a drinking establishment beckoned him. Fuck it! This was good enough. He pulled into a flat area of dark sagebrush. After so many years he'd learned it really didn't matter where he parked. His life wasn't going to change overnight. One parking place was as good as another. He was just marking time and he knew it. One place to die was as good as another.

The lights were switched off and he stumbled towards the rumpled bed at the rear of the motor home. He wondered if he would see the dawn and unconsciously snorted to himself. Who gave a shit?

"Now you goddamn listen to me!" Frank Frederick was several steps behind his wife who was stomping through the dust as though she had a destination in mind. The sun had barely broken the horizon when she spotted the sign for Charley Yee's souvenir shop.

"Now, listen, I don't give a shit what kind of junk he has for sale, you can't buy any. I mean it." Frederick was half-yelling. As they neared the hogan, the ex-FBI man caught up with his wife and breathlessly repeated, "Not a goddamn thing. Got it?"

His wife ignored him, as she always did. She didn't have to be told she couldn't buy anything. She was painfully aware of that fact. They were living so close to the financial edge she even had to ration the Spam sandwiches. She totally understood their life-status and it pissed her off.

She planned on giving an Oscar-winning performance as an out of control spendthrift just to drive her husband's blood pressure up. She couldn't spend anything, but that didn't mean she couldn't have a good time.

They stood just inside the doorway of the crude hogan for a

few moments waiting for their eyes to adjust to the dark. When they did, Frank visually swept the interior in a matter of seconds. He made his mind up instantly.

"Come on. Let's go. This is all junk!" Frederick didn't bother lowering his voice. It sounded loud in the small, dark interior.

Frank Frederick had just turned to leave when a short, thoroughly desiccated visage of a man appeared from behind the blankets at the back of the room. A loose-fitting buckskin vest draped over a denim shirt faded nearly white. Traditional high-topped Apache moccasins broke the bottom of twice-cuffed jeans which dragged on the packed dirt floor. A cloth headdress resembling a turban with a single feather covered his head. Long hair, more gray than black, flowed well past his shoulders.

The face matched the buckskin vest. But, it showed much more age, much more exposure to the desert sun. His lips parted in a gentle, almost serene, smile exposing perfectly-spaced, but worn and yellowed teeth.

"May I help you?" The voice matched the smile. "I am known as Charley Yee."

"Nah, we're just lookin'," Frank Frederick snarled as he headed for the door. Then his wife spoke. She was holding a ceramic box and smiling.

Frank Frederick recognized the ploy. This time he wasn't going to let it work. He wasn't going to let it piss him off. He tightened his fists. Then he realized she had already pissed him off and she had accomplished her goal, which pissed him off even further. He resolved to play along and let her pretend to shop. He couldn't let her know she'd already won.

Frederick tried to play the game and pretend to look at the meager merchandise but he lost interest immediately and began snooping around the rest of the structure.

He stepped behind the blankets separating the back of the hogan from the front. Charley Yee's lifetime accumulation of assets lay in a humble heap against a near wall. A low bench covered with a threadbare Navajo blanket appeared to be his bed. His clothing and other belongings hung from pegs and nails in a random pattern. It looked like a poorly-organized garage sale. Frederick smiled a wry smirk. He had finally found someone who owned less than he did. The thought didn't make him feel any better about his own situation, but it at least gave him someone to look down upon. That was worth something.

He shifted his eyes to the shrine. It stood in a garish grotto framed in an arch made of sun-bleached deer antlers and triangles cut from every conceivable material and source, billboard to filling station sign.

The arch framed an elevated pulpit on which a squarish outline stood. Frank Frederick first took it to be a collection box. He snorted at the idea of anyone wanting to contribute to such a worthless concept. As he moved closer, however, something looked familiar. As each detail of the box worked its way into his mind it became a key which unlocked tiny memory vaults. Vaults which had been sealed and studiously ignored for nearly five decades. For half a century.

As his eyes focused on the shape and details of the box, a part of his mind recognized it. Then just as quickly, he dismissed it.

It couldn't be! It would be entirely too incredible!

As he closed in, his eyes raced from edge to edge, corner to corner. He compared each detail with those so deeply etched in his mind's eye so many years ago. His breath caught in his throat. He could hear his own heartbeat echoing off the domed sagebrush ceiling of the hogan.

Trembling old fingers reached out and touched the fluorescent triangles in a circle affixed to the front of the box-shrine. He dropped to his knees in front of the shrine and fumbled for his reading glasses.

His fingers shook as they hooked the cheap frames over his squat nose and around his ears. He leaned close and read the inscription on the small, brass tag so painstakingly inlayed into the lower corner of the shrine's cover.

He read the first small group of letters. A flash went off in his mind and his body went weak all over. This was it! The inscription read, "Trig. Assbly. XK-104, Mk. II, Mod. 1-HC, Los Alamos Atomic Laboratories."

This was it! This was it! Frank Frederick's overloaded mind repeated the phrase over and over in a delirious, endless loop.

The box was closed but the latch was open. Frank Frederick was so weak with excitement, it was all he could do to raise his arms to touch the lid. Was it there? Would the item which had haunted and eluded him for his entire adult life actually be there?

"Sir, you also worship my gods?" The voice from behind was soft and tranquil but Frank Frederick was so deep in his own trance it made him jump.

His head turned slowly and he stared up at the bony image of Charley Yee with wide, vacant eyes. He spoke in an awed, incredulous voice.

"Where, in God's name, did you get this?"

Charley Yee smiled sincerely. No one had ever shown such reverence for his shrine or appeared to have the same connection with it as he. He sensed a camaraderie with this white man on his knees in front of his shrine.

He answered as simply and as honestly as he could. "It was given to me by my gods in a vision."

Frank Frederick was still staring at him. As the words slowly formed a coherent sentence in his mind, he knew it was not the answer he wanted.

"No, I mean it, old man. Where did you get this?" Frank's voice had lost its awed tone and was closing in on demanding.

Frank then realized it made no difference where it came from. It was only important that it was there. That he had found it. That the single most emotionally and professionally damning artifact in his life was once again in his possession. The nightmare was over.

He turned his back on the puzzled old Indian and hooked a trembling finger under the shrine's cover. He pulled. The side opened easily. Frank Frederick took one look and fell back into a sitting position.

"Shit! Goddammit!" Frederick coughed uncontrollably for a full minute then looked back up at the case to make certain his eyes weren't lying.

The suitcase-sized case was empty. The wooden brackets in each corner showed where they had been carefully crafted to hold a cube shaped object. But the object was gone. The handling case was there, but the assembly was missing.

Frederick snapped around to face the Indian, jumping to his feet as quickly as his aging body would allow.

He grabbed Charley Yee by the shoulders and stooped to put his face right in front of the old Indian's. Now his voice was on the edge of a full-blown shout. "The metal box that was inside it! Where is it? Do you have it? Where..."

Charley smiled gently and slowly put a finger to his lips short-stopping Frederick's impending tirade. "Sir, as you must surely know, the object inside belongs only to the gods. I left it with them and under their protection. They spoke with me in their special tongue and said they would forever keep it safe. So, it is with them. I go to visit, when the gods tell me, but it is in the Mogollon, with them"

Fifty years of frustration rushed to the surface of Frank Frederick's mind. His first impulse was to shake the location of the box's contents out the Indian. But the coughs stopped him.

May Frederick stepped through the blankets just in time to see her husband bend over in front of the worried-looking Indian and start coughing violently.

He staggered outside and reached for his ever-present inhaler. It wasn't there. May Frederick came outside just in time to see his hand searching his pockets. She knew what he wanted and she smiled.

Slowly she reached towards her purse for his spare inhaler. She was in no hurry. Frank Frederick saw what she was doing and angrily ripped the purse from her hands.

He leaned against the splintered outside wall of the hogan and felt the life-giving mist working its magic on his inflamed tissues. His mind was whirling around an entirely different issue. The coughing was a minor irritation.

The handling case was in the shrine. And the Indian knew the location of the assembly. He was close! So terribly close! Frederick staggered towards the motor home. For the first time in five decades he felt a flicker of hope in his heart.

Five

Marilyn Tipton smelled of peaches. And the sweet powder she always used after her bubble baths. The aroma settled around Sam Tipton like a warm, familiar fog. Her long auburn hair flowed down over him and he felt the smoothness of her hands as they gently explored his body, her nails occasionally touching to leave a trace of electricity in their path.

Her body was a warm presence as her legs gripped and guided him. The lovers flowed together until Sam and Marilyn Tipton moved as a single, loving entity. Their languid love-making created a melody with a rhythm which became faster and faster.

The rhythmic cadence built in intensity then, without warning, became sharp and harsh. The melody became discordant and laced with pain. Each time she moved, he felt a stabbing pain and heard her voice biting into him hard and coarse.

But it wasn't her voice. And it wasn't her pain.

"Tipton! Sam Tipton, you fucking drunk, wake-up!"

The rhythmic pain continued until Sam Tipton's eyes slowly ratcheted open. His eyeballs made an imagined grating sound as his eyelids ground open. The morning light poked at them with fiery barbs. He started to close them again, but the voice and the stabbing pain wouldn't let him.

"Get the fuck up, I need that goddamn gear! You're costing me money!"

More stabbing pain and Sam turned his head, not yet certain where he was. Or which life he was living. Then he remembered: How long had it been? Ten years? An entire decade had slithered down the tubes since Marilyn. Since Melissa. Since returning to Arizona. To the rest of the world, a new century was just poking its ugly head over the horizon. He couldn't have cared less.

His head slowly turned the other direction.

The sun burned behind the outline of a man reaching in through the missing window of the dilapidated vehicle with a gold-tipped walking stick. The stick was jabbing him in the ribs. Sam wasn't certain which irritated him more, the pain the stick was causing, or the man's presence.

Summoning his dwindling strength, he rolled up on his knees

in the junk-strewn back of the old Willys and tried to focus on the intruder. Sam had to fight to maintain his balance on the layer of dust-covered mechanical debris that had long ago replaced the back seat. The near-derelict vehicle looked the way Sam felt.

The stick jabbed at him again. A last time. In a single, swift motion, an irate Sam Tipton grabbed the stick, slamming it against the rusting window frame. The black wood splintered and he jabbed back through the window at a sagging, puffy face with the broken half.

Tipton found his voice, "Mandell, you rotten mother-fucker, you poke me with that goddamn thing one more time and a team of surgeons won't be able to get it out of your ass!"

As the words left his mouth, Sam Tipton felt the pounding in his head. It was going to be another of those mornings. He pivoted on his heels to sit crossways on the cluttered floor. He looked through a glassless window at Eddie "Mad Dog" Mandell. The stubby, round figure was bent over examining the jagged stub of his walking stick with incredulous eyes.

"You'll pay for this!" Mandell whimpered. "It was my father's and..."

"Shut the fuck up, before I crawl out of here and pound the shit out of you! Just shut the fuck up!" Tipton rubbed what was left of his eyes with the heels of his hands, as he spoke.

Half crawling, Tipton made his way over the scrap heap in the back of his 1951 Willys Overland. He caught himself just before falling out the back. The tailgate was missing leaving the entire end of the station wagon-like vehicle open to the surrounding desert.

Dangling his feet over the mangled rear bumper, Tipton looked around. It wasn't the first time the morning sun had found him crawling out of the Willys in back of Roberta's saloon and not-so-fine eating establishment.

"I need that goddamn..." Mandell started.

"You'll get your goddamn gear," Tipton snapped. "Now shut up. You're ruining the best part of the morning!"

"It's noon already," Mandell pointed out.

"Close enough," Tipton said, "now shut up while I enjoy it."

He used both hands to comb his long, disheveled hair back from his face. Some of the hair got caught in the ragged, graying beard covering his face. He looked at his hands and sniffed. He wrinkled his nose.

"Jesus!" he muttered quietly. "It's definitely time for a bath!"

As he dangled his legs off the back of the Willys, his faded denim shirt was half unbuttoned and hung loosely over once broad shoulders, their still strong muscles wrapped tightly over the visible bony structure. His deep green-brown eyes worked at focusing and his hair dangled in greasy strands to his shoulders. It was usually held back in a pony tail, but the mornings-after found it living a life of its own, going any direction it pleased. One leg of his grimy jeans was caught in the top of a scruffy cowboy boot worn nearly through in spots. The Sam Tipton of Washington, D.C. had completely disappeared.

"Tipton..."

"Yeah, yeah, I know. Your goddamn gear. Let's go."

As he spoke, Sam Tipton forced himself to stand and walked unsteadily to the dented driver's side door. In an instant, the rumble of the Chevy V-8 from the dual pipes showed the Willys felt much better than Tipton did. With power running through its rusting bones, the sagging old vehicle took on an entirely different personality. It sounded proud, with a hint of attitude.

As the two-car caravan slowly wound its way down the main, and only, street in Pitacho, Tipton noticed the roof of the old cut-stone bank had finally caved in. He found it sad the old building had given into time and the elements. He had been watching it sag, along with so many of the other abandoned buildings, since he found himself in Pitacho. Whenever that was.

Even he wasn't certain when he first came to town. One morning he woke up and there he was. And there he stayed.

When a teenager, Pitacho had been one of Tipton's regular haunts. A place to go when he didn't want to be found. His return made perfect sense. It had been a part of his world few knew existed. When he wanted to vanish, all he had to do was drive that twisting, seldom-traveled road that connected his dad's ranch with Pitacho's precarious perch on the edge of the mesa.

In Pitacho Tipton could revisit his past with no one knowing he was there. There he was just another drop-out among a crowd of drop-outs. He could disappear for as long as he liked. Or as long as he survived.

The clear air was beginning to make him feel better. He mentally upgraded his condition from shitty to simply terrible.

An elevated concrete sidewalk, most of its broken slabs meeting in awkward angles, bordered both sides of the street. The entire town, once a small, but proud, copper mining center, was reduced to a sad string of sagging storefronts, broken glass and unhinged doors, which stopped abruptly when both the elevated sidewalk and the cracked concrete road ended. This was the signal that Tipton had come to the edge of town. From there on, the road was a sandy scar running between knee-high clumps of sage-covered debris which had once been buildings. Gravity and the elements were working on those few still standing.

Several adobes were slowly being returned to the desert by winter rains. Their losing fight was symbolic: the town and its population were also losing their battle with the desert.

The old Willys circled around behind a large, square adobe structure. Tipton looked up and made a mental note to plaster up a crack beginning to form over the large freight door.

He hadn't the foggiest idea who actually owned the ancient building. For seven or eight years, however, he had called it home and considered himself its custodian. Or its curator. He wasn't certain which. During that time not a single soul had questioned his occupancy. With only one out of every ten buildings in town occupied, squatting was an accepted practice.

Tipton tugged on a castle-like wrought iron ring and the heavy timber door opened. As the cool darkness of the high-ceilinged old building flowed over them, a long soulful note from a bending guitar string raced past, as if escaping the dark for the light beyond. The note stopped abruptly.

"Hey, Cowboy, I thought we'd lost you again."

Joseph Longfeather slid down off a workbench and laid the Fender Stratocaster against the amplifier. As he spoke, he ran a hand through his glistening black, shoulder-length hair. Though slightly shorter than Sam, his shoulders appeared twice as wide. His torso tapered rapidly to the silver concho belt in his tight-fitting jeans. His naturally dark skin set off the bone and leather choker circling his massive neck and made his bright blue eyes look out of place in what was obviously a Native American face. They were the color of the turquoise in his belt buckle and the legacy of a much-revered cavalry captain great-grandfather.

"Nope, just another long night and early morning at Roberta's," Sam explained.

"Hair of the dog..." Tipton scooped a half-empty Jack Daniel's bottle off the workbench, twisting the cap as he did.

Joseph Longfeather frowned. His friend was fighting a battle and he wasn't winning.

"What's Mad Dog want?" Longfeather exchanged his frown for a grin, as he gestured towards Eddie Mandell. He knew the third-generation mine owner hated the nickname they had hung on him. That was reason enough to use it as often as possible.

"Longfeather, stop calling..."

"Mad Dog wants his goddamn gear," Sam snapped. "Stop whining, Mandell, or we'll stop fixing the stuff your gorillas keep breaking."

As he spoke, Sam walked off to one corner of the shop. He began unbuttoning his often-mended denim shirt.

Eddie Mandell said, "Look you guys, stop giving me shit or I'll find someone else to do our work."

"Forget it, Mad Dog. You tried that, remember? Drive a hundred miles then find out the part doesn't fit. We're the best and you know it. Besides, if your old man found out you switched, he'd cut you off." Sam grinned and continued undoing buttons.

He loved picking on the round-faced jerk. Mandell's dad and grandfather had both been mine owners. But they had come up the hard way, with a pick in one hand and dynamite in the other. Mad Dog had been born into it. Only his dad's mine accident kept the old man from shipping the kid off to Los Angeles where he couldn't do any harm. And wouldn't embarrass the family.

Eddie Mandell really wasn't such a bad guy, it's just that his presence was so irritatingly normal. Normalcy in Pitacho stood out like a candle in a dark room. On top of that, he was the only person in town who wore regular pants, not jeans, and no one had ever seen him in boots. Some referred to him as the desert dork.

Mandell inspected the large gear Longfeather had laid on the bench in front of him.

Sam pulled his shirt off and unhitched a tarnished, brass US cavalry belt buckle holding up his soiled and faded jeans. The buckle was one of Sam's prized possessions, a gift from the Longfeathers. It had belonged to the long-ago cavalry captain.

Sam took another long pull on the bottle. He gritted his teeth as the brown liquid burned its way down. He started pulling his pants down.

"Tipton, what the hell are you doing?" Mandell's voice went up half an octave.

"I'm taking a bath! What's it look like?"

The underwear landed on a dusty workbench with the rest of his clothing and he stepped out into the sunshine. The light made his pale body glow.

He reached for a garden hose hanging on the outside wall of the adobe. Mandell saw the rubbery blue scar running down one side of Tipton's back and felt compelled to ask its origin. He tried not to look at the shaggy, naked man as he spoke.

"That's a hell of a scar Tipton."

Sam Tipton didn't have to feel the mottled surface to know it was there. He could no longer feel the flames as they bore down on him and he couldn't remember the fireman dragging him from the flaming living room. He remembered nothing but the soul numbing pain that wouldn't leave him alone. The scar was minor. That was just a reminder of the physical pain.

"Just something to remind me I used to have a life, Mandell. Something you wouldn't understand," Tipton replied.

Tipton spoke as he held the hose over his head. The hose ran up to a large, rusting steel tank sitting on stilts next to the building where it collected rain water off the roof.

Mandell wasn't satisfied, "Just another of your drunk nights, huh? What..."

He stopped mid-sentence as Longfeather clamped an iron hand around one of Mandell's fat biceps. The hand-shaped bruise wouldn't go away for weeks.

"Shut up!" Longfeather's voice was quiet, barely a whisper. Mandell couldn't mistake the message.

Tipton ignored him and stood with the bottle to his lips. The other hand held the hose over his head. The water ran off the long hair, repulsed by the coating of dirt and grease. Eventually, with a little coercion from a bar of soap, it soaked the hair.

"Hey, Cowboy! Lookin' good!" A female voice drifted from a passing pick-up truck. A toothy grin filled the window and a hand waved.

"Hey, darlin'!" Tipton shouted back with both hands in the air. He presented the passer by with a full frontal view.

"Always pays to advertise," he said looking over at Mandell. Then his eyes traveled up and down Eddie Mandell's pudgy outline and he modified his statement, "Usually, anyway. Whew! Disgusting image!"

Longfeather laughed. Mandell didn't.

Six

"**Leave me the hell alone!**" Frank Frederick yelled at his wife.

Shirtless, he lay across the back of the motor home on the makeshift bed, an ancient albino possum flopped onto a wrinkled nest of blankets. His eyes were closed. A cold can of beer was pressed to his sweating forehead as he shouted at his wife.

"I've got some thinking to do. Read something and be quiet."

A free hand whipped a magazine the length of the RV. He didn't bother raising his head. The magazine was still fluttering to the floor when May Frederick snorted and stomped through the door into the afternoon sun.

The old man thought hard. He knew he had an opportunity, but he wasn't certain what kind. If the old Indian was right and he had the assembly, it would erase the clouds which had hung over him for a lifetime. It would clear his reputation.

His eyes flickered opened. He stared at the cracking insulation of the motor home's ceiling. He then surveyed the rest of the crumbling, four-wheeled remains around him.

What good would a clean reputation do now? Who would give a shit that a mistake made in his youth had been rectified? He'd learned a lot about the realities of life since then. One of them was that a great reputation doesn't put beans on the table. Or replace a stinking, shit box on wheels with a house above a serene, beach populated with golden bodies in string bikinis.

The time for idealism was long gone. You can wrap yourself in the flag, which might make you feel good, but it won't keep out the cold. Another asthmatic cough tried to work its way up his windpipe. A quick shot from the inhaler squelched it. Frederick wanted to keep out the cold. More than that, he wanted a future, not a clean past.

The Indian says it's in the Mogollon, the voice in Frederick's head repeated for the hundredth time. In the Mogollon! He remembered how the Indian had said the word, with its Spanish pronunciation. It wasn't pronounced the way it was spelled. "Moag-ee-yoan" was the closest Frederick could come in his mind. Which was close enough.

The Mogollon Rim rambled on for hundreds of miles. Hundreds of miles! Where in the Mogollon? Where? Only Charley Yee and his mythical god knew. Frederick smiled inwardly. Charley Yee may know where it was, but he sure as hell didn't know what it was. In Yee's most stupefied condition, with peyote visions dancing up and down main street, he wouldn't be able to imagine what it was.

Frank knew what. But he desperately needed to know where. Charley Yee was the key.

This time Charley Yee had company for his sunset ritual. A fellow worshipper.

Frank Frederick stared at the sunset beside the slowly-rocking Apache and hid his desires behind what he could remember of Bureau training. He was there to get information which meant befriending the old Indian. He would become one of the worshippers at Charley Yee's Shrine of the Mogollon. He could fake being religious. He was an FBI-trained atheist with a stomach full of Spam. He was the perfect combination for worshipping anything or anyone.

"So, Mr. Yee, how long ago did the gods visit you and make you the keeper of the shrine?" The setting sun glistened off the amber bottle, as he passed it across to his fellow worshipper and drinking partner. He tried to make his voice sound reverent. In Charley Yee's condition of advanced, but very reverent, inebriation, it probably didn't make any difference.

"It was on the third day of my vision quest." The elderly man remembered, as if in a trance. Much of the trance had come out of the bottle. Frank Frederick faked drinking each time it was passed back to him. Not an easy thing to do, considering how badly he wanted a drink.

"They appeared from nowhere. They roared down and breathed upon me before using fire to carve a home for themselves in the Mogollon." The old Indian's voice trailed off as he stared at the setting sun.

Frank Frederick's mind was screaming. Where, goddammit, where? He contained his thoughts. His mouth was shaped in an understanding smile. He was working hard at maintaining his cover. It had been a long time.

The bottle was passed to Charley Yee. Long pull on the bottle. He brightened, as he remembered.

"I was so scared. But I knew. I knew what the gods were saying to me. I had to follow them. My life was theirs."

His eyes never left the setting sun. As the sun slowly worked its way towards the horizon, the bottle repeatedly worked its way to his waiting hands. Eventually Charley Yee began to set right along with the sun.

"Mr. Yee," Frederick's sincerity sounded forced, even to him. No problem. He was certain the high priest of the Mogollon was too far gone to notice, "I would like to help your gods and continue your work at your shrine."

Frederick reached inside his jacket and pulled out a small wad of bills. It was mostly ones with a ten on each side. It was all of the cash he had until his next social security check. His total cash on hand was ninety two dollars.

"I would like to give this directly to your gods, if I could." Frederick looked at Yee and waited for an answer.

Yee stared at the horizon. Silent.

"Please, give me directions. I'm certain they would appreciate it, and I want desperately to meet them."

Still no response.

Charley Yee slowly turned his head and looked directly at Frank Frederick, his newest, and only, convert to his religion.

"The gods see only me." A trembling hand came up to take the money. Frederick was faster and quickly withdrew it.

"Give me the money and I will give it to my gods." Yee's voice had lost a bit of its reverent edge. He had to eat too.

"No, goddammit, take me to your gods!" Frank was losing patience. "Come on. Your gods will like me and the cash I bring them. All gods love cash. That's what makes them gods."

Yee frowned.

"Now come on, Yee..." Frank had started to yell, but stopped when the self-proclaimed shaman rose unsteadily to his feet.

In a quiet, but stern voice, Charley Yee said, "I will speak no more to you about my gods."

Before Frederick could say anything, the Indian had disappeared back inside his hogan, leaving him alone in the rapidly gathering dark.

"Goddammit," Frederick muttered and he rose to make his way back to his motor home. As he walked, a plan began to develop in his mind.

He studied Roberta's lights. He had to find a telephone.

Brad Anderson had trouble locating the ringing telephone at first. As he fumbled it to his ear, he glanced at the clock on his wife's side of the bed. The glowing numbers said it was 10:30 PM. He had barely fallen sleep.

He was thinking it must be something important for someone to call at that time of the night. It damn well better be something important to wake him up.

He didn't recognize the voice on the other end until it identified itself, "Frederick! What the hell are you doing calling this time of the night? We have nothing to discuss at any time, much less this late!"

His voice was a harsh whisper. He didn't want to wake up his wife because of some over-the-hill agent who was anything but a friend. He wasn't an enemy, but Frederick was one of those people he'd rather forget he ever knew. After Anderson moved into FBI headquarters he found it to his advantage to distance himself from certain elements of the Bureau. At that point he began to realize he was destined to be more than simply an agent. Frederick was just that. A simple agent and not a very good one.

He listened for a second then responded.

"Look, Frederick, let's not play games. I wasn't even with the Bureau when that...Wait, hang on a minute!"

Bradley Anderson swung his legs from under the covers and hurried for the master bath without even looking for his slippers. As he passed the windows, he glanced out. It was raining hard. He grimaced. The D.C. beltway would be a bitch in the morning. He hated commuting into downtown Washington in the rain.

The bathroom door securely closed behind him, Anderson put the lid down and sat on the commode. He left the lights off and the portable phone glowed unnaturally bright in the pure dark of the windowless bathroom.

"Okay, let's start over." His voice was cold and formal.

He listened for several minutes before saying, "Yes, I remember the case. It would be hard to forget, but it has nothing to do with me. You fouled that up long before I was joined the Bureau.

"Look, Frederick, I don't know who told you that...No, I'm not for sale. I don't care what you think you found out...I'm not dirty," Anderson's attempts at formality were slipping. "Goddammit, you're pissing me off!

"I'm going to hang up now." Anderson's voice had gone up

a pitch. He was irritated. And nervous.

"No...I'm hanging up right now unless you can give me a good reason I shouldn't."

Anderson shivered and pulled a towel off the rack behind him to drape over his pajama-clad shoulders.

"Repeat that...No, I mean it!" Anderson said, "Repeat that and, no, I'm not recording it. I'm sitting in the bathroom in the dark, freezing my...freezing to death, listening to some alcoholic ex-agent with delusions of grandeur. Now, repeat what you just said, so I get it straight!"

He listened for thirty long seconds.

"How do I know you have it...You're telling me you have the HC? You have Cobalt Blue?" He was surprised he could remember the assembly's code name.

Frederick droned on on the other end of the line.

"No, I'm not interested. Not in the slightest." Anderson was trying hard to sound emphatic. "That's old news. However, just in case I need to talk to you, how do I get a hold of you?"

"Come on, give me your number. Don't play games with me." Anderson looked at the phone and cursed himself that caller I.D. didn't work on his portable.

"Look, Frederick, I'm not interested but give me a call back in two days just in case I change my mind...no, I'll make it worth your while, anyway."

The phone went dead in Anderson's hand and he stared at it in the dark. Cobalt Blue! This was too big for him, but he knew someone who would probably be interested. The keypad glowed in the dark and his mind spit out numbers only he and a very few other people in the world knew. Even the phone company didn't know who actually picked up the phone.

The line was picked-up and Anderson began speaking, "Sir, it's Anderson...yes, sir, I'm sorry to call you so late, but I thought you'd want to know as soon as possible. Remember Cobalt Blue?...Yes sir, that's the one. I have an ex-agent who claims to have found it and he wants to deal for it. No sir, he sounded positive and I'm inclined to believe him. He's supposed to call back day after tomorrow. In the meantime, if you're interested, I'll gather what data I can on the project."

Anderson listened for a full minute before speaking.

"Yes, sir, I'll keep that in mind. After we have more information, you can make your decision....

"Yes sir, we still have several men we can trust. You know all of them from past operations."

"Yes, sir, I know it's a closed case, so I'll have to be careful."

"Yes, right now, you and I are the only ones who know this. Us and the ex-agent I mentioned."

"Don't worry sir, I'll do the work myself and won't involve anyone else until we are certain how real his story is."

"Have a good night sir."

Bradley Anderson silenced the phone with his thumb and sat and stared at it for a few seconds. Dozens of thoughts flowed through his head.

Cobalt Blue! A half century later it shows up. And it was almost in his hands! Amazing!

As he walked silently to bed and backed under the covers, scenarios wrote and re-wrote themselves in his mind. Cobalt Blue! Absolutely amazing! He felt another serious career move coming on.

Seven

Having negotiated the price of Tipton's machine work on the gear down to less than a third of what it was worth, Eddie Mandell moved on to the next item on his day's agenda.

"I almost hate to ask this," the Mandell kid, who was actually over forty, said, "but I need to hire you to fly me up to Flagstaff before it gets too dark and you get too drunk."

Sam grinned. Mandell was a lousy passenger. One pass down a narrow canyon and Mandell would dirty his underwear.

"Sure Mad Dog." Sam was using what was left of his phony Washington smile, "Do I have to wait in Flagstaff for you?"

"No, I'm picking up my new Cadillac," Mandell replied.

Longfeather and Sam laughed in unison. Mandell already the owned the only new car in a twenty mile radius. "New" wasn't something found often around Pitacho.

Longfeather braced himself against the old ex-military L-5 Stinson's wing strut and hung his head in the open window to get it out of the prop blast of the running engine.

"Hey, bro, I'll be gone when you get back. I've got a week's gig in Vegas. You going to be okay?" Longfeather yelled. The noise from the engine made Sam miss the concerned tone of Longfeather's question.

"Hey, I'm always all right, you know that!" Tipton shouted.

The Chiricahua Apache's face softened as he looked Sam Tipton straight in the eyes, "No, goddammit, I mean it! You've got me worried."

Engine noise made conversation nearly impossible.

"Hell, man," Tipton shouted, "I've got myself worried. We'll talk about it over a drink sometime."

Sam reached out of the cockpit and warmly squeezed the back of his partner's neck. Then he grinned his loony "yes I'm crazy" grin and started buckling his belts. Longfeather didn't feel like grinning.

Joseph Longfeather stepped back as Tipton blasted the tail around to take off. Longfeather's eyes swept the airplane from one end to the other. It was hard to stop being a crew chief.

He'd done the same thing for his blood brother a thousand times in another life. In that life they had both been kids wearing Marine fatigues and the airplane was a hulking F-4 Phantom, not a sagging, World War II Stinson observation airplane. The airplane, found abandoned during one of their many desert scrounging trips, was older than either of them.

The two men had been more than friends almost since the day they were born. Tipton's father and Longfeather's mother both lost their spouses early in life so they raised their kids as one big family. As he watched Sam's long hair and beard blowing in the propeller slip stream, Longfeather realized, as he often did, that he loved his friend. And with love comes worry. Longfeather knew Tipton had a problem and it wasn't getting any better.

He stepped back, as Sam brought the power up and carefully guided the airplane through the junk pile of machinery, rusting antique cars and derelict airplanes.

Longfeather watched the airplane lift off the abandoned stretch of road behind the adobe then, abruptly, drop out of sight over the edge of the mesa. The Apache laughed out loud. Tipton was already messing with Mandell's head. Mad Dog would be lucky if he got to Flagstaff without displaying his lunch on his ill-fitting silk shirt.

The clear air at that altitude exaggerated the golden hue of the setting sun, giving it a thick, almost syrupy texture. It coated everything in sight.

Sam looked down and watched shadows deepen, their edges clearly defined by each small valley or arroyo. The sun angle flattened still further and dying rays skipped off the high points. Barren hilltops turned pure gold. Hollows went dead black.

With Mad Dog Mandell happily sniffing the upholstery of his new car far behind, Sam Tipton eyed the rapidly-changing light show below. He couldn't resist the invitation. He eased the nose down, bleeding off altitude to become part of the sunset.

As the airplane settled into a narrow, rocky canyon, Sam felt that old feeling. His mind was somewhere out in front of the airplane. It was snaking down the twisting, aspen-lined canyon, plotting the path he must follow to keep from becoming an insignificant splotch against a cliff. Left, right. Up, down. All at the same time. His mind was that of the red-tailed hawk. The airplane ceased to exist and his mind raced down the canyon completely unencumbered by the mechanics of the rattling old machine around him.

He pulled up and dropped over the crest of a gentle, tree-covered ridge and found himself between tall cliffs racing towards the open end of a box canyon. The sun fell a few more degrees and the shallow canyon gathered the light, its grassy floor becoming a luminescent green. At the far end, where the valley fell off the edge of the mesa, the light accented straight lines which broke the natural flow of a cliff. Man had been there before. Nature never makes a straight line.

As he closed on them, the lines quickly constructed themselves into a tall, stone structure. His mind first identified it as an ancient Indian cliff dwelling. In seconds, however, it became a building of much later vintage. A limestone mine building turned gold by the sunset. Sam reduced power and banked around to keep the building in sight.

Something about the old building touched Sam. It stood alone, but proud. It had watched thousands of sunsets and, judging from its isolation and age, Sam knew it had watched most of those sunsets alone.

The sun dipped another few degrees and shadows raced beneath the old airplane to invade the valley. Darkness was minutes away, so Sam bent the Stinson around and pointed its nose towards Pitacho. It had been a long day.

Tipton felt his way through the adobe's darkness, eventually finding a large switch. It made a loud clacking sound and light bloomed from one corner of the shop.

He dropped heavily down on the end of his cot, one hand unconsciously caressing a clear plastic bag sitting on the cedar stump night stand. It held a pair of shined boots.

He stared at the boots for a second. The shine had been fresh ten years earlier. He pictured Marilyn's hands as they expertly brought the leather to a low, pleasing gloss. They hadn't been worn since that day. And they hadn't left his sight since that day.

He hit the switch again and flopped back onto the cot to stare into the darkness overhead. Then, for no reason, the old mine building in the hills presented itself in Tipton's mind. The image didn't go away until sleep took its place.

Eight

Secretary of Commerce Foster Ward stood at his office window enjoying the view. It was a good view, not a great view, but a good one. Certainly better than the Secretary of Transportation's, but not as good as that enjoyed by the Secretary of Defense. Being in the corner office let him view the Smithsonian Mall at an angle between two marble and glass office monstrosities. Looking the other way, he could catch a glimpse of the capitol building.

Not a bad view at all. Having that kind of view in D.C. was another way of signaling the world how much power he had. At least he had power for another two years, at which point this particular President would be out of office and out of terms. Being a political appointee had its downsides. It had been nearly six years, but not long enough for Secretary of Commerce Foster Ward to feel secure in the financial future he had so painstakingly built for himself.

He had to keep working on that future. The day the next President was being inaugurated, Foster Ward would be crossing the Gulf of Mexico at 30,000 feet, heading south, very far south, to enjoy the fruits of his extra-curricular activities. Even as a Senator, he'd seen the opportunities. And he had seized them. As Secretary of Commerce, he had even more opportunities. He knew who had what to sell. He had access to the information because it was part of his job. He saw the information. He took the information. He sold the information. If this Cobalt Blue thing worked, his future would be secure. Soon it would be adios to politics. Hello to well-financed, high-profile retirement.

Hands folded behind him, the tall, graying ex-Marine pilot rocked gently back and forth onto his heels. He'd been smart to turn down the offer to run for vice-president. It would have slowed him down too much. It would have focused too many eyes on him too much of the time. No, Secretary of Commerce was just right.

He was the uncle everyone depended upon to do a certain job, but was too "slow" to be included in serious family discussions. That suited Foster Ward just fine.

The office intercom buzzed. A firm female voice announced, "Mr. Anderson to see you, sir."

"Send him in, Susan."

He heard the oversized, polished walnut door behind him open, but didn't turn to look. He continued to enjoy his view for several reasons. First, by not acknowledging the visitor immediately, they knew he was in charge. It put them in their place. He smiled again. In this case, the visitor was his chief of security, Brad Anderson. Anderson had been in management at the FBI when Ward found he shared his own unique view of financial security and how to attain it. Ward hired Anderson away from the Bureau but was always careful to keep him in his place, as one would a well-trained, but potentially vicious guard dog.

Slowly Ward turned and motioned towards a conversation area. Anderson sat down on the glossy leather couch facing the coffee table. Ward dropped into the matching arm chair next to it.

"Okay, Anderson, what do we have on the Cobalt Blue thing?" Ward didn't waste time. "If this is a real deal, I want to move on it, right now."

Ward leaned forward in his chair to make sure Anderson understood his next statements. "Although it wasn't designed as a weapon, Cobalt Blue could well be the most effective tool a terrorist ever had. It's small enough for a person to easily carry and powerful enough to totally erase a square mile for eternity."

He paused for effect, "And I want it."

Ward's eyes were staring into space above Anderson's head. He was seeing his future. "I, we, can make a fortune with this. This will easily be the biggest deal we've ever made. I, we, can retire with this one."

He returned his stare to Anderson, "I know any number of overseas terrorists and right-wing political groups that would pay millions for Cobalt Blue. Millions!" As he said the words, his voice couldn't hide his excitement and he didn't try.

Fixing Anderson with his eyes, Ward asked, "Now, where is this thing and how soon can we get it?"

"I wish we knew more than we do right now. Our contact swears he has it. But, I don't know whether we can trust him or not. When he was with the Bureau he was much less than perfect, but he also knew how to work the angles. Another point in his favor is that he wouldn't have called me unless he had something solid. Besides, he didn't try to squeeze me for money. He wasn't going for quick cash and he wouldn't tell us where he is. So he sounds serious."

Anderson glanced down at some notes he had scribbled from Frederick's file before continuing. "He was trying to be cute, but he's been out of the game too long. He didn't realize how easy it is for us to back track phone numbers. He called us from a pay phone in an obscure town in Arizona. I'm assembling a crew right now to pick him up."

Secretary Ward leaned his head against the high back of the arm chair. His eyes were closed, but he was listening intently. The fingers of his left hand idly twisted the Annapolis ring on his right hand. He was unaware of the habit.

"What are the chances, if we find this thing, of it still working?" Ward didn't change position or open his eyes as he asked the question. The ring was still twisting.

"Sir, my people tell me that because it was a test unit, it was designed to be extremely simple and entirely mechanical. There seems to be no reason it shouldn't still work. This assumes it wasn't damaged or anything."

Ward slowly raised his head and opened his eyes to look directly at his chief of security and said, "If this thing works, or even looks like it might work, it's worth a great deal of money. More than you can imagine and I have several buyers in mind."

Anderson leaned back and spoke slowly, "Aren't you worried, they'll bring the unit back here and use it in D.C.?"

Ward smiled, "Oh, there's always that possibility." Ward's voice was whimsical. Amused. "Most of the people I am dealing with, however, are more monetary oriented. Their goals are money, not politics. Most of them anyway. They are more likely to shut down a rival company's mining operation. Or maybe disrupt the gold market by erasing a huge gold reserve. However, if it is headed to our own backyard, I'm certain they'll give us ample warning so we can be on a goodwill trip somewhere." A soft chuckle escaped his lips.

He stared through Brad Anderson as he thought for a second. "The crew you're sending? Make certain they don't know exactly what the apparatus is. But, make very certain they know how much they'll be paid if they're successful. We want to give them an incentive to succeed."

Leaning back in the chair, Ward closed his eyes and continued. "With any luck, we won't need your crew again. Once Cobalt

Blue is in our hands, arrange to have them removed. When this is all over, I want only you and I to know anything about Cobalt Blue. There will be no witnesses. No one."

With that, Ward rose and walked quickly to the window to renew his appreciation of his view. Anderson took the cue and moved quietly out of the room. Hand on the doorknob, he remembered the Secretary's emphatic tone about there being no witnesses. Subtle worry lines formed slowly on his face.

Ward let his gaze slowly swing west towards L'enFant Plaza. He began working on plans to reduce the final number of witnesses to zero.

Nine

The quarters scattered across the dark phone booth's floor like a bunch of chickens with a coyote in their midst.

"Goddammit!" Frank Frederick was completely out of patience. "Wait a minute, operator, I dropped my damn change! Yeah, I know, just hang on a minute. Just a goddamn minute!"

Frederick was so frustrated he was on the verge of screaming. In desperation, he let the phone dangle and got painfully down onto his knees to pick the quarters off the dust-covered pavement. The booth's light looked as if it had died sometime around 1950 and only the light from the parking lot helped him ferret out maverick quarters.

He was cursing himself for not thinking to call overseas in the first place. The call to Anderson in Washington had been a waste of time. This one would not be. Although he hadn't spoken to the terrorist known as Kwan for many years, Frederick knew he would be in the market for something like Cobalt Blue. And there was no mistaking Kwan's intentions. He always did what he said he would. That was definitely not the case with the assholes in Washington. They were small-time punks compared to Kwan.

Frederick captured more quarters and yelled into the dangling receiver, "Here, I'll give 'em to you as I pick 'em up."

Still on his knees, he reached up and shoved an endless stream of quarters through the slot until no more lay beneath him.

Struggling to his feet, he cradled the phone in his neck.

The flat, uninvolved voice of the overseas operator told him his call was going through. Frederick glanced around the abandoned filling station. A finger was stuck in his ear to block out the interstate traffic noise overhead. He congratulated himself for thinking to drive out of town to make the call. People might have noticed him feeding a bucket of quarters into the phone in front of Roberta's.

A quiet woman's voice answered the phone in a language Frederick wasn't certain he recognized. It made no difference.

"English! Speak English. Is Mr. Kwan there?" Frederick was impatient but still smiled. He knew his man's name wasn't Kwan, but that's what Frederick knew him as.

The answer came back in English with a lilting Asiatic accent. Frederick couldn't place the accent either. The female said Mr. Kwan wasn't there, but she'd give him a message if she saw him. Who, the voice wanted to know, was calling.

In Frederick's mind the image of the speaker alternated between being an oriental porcelain doll with the features and demeanor of a trusting child to a sly faced, Asiatic dragon lady.

She'd give him a message, when she saw him! That phrase told Frederick the number was still good.

"Tell him Frank Frederick called and remind him of our dealings in a small cafe´ in Nogales, Mexico. I'll be waiting." He read off the number on the pay phone, the voice thanked him very politely and the line clicked silent.

Frederick looked across the parking lot. An oily puddle was beginning to develop under his sagging RV. He leaned against the dirty glass, his hand resting on the phone.

He figured it would take two minutes for the phone to ring. It took less than thirty seconds.

Frederick yanked the phone off the hook, "Ah, Mr. Kwan. How nice to talk to you. Yes, it has been a very long time."

The voice at the other end was courteous and very cool. "Why," it asked, "are you calling me after so many years?"

Frank Frederick didn't like his attitude, but chose to ignore it. There was too much at stake. "In Nogales, you said if I had anything you might be interested in to call, so I'm calling."

The voice wanted to know what made Frederick think he had something Mr. Kwan would want.

"Listen, I know you and your business better than you think I do and believe me, this is something right down your alley," Frederick said.

Remembering that it wasn't his money paying for the call, Frederick took his time in describing the assembly which had been code-named Cobalt Blue. He went into great detail as to how it was designed and built and the circumstances under which it disappeared. He forgot to mention the part his own negligence played in its disappearance.

He also neglected to say that he not only didn't have it, but didn't even know where it was. He told himself, however, he'd soon have it in his possession. It was only a small stretch to say he had it.

"Come on, I'm not going to name a price," Frederick said,

"This thing is priceless and you know it. If I had a brain in my head, I'd hold an auction. You aren't the only game in town, you know."

Kwan hadn't hung up during the protracted explanation and had said little. Frederick liked that. It meant he had him hooked. The tired ex-agent was feeling confident enough to push the negotiations a little harder.

"So, if you want it, name a price and, if it's good enough, it's yours. If not, I'm gone and you'll never hear from me again."

Frederick fidgeted as he listened. His wife was sleeping in the RV. The last thing he needed was her staggering across the pavement and screaming at him through the glass. He'd already decided that whatever Kwan said, he'd ask for double. If Kwan hesitated, he'd hang up immediately, wait one day to give Kwan time to reconsider and then call him back.

Then the educated voice with only a trace of accent made Frederick an offer. The ex-agent couldn't see his own eyes open in amazement and he couldn't stop himself from blurting the words. "Four million?"

The words leaped out before he even knew he was going to say them. He was prepared to bargain for a hundred thousand dollars and would have taken half that. Then Kwan offers him four million!

Instant cold sweat on his face and under arms. He was in over his head. Four million dollars and he hadn't even started negotiating it up. Jesus!

He held the phone up in front of his eyes. He half-expected to see Kwan's sinister smile through the receiver. Jesus! Four million bucks! He slammed the receiver back on the hook and fell back against the door of the phone booth. The night was cool, but he was sweating all over. Goddamn! Four million dollars!

He struggled with the door, finally getting it open. Then the phone rang and he jumped so hard he squirted the rest of the way through the jammed door. Then it rang again. And again.

Frank Frederick tried to shut his ears to the ringing as he walked quickly towards the dark RV. Four million bucks! The words kept ringing through his mind. Jesus!

A phone was still ringing in a dark phone booth in Arizona when an average-height man of indeterminate age, thirties possibly forties, ran the palms of both hands down the sides of his head. Small refined features. Tight skin. No facial fat of any kind.

The long hair smoothed to a gloss-black surface as the hands passed. The phone receiver lay on his desk, the ringing clearly audible. He swiveled his chair around to face a computer keyboard behind him. Fingers danced on the keys. He waited a few seconds. Green letters poured onto the screen. They contained the address of the Arizona pay phone at the other end of the ringing. The Asian man known as Kwan smiled. Close enough.

He touched a brass button on his desk. Instantly an oriental rice-paper panel slid open and a smiling young girl stepped through. She kept her almond-shaped eyes focused on the floor. Her hands were clasped in front of her kimono.

"Phoenix, Arizona with the usual." The girl understood completely and backed quickly out the door. It slid silently shut behind her.

Kwan leaned back in his chair and smiled. It had been a long time since he had visited the American southwest. Like so many of his countrymen, he had a fascination with the area. There was something of the samurai in the image of the lone cowboy fighting for right. There was also something of his culture in the other side, in the dark side of the cowboy legend. Where there was good, there was always evil. The interface between the two was where huge profits were made.

Frederick was a fool. But a fool with an artifact worth retrieving. And a fool who would be unable to resist the bait he had dangled. Frederick would call again. And Kwan would be ready.

Ten

Roberta Rodreguez stood behind the bar and peered through the smoke at the noisy crowd. It was her domain and the regulars all knew that beyond a shadow of a doubt. The newcomers, what few there were, found that out quickly enough.

At an even six feet, Roberta was hard to miss. Especially since the four-plus decades since her birth had been spectacularly good to her. Her jeans worked hard at containing tightly curved hips and the sleeveless denim shirt had to be oversized to enable it to house a Rubenesque bustline. The worn, leather biker's vest with the Harley-Davidson emblem embroidered on the back couldn't be fastened in the front, even if she tried. The vest hung to her hips with an interruption on the right where the well worn cocked-and-locked .45 Colt automatic rode high on her hip.

Her full, black hair accentuated her olive skin and features which captured the best of her Navajo and Hispanic heritage. The hair flowed easily to her shoulders over her ears, partially hiding the jagged, vertical scar just behind her left cheekbone. That was the reason for the .45. No man would ever harm her again, and that man would harm no one again.

She smiled a warm and very wicked smile as she spotted a familiar form materializing out of the dark.

"Hey, Cowboy, you're lookin' good. Heard you took a bath." As she spoke, she reached quickly across the old oak bar, its top polished ebony smooth by a century of sliding shot glasses. She grabbed Sam Tipton by the front of his shirt and pulled him halfway across the bar.

"Would I be interested in the reason you cleaned up, Tipton? Somethin' you might want?" Her voice was deep and sultry.

Her coal black eyes were dancing as she held Tipton's face a few inches from her own. Sam was amused. The invitation was clear and a dusty cowhand on the next stool laughed out loud. He elbowed a gnarled, graying friend wearing a ragged, straw cowboy hat and they laughed together. They hid their jealousy well.

Tipton ignored them and kept his eyes locked on Roberta's, their noses nearly touching. A quick smile played at the corners of his lips. He had trimmed his beard back to a socially-acceptable length and his usually wild and ratty hair was pulled back into a short ponytail. He called it his Sunday-go-to-meeting do. Most of all, he didn't stink. Tonight, he liked himself for a change. He knew that would probably change by morning, but for the time being, he was satisfied.

"Well, darlin'," Sam's eyes were flicking back and forth, flirting with Roberta's, "now that you mention it, yes there is somethin' I want."

He smiled softly and both hands came around to cradle Roberta's head, his hands sliding dove-tail fashion into her hair. By this time, drinks at the bar were forgotten and every face within earshot was focused on the couple playing obvious, and very public, love games. The patrons were so enthralled by the display, they were forgetting to talk and a subtle wave of silence settled first at the bar and rippled back across the floor.

"Yes, Mister Tipton?" Roberta tilted her head slightly, her lips brushing Tipton's nose as she whispered, "And what would that be?"

Ears the full length of the old industrial building-cum-desert-saloon, craned to hear the barkeep's throaty whisper and the expected answer.

Sam Tipton tightened his fingers in her hair and drew her to him. Their lips met in a long, hard, screen-worthy kiss. Then he firmly yanked her face back and stared at her. Her eyes were smoldering and setting fire to every male heart in the bar.

"You know what I want, woman!" His stage whisper was demanding and Roberta Rodreguez nodded. But, he had to voice it for her to obey.

"Two enchiladas, one beef, one chicken, and a gallon of Cervesa."

"You got it, Cowboy!" The dark-haired temptress whirled to disappear towards the kitchen. An entire room full of horny bikers and desert rats was left hanging in mid-air. A collective sigh filled the saloon and the roar of conversation and drinking immediately returned.

Sam slowly turned around on the bar stool, a beer in his hand and a greasy empty plate on the bar behind him. The subtle glow was building at the base of his skull indicating the second pitcher of beer was just beginning to work its magic. He idly watched the crowd and noted a squat, older man stepping through the door. The man wore the flowered-shirt uniform worn only by tourists. A dumpy old blonde, obviously irritated, followed a few seconds later. She studied the floor as if trying to decide whether to shuffle through the layer of peanut shells or pick up her feet and crush her way through. The man was in a hurry. The woman wasn't. The Fredericks were a painful couple to watch. Some relationships should never be continued and it took Sam only a few seconds to recognize the signs.

"That's some way of ordering food, mister."

Tipton turned his head at the voice. He recognized the round, smooth-cheeked, mid-thirties face only because he'd seen it at the bar several times in the last month. It didn't belong to one of the regulars. A hand was stuck out in his direction, a practiced grin behind it.

"Hi, I'm Ted Fowler. Real estate's the game." Sam took his hand and nearly laughed.

"What in the hell are you doing here, Fowler? Slumming?" Tipton replied.

As he spoke, Sam surveyed the cheap, poorly-fitting sports jacket and even cheaper, even more poorly-fitting toupee. The image of a squirrel's nest flitted across his mind. He smiled. Nope, this guy wasn't slumming. He was at his correct social level, but definitely out of his social element. The plaid jacket couldn't have stood out more amongst the jean jackets, leathers and cowboy hats, if it had been on fire.

"No actually, I'm prospecting," Fowler said.

"You don't look like no damn prospector." Sam laughed again. There were probably a half-dozen real prospectors in the inebriated crowd and none of them wore plaid jackets. Most were desert-worn shadows and looked worse than Sam on his very worse day. The desert does that to people who go looking for dreams where there aren't any.

"No, I'm just looking for real estate, land, that type of thing. Say," Fowler made an effort to engage Sam with a serious look, "you wouldn't have any land to sell would you?"

This time Sam couldn't help himself. The beer had lubricated his inhibitions to the point the laughter came out with a slight hysterical edge to it. It started as a giggle and blossomed into a long, belly laugh. Sam Tipton was in the process of disappearing to be replaced by his hops-fueled alter ego.

"Hey, Roo-berr-ta!" Sam threw himself across the bar and

grabbed her hand, pulling her into the conversation. "This guy wants to know if I have any real estate to sell!"

He was laughing uncontrollably.

Roberta recognized the signs. Her favorite patron was getting heavily into Saturday night. She reminded herself to take his car keys in a few minutes.

"Tell him, Roberta. Tell him what a land baron I am!" Sam couldn't stop the residual giggles.

Sam turned to face Ted Fowler, real estate magnate in the wrong place, and said, "Fowler, look around you. You stupid fuck! This entire damn mountain is probably for sale, if you could find the owner, that is. It's all fucking worthless!

"Hey, Roberta!" Sam's voice soared to the far end of the bar where the shapely barkeep had moved to rack up glasses. "Do you even know who owns this dump?"

Roberta Rodreguez ignored him.

"Fowler, I'll bet there aren't five people in this damn town who actually own the places they live in. Shit, I'm squatting in the square adobe at the end of the street and I'll guaran-goddamn-tee you no one knows who owns it or the land it sits on."

Sam was feeling the beer and grabbed a third pitcher. Ignoring his glass, he took a long pull directly from the pitcher. He stood and loudly addressed the assembly of bikers and desert dwellers, "Hey, ev'y body! Ted Fowler's a real estate man. And he's full of shit! And he thinks we have somethin' to sell!"

His voice rose to a high, hysterical, slurred wail. "Ted Fowler's totally fucked!"

In a flourish, Tipton whirled and snatched the toupee off the astounded real estate man's head. "He's fucked! And he's bald!"

Tipton was laughing hysterically and pounded the top of the bar with the palm of his hand. Each time he hit it, spilled beer spurted out in all directions.

Ted Fowler was bright red with embarrassment and jumped up several times trying to retrieve his toupee from Tipton's up-stretched hand. Finally giving up, he stomped through the crowd. Stopping at the first biker he passed, he whipped out several one-hundred dollar bills.

Shoving the bills in the brutish biker's face he said, "It's yours if you smash that drunk's goddamn face in."

The biker sneered at the real estate man, his bloodshot eyes traveling up and down Ted Fowler's short frame. "Fuck off little man, I don't like you! Your jacket either. But, your wig's cute."

The biker roared with laughter and an embarrassed Ted Fowler pushed his way through the laughing crowd and out the door. He nearly knocked Crazy Charley Yee off the front porch as he stormed out.

Frank Frederick sat in a far corner table, unaware of Tipton's rapidly deteriorating sanity on the other side of the crowd. His mind was elsewhere. Images danced across his mind. Some were old, nearly fifty years old. Others were as fresh as that afternoon. A lacquered, birch carrying case figured prominently in each. Frederick barely tasted the beer as it ran down his throat.

May Frederick pushed her rickety chair back against a cut-stone wall and did her best to rise above it all. She nervously flicked at her dress with the back of her hand, trying to keep the peanut shells off her lap. Her husband threw them in every direction each time he reached into the big pile of whole peanuts resting in the middle of the table. She watched with disgust as the tall, female barkeep drifted from table to table with a huge tin grain scoop full of peanuts. She stopped and replenished a table each time she spotted a pile that was running low.

This was not May Frederick's kind of fun. She frowned at her husband. In the best of times, she seldom conversed with him, but the general din combined with the country music blaring from an unseen juke box made thinking, much less conversation, impossible. She was not a happy woman.

Frank Frederick didn't notice her mental state and wouldn't have cared if he had. Charley Yee and Cobalt Blue was all he could think about. He barely heard the roar of the crowd around him. Bikers, miners, Indians and cowboys. All of them drunk. He didn't care about them either.

"Hey, May," Frank Frederick yelled, but not loud enough for his wife to actually hear him. "We're going to stay in this town for a while. I think I like it."

May Frederick couldn't hear him but knew she didn't like what he was saying because he had a half-smile on his face. She dismissed him with a brief wave of her hand.

"Yeah, okay, Frank. Whatever!"

Sam Tipton leaned forward with both hands above him against the wall. A high pressure golden stream played on the corroded surface of the urinal trough in front of him.

"Aaahh!" The pressure release sent little pangs of joy shooting through his muscles. He'd often said the rush of a much-needed piss was one of the truly underrated physical pleasures of life. At that moment he rated it well above mediocre sex and on a par with great sex.

"Yeah, man, I know what you mean," the big biker said from the position next to him.

Sam had been caught up in his own pleasure and hadn't heard him clearly. He turned. "Say, what?"

"Hey, you fucking drunk, watch what the hell you're doing!" The biker danced out of the way of the waving stream of recycled beer. He stared with disgust at the moisture running down his leather pants. He hadn't moved quickly enough.

"You stupid mother-fucker!"

Sam's urinary revelry was rudely interrupted. In seconds he found himself outside what laughingly passed as a restroom at Roberta's, headed for the rest of the Saturday night crowd with his pants still unzipped. The biker swore loudly and continuously as he dragged Tipton by his collar and belt like a big, limp scarecrow. The laughing crowd parted to let them through.

The beer had reduced Tipton's ability to express himself to the universal grin of the totally wasted. He didn't even feel himself being dragged through the front door.

"Get the hell out of the way, you fucking crazy Indian!" The biker elbowed Charley Yee out of the way and put his considerable bulk behind hurling the giggling form of Sam Tipton off the curb and into the street. Tipton landed hard, but was too limp and numb to actually be hurt.

Charley Yee leaned against the post and smiled down at one of his few friends, as Sam Tipton rolled over to lay on his back in the street. Then, still giggling, Tipton struggled to his feet and tried to focus his wavering eyes on the Indian.

"Hey! Charley...Let's go get drunk!"

Charley Yee stopped smiling long enough to sit down on the curb where he could observe his friend more closely.

"You're already drunk," Yee pointed out. Tipton was one of the few who commanded the Apache's attention when he spoke.

"Charley, what're you talkin' about? How drunk is drunk?" Tipton asked.

"Look at me, Charley, I'm still standing. And look in here!"

Sam Tipton had both index fingers pointing down on the top of his head. His words slowed and ran into one another as he said, "Look in here, Charley. I'm still thinking. My goddamn brain's still working. It still hurts, Charley Yee!"

His voice thinned as the imagined pain worked its way into his words.

"It still hurts to think, Charley. And I don't want it to hurt," Tipton half-whined."So, there you have it, Charley Yee." Sam Tipton skipped over the momentary glumness and smiled brightly. He was standing still but weaving like a spindly tree in a soft breeze. "My head's still working. I'm still standing. Therefore, I'm not drunk. At least I'm not drunk enough.

"Time to gets some more." Sam tried aimed one foot at the high curb, headed in the direction of the door. "Time to gets...."

His legs gave out and Sam Tipton sagged towards the curb. Charley Yee's arms were there before he hit.

Fighting to stay upright, the two struggled towards the alley leading to Roberta's back lot, Crazy Charley Yee said, "Night's over Cowboy Sam. Time to sleep it off again."

It would not be the first time Charley Yee had put his friend to bed in the old Willys. He knew it would not likely be the last.

Ted Fowler's fingers drummed on the desk as he waited for the phone to answer. Globe, Arizona wasn't a big town, but even its Gila County Assessor's office was bound to be busy, so he'd wait. But, he was impatient. He worked on weekends prospecting for cheap land, so he was usually late getting into the office on Monday. But not this Monday. He had something he had to do. He was going to mix a little pleasure with a lot of business.

The fingers of one hand rested on a county tax plat book. The data block in the corner identified it as covering the area around Pitacho, Arizona.

A voice answered.

"Stephanie, this is Ted over at Fowler's Real Estate. Yeah, I'm doing fine. Great! Listen, I need you to run some ownership and tax status checks for me, when you get the time."

He droned on for several minutes giving block and lot numbers, then listened for a few more minutes. While he waited, he played nervously with the back edge of his toupee, making certain it flowed into what little natural hair was left. The hair piece was his spare and it had never fit right. Thinking about the loss of the old one still made the back of his neck burn and turn red.

"Yeah, I know they are old and some may have gone for tax sales. I need as many current owners as you can find me. Also, if any are in default, I need that too.

"Great! Great! Okay, just print them out and I'll be over later this morning. Oh, yeah, I need the dates of the next tax sales, too.

"Oh, no, no great rush," he lied, "but I would appreciate what you can do for me."

Ted Fowler smiled as he hung up the phone. He needed a big old adobe building like he needed another belly button. But, what the hell. Why not mix a little business with his pleasure.

Eleven

Frank Frederick sat in a far corner of the large, open expanse that was Roberta's and watched her. He admired the tall girl's spunk. And her body. Her drinking establishment was becoming a nightly stop for him.

Frederick had to look hard to study her outline in the dim lighting. The old, industrial tin shades with their small, yellowed bulbs hung low overhead. They kept their light close to the floor but were hard pressed to illuminate even a small part of the large floor area. Stray bits of light escaped to the two-story ceiling helping Frederick guess the age and purpose of the building.

It obviously hadn't been intended as a bar.

Massive wooden beams ran from front to rear. They were intersected once in the middle with an equally massive girder supported on stout wooden posts. The posts were as big around as any of the drunks milling aimlessly among them. Above the beams he could barely make out the remains of industrial fittings which had ceased serving their purpose many decades earlier. A mill? Possibly a blacksmith or iron-working facility?

The floor beneath the thick layer of peanut shells was as stout as the rest of the building. Broad, heavy boards, their surface polished into an uneven gloss by decades of machine oil and heavy boots. The surface as solid as concrete. The floor would outlast every breathing soul standing on it.

The seventy-one-year-old ex-agent was enjoying the solitude of being in a large boisterous crowd alone. Amidst the general din echoing off the massive stone block walls was a loud, personal silence. A sound which normally intruded on his every thought wasn't there.

May Frederick had discovered a TV set at the rundown little general store on the edge of town. The store's owner, a small, bewildered-looking old Italian, claimed to be an ex-advertising executive from Secaucus, New Jersey. Frank believed him. The claim was too outrageous not to be true. Frederick didn't care where he was from. As long as he was willing to put up with his wife and her sit-coms, he could be from the moon.

Frank Frederick leaned back in his chair. He was as relaxed

as he had been in months. His feet rested easily on an ancient oak bent-wood chair. His hands were cupped around a cold beer which rested comfortably on his rounded belly. As relaxed as he appeared, however, a whirlwind of thoughts raced through his mind. Charley Yee. Cobalt Blue. Charley Yee. Yee was the reason he had selected that particular chair at that particular table. By leaning back, he could look through the open front door at an angle and watch the old Indian as he sat on the curb celebrating.

Charley Yee was, alternatively rocking and drinking. He stared at an invisible horizon where the sun had set. He was in a world of his own and unaware he was being carefully studied.

Frank Frederick was thinking hard. Scheming. Planning. Developing and rejecting scenarios that would give him the location of Charley Yee's "gods." Frederick told himself an inside joke and smiled: If Yee's gods were spending their time around Cobalt Blue, it wouldn't take much for them to become ex-gods.

As he thought of the assembly, he couldn't help but feel a glow deep inside. It was so close he could almost smell it. He felt its presence. But where? Frederick eyes seldom left the form of the rocking Native American who held the key to his future.

He had a plan, but he would need help. Glancing around at the crowd, he tried to identify someone he could trust. Not an easy task. As his eyes roamed the room, he couldn't help wondering at the disparate nature of the crowd. There was an equal mix of cowboy hats, biker's bandannas and long black hair with Native American adornments. He was an outsider and thoroughly aware of his status. They barely looked at him when he walked through the door, but he could read their thoughts in the fleeting stares each of the regulars aimed at him.

He would have to go elsewhere for help.

But, maybe not.

Frederick's view of Charley Yee was momentarily blocked by two young men. He recognized the look. They stood out in the bar as much as he did but for entirely different reasons. Short and muscular. Close cropped black hair. Sleeveless tee-shirts and wide bandannas around their heads. They gave up their identity by simply walking in. Street punks. Big city street punks.

They swaggered through the crowd. Banty roosters feeling their oats. They aimed themselves at the empty table next to Frederick. Frederick could see what they couldn't see behind them. Cowboy and biker alike laughed after the two had passed. They had not gone unnoticed and had not inspired universal affection towards themselves.

One yelled at Roberta as he swung his leg over the chair back and dropped into place. The other spun his chair around and rested his chin on the back as he chattered in rapid-fire Spanish. Frederick didn't have to see their pupils to know they were wired. Speed knows no racial or cultural boundaries. It effects everyone the same.

"Eh, senorita, dos Cuervos." The short one laughed and started to slap Roberta on the rear. She grabbed his wrist and stared him down. He laughed the quick nervous laugh amphetamines inspire and looked over at his buddy. They both cracked up as if enjoying some hilarious private joke. Roberta dropped his arm and disappeared after their drinks.

Frederick liked what he saw. No one in the bar knew or liked the two and it would probably be the last time they would be there. They may be the help he needed to make his plan work.

"Hey, hombres, se habla Anglais?" The retired agent's voice cut through the noise. Frederick never claimed to be a linguist but he could order beer and sex in at least a dozen languages.

The two looked over at a pale, overweight old man and laughed their high-pitched laugh.

"Hey old man, do you speak Spanish?" The voice had only a trace of accent but liberal doses of sarcasm. "What you think, old man? We're so stupid we don't speak English?"

The youth was right. His English was much better than Frederick's Spanish.

Roberta arrived with their tequila and Frederick slapped a ten-dollar bill down on their table.

"Theirs are covered."

The young Chicanos showed no indication they had heard him but threw back their drinks before Roberta had disappeared from sight. They slammed the empty glasses upside down on the table in unison.

"Hey, old man, what you do that for?" The younger, and smaller, of the two asked. He looked to be barely out of his teens but was doing the talking for both. The other's eyes were constantly swiveling around watching the crowd. Frederick recognized the gang tattoo on the backs of both left hands.

"Let's just say it's the opening for a business offer,"

Frederick said.

"What makes you think we do b'ness with you?" The kid asked. "Besides, you smell like a cop. How about it, old man? You a cop?"

Frederick smiled and actually managed a small laugh, "No, I'm just a guy who needs a little help."

"What kind of help? We don't sell drugs to no people like you. It's bad for b'ness."

Frederick laughed again and signaled Roberta for another round. The young Chicanos relaxed a little, but never let their guard down.

As the drinks arrived, Frederick swiveled out of his chair to the empty one at their table and leaned forward to spell out what he needed. He laid most of the cash he had left for the month on the table and the youths broke out into wide, intense grins. Between the cash, the tequila and the drugs, they couldn't have stopped grinning, if they tried.

They liked the plan and would play along. This time it was Frank Frederick's turn to smile.

Sam Tipton caught an old guy's reflection in the bar mirror out of the corner of his eye. He stood out from the crowd and looked familiar.

As soon as he saw the reflection, Tipton made an instantaneous judgment. Sagging posture. Dull eyes. Drooping features. Tipton painted a mental picture of another's sad future. He was looking at a man in decline. Then he made yet another discovery: The face looked familiar because it was his own.

He laughed at the mistake. The lips in the mirror curved into the shaggy beard and he realized he didn't like the image. His mind had unwittingly painted an ugly self-portrait.

He squinted in the uneven light, and studied the man in the mirror, and tried to rationalize: the face wasn't that of a lost man. It was the face of a man in transition. A man recovering from a great loss. But, maybe he was just seeing what he wanted to see.

Face to face with himself, he realized that admitting a problem existed was the first step towards a solution. And he was freely admitting it. He had a drinking problem. That was the most important step. He had to start someplace and this was it! New resolve surged through his system. This night would end with him still standing. This would be his first step in a new direction.

He looked down at the drink in his hand. He'd finish this one and that would be it. Just this one.

"Hey Indian, we want your Gods!" The words skipped along so quickly even Jose Cuervo hadn't been able to slow them down. Amphetamines move at their own, unstoppable pace.

Hands on hips, the Hispanic youths stood in front of Charley Yee and Sam Tipton. They glared down at the pitiful-looking pair. The Apache and his friend were sitting on the curb, arms over each other's shoulders as they rocked in unison. A slow, mournful chant came from the inebriated Apache's barely moving lips. Tipton occasionally joined in with a bourbon-slurred "Yeah, brother!" or "Hallelujah!"

Frank Frederick leaned against the wall just inside Roberta's door, watching from the shadows. His plan was just beginning. He liked what he saw so far.

"Hey, Injun, what you doin'! Look at us!" The smaller of the two hissed at Charley Yee. The youth wavered slightly and his lips were contorted as they spit the words.

Charley Yee ignored him and stared at the far horizon.

The Chicano's forearm muscles danced as he impatiently clinched and unclenched his fists at his sides. The speed racing through his system had every muscle, every nerve on edge. He was unable to stop his eyes as they moved in jerky circles around Yee. His speed-frazzled nerves were irritated by everything. Even Roberta's always-welcomed neon bothered him. It especially irritated him that a scrawny-looking old Indian wasn't doing exactly what he wanted. How dare him! Back in the Barrio, everyone knew who was boss. His mind raced, his thoughts focused on this single Indian who didn't seem to realize who stood in front of him.

Sam was leaning against Charley Yee when the smaller Chicano motioned to the Indian and stepped back. His "bodyguard" stepped in, grabbed Charley Yee's loose-fitting old shirt and jerked him to his feet.

Tipton was caught unawares. He fell momentarily to the curb before scrambling awkwardly to his feet. He tried to focus on the sight of the larger Hispanic shaking his friend like a rag doll.

"Hey, you little shit..." Tipton stepped clumsily forward and tried to pull the two apart.

The Hispanic didn't even let go of Charley. He shot his left hand, palm open, into the middle of Sam's chest. Tipton fell into a backwards trot and landed in a heap on the sidewalk.

He sat up and re-focused his eyes. This time he saw the hand flashing back and forth. He heard the unmistakable sound of skin meeting skin as the Hispanic repeatedly slapped the old Indian across the face. After each slap, he'd put his nose to the Indian's face and scream at him.

The words made no sense to Sam. They wanted Yee's Gods. His numbed mind answered, what gods? Charley made up his own gods. Who wanted imaginary gods? Were these two Mexican kids crazy? Why were they hurting Charley?

Sam Tipton lunged off the curb, throwing himself at the Chicano youth, intending to hit him in the face with his fist. He stumbled across the street, right hand cocked back in a Keystone Cop pose as if to swing. The kid glanced at him and laughed. His free hand lashed out, his fist caught Sam directly in the nose and stopped him in his tracks.

The fist grew larger and larger in Sam's vision as if in slow motion. Then he was laying on his back. His view of the scuffle was transformed to an upward angle with the two outlined against the black night sky. The garish orange and blue neon painted them in grotesque shadows.

He lay on the gravel-strewn concrete, tasting his own blood running. He tried to get up, but his muscles wouldn't listen. Fists flashed and his friend cried out. Then Sam Tipton, ex-Marine, ex-engineer, ex-husband and father, saw the kid looking down at him between swings. He was laughing at him.

Sam saw himself in the kid's expression.

Sam Tipton wanted to help Charley Yee, but couldn't. He was incapable. And he knew it.

Frederick watched and smiled. He loved the way it was working out. The Indian and his drunken friend were getting the hell beat out of them. This was his chance. Most of Frederick's available cash was stashed in the small Chicano's back pocket. He couldn't stop grinning because that cash had bought him a winning ticket to the fight in progress.

The cash had bought him the chance to be a hero. To walk into the fight, throw a few fake punches and chase the tough guys from the city back to the Barrio, Charley Yee would have reason to thank him. And reason to trust him.

And reason to eventually introduce him to his gods.

Frederick glanced around the bar. The din of desert rats enjoying themselves overpowered Charley Yee's incoherent cries for help. Not a soul had noticed the commotion in the street. He smiled as he stepped through the door. He straightened his back as much as his years would permit and stepped off the curb. He was prepared to be the hero.

What he was not prepared for was the small, fast fist that materialized in front of him. He had just enough time to see the wild, dark eyes of a young man with far too much tequila mixed with his amphetamines to know what he was doing. Then the lights went out. It had seemed like a good plan at the time. But it hadn't worked.

As he lay on his back, Sam Tipton saw the old man stride into his field of vision. He idly watched as the other Mexican dropped the old man to the pavement with a single punch.

Tipton couldn't take his sagging eyes off the fists as they arced towards Charley Yee's face and into his stomach. His friend wanted to fall, but the Chicano held him up and kept hitting him. And hitting him.

Yee's screams filled Sam Tipton's head until the only sound on Earth was his own heart and Charley Yee's pleading voice.

His mind was so full of Charley's pain he barely heard the explosion of Roberta's .45 as it lit the night sky over her head. Then the huge pistol was pressed hard against the frightened kid's forehead. She removed it just long enough to fire another round into the air. Before she could bring it back down both of the Barrio punks were running hysterically down the street. A dark, wet stain spread down the pants of one.

Tipton's eyes swiveled around and saw the entire population of Roberta's standing on the curb. Some winced as Roberta and a cowhand helped Charley Yee to his feet and helped him into the bar. A few glanced at Frank Frederick stumbling down the street towards his RV. Some laughed at Sam Tipton laying in the street.

Then they were gone. Nothing but backs visible, as they pushed back inside. The entertainment was over.

Sam Tipton lay in the middle of the street covered with dust and his own blood.

The next sound he heard was his own voice screaming curses at himself while staggering between the buildings towards

Roberta's back lot. He wasn't so drunk that he didn't know he had let a friend down and he hated himself for it. He wanted to run away but where could he run that he wouldn't eventually come face to face with himself?

Roberta stepped out on the sidewalk just in time to see the old Willys sliding sideways through the dirt as Tipton riveted his foot to the floor. Even in the dark, the cloud of dust erupting from the alley in his path was clearly visible. The box-like old wreck leaped into the air when its big tires hit the concrete edge of Main Street. It bounced once then disappeared down an alley on the other side. The vehicle's lights reappeared briefly as it clawed its way up the incline behind the crumbling town. Then it was gone. Only the roar of its dual pipes echoing out of the dark said it was out there. Then they too were gone.

The tall saloon-keeper watched until Tipton's lights disappeared up the seldom-used dirt road she knew led up the mesa towards the rim. She frowned and stepped back inside. Charley Yee was badly broken up and would need her help.

Twelve

Tipton cursed the old truck. He cursed the rotten road. He cursed the hard, full moon staring down between the trees. He imagined it watching. And laughing at him. He stepped on the gas harder. Rocks and dirt spewed from under the old Willys, but it wouldn't move. Even though his brain was numb and barely able to function, he recognized a tree was laying across the road. And he recognized that no matter how much of the dark, rocky road his tires spit out behind him, he couldn't push the tree out of the way. So, he cursed the tree.

His headlights could see no further than the tree which, by then, was welded to the front bumper. The old vehicle had tried to be the little Willys that could. But it couldn't.

"Goddammit!" Sam cursed. Beaten by a lousy tree! Beaten again. Goddammit! The moonlight reflected off the rotting trunk. Just another dark barrier on life's rocky road.

"Jesus, goddamn Christ," Tipton mumbled to the world in general, "are you ever going to stop fucking with me?" If the gods were listening, they gave no indication.

"Okay, if that's the way it's gonna be!" In a single drunken motion Tipton switched off the engine, killed the lights and tumbled out to land in an uncoordinated heap on the road.

The moon painted his surroundings in silver and black shadows. Nothing had solid form. Standing dead trees from an ancient forest fire were scattered amongst the living and they danced in his vision as slim, gray ghosts.

The road was a vague, rude gash on the mountain's side. The moon refused to give it color because it was so overgrown and undefined. In its best day, it hadn't been much of a road. After decades of non-use, its legacy was nothing more than a narrow, rock-strewn path through the high pine forest. The moon shimmered off rock faces where miners of another time had blasted rock noses away to create a shelf for their road. Ground water seeped through the jagged scars. The Earth's own bodily fluids reflected the pale moonlight.

Tipton staggered around behind the Willys. He leaned against it and stared over the edge. Falling construction rubble had scraped a wide path through the trees several generations before. The moon's light couldn't penetrate the dark below. Seized by the urge, he unzipped and sent a golden stream out into the dark. He laughed uproariously when the moon turned it a sparkling silver. It disappeared from sight long before finding the ground.

"Crazy bastards!" His voice was slow and deep in his throat. It grumbled along barely audible above the cool silence of the night. "Didn't know shit 'bout building roads."

"Here, catch this!" His voice pierced the night in a hollow, uneven wail as he pitched a rock into the darkness. The sound of it hitting other rocks far below didn't come back to him for many seconds. He laughed.

"Yo, watch out, ol' Sam! You could definitely bust your butt down there!" He laughed again and grabbed the side of the truck for balance as one foot slipped. A dozen small stones rattled down the incline.

"Sure don't want no busted butts 'round here!" Sam kept his hold on the drip rail and slowly, one hand after another, worked his way to the open rear of the Willys and crawled in.

At that altitude the night air was cool and clear. And strong with the scent of pine. The moon's craters stood out as pale blue scars against a silver-white skin. Smooth plains bounced back much of the sun's light. Some of that reflected light flashed through thousands of miles of dead space to fall upon an old mining road which crept up a remote section of the Mogollon Rim.

When the light had started its journey, it was sun bright and hot beyond measure. Converted to moonlight and reflected down to northern Arizona, it became cold and lifeless. Very much like the creature huddled in the back of the old vehicle below.

As the temperature fell, so did Sam Tipton's desire for life. He had been there. He knew life. As he stirred in his sleep, his eyes fluttered open for a second. He saw the clear, clean outline of the moon watching him and he smiled.

His lips moved slowly and quietly, his soft words barely making it outside the open rear of the Willys.

His eyes fixed momentarily on the benign face of the moon and he whispered, "Hey, baby... Yeah, I love you too. And I'm coming. Just wait. Just a little longer. I'm coming."

Then his eyes fluttered closed.

Thirteen

A gray East Coast drizzle slithered down the glass panels of the French doors. They led out to a small garden adjacent to the equally small, but luxurious, oak and leather study.

Secretary Ward scowled as he shifted his attention from the cold outside to the cold inside. Cradling the telephone in his neck, he knelt down and pushed another split log into the fire. Hopefully it would catch quickly and dispel some of the chill.

The ringing in his ear stopped abruptly, replaced by a guttural female voice. It announced the name of the company in a tone so devoid of emotion that Staffelwerks, GMBH would have been better off using a computer. The voice matched the dreary atmosphere outside in the garden.

"Herr Steitz, please. Tell him Mr. Draw is calling." Ward knew the code name would hardly stand up to CIA scrutiny. It was probably unnecessary, but he didn't want his name floating around in the mind of a teutonic secretary who probably never cracked a smile and never forgot a name.

"Ah, yes, Herr Steitz, how good it is to speak to you. Yes, it has been a long time. Oh, I'm glad to hear your last purchase worked out so well for you." Ward poked at the fire as he spoke, bored with the preliminaries. He knew as soon as Steitz heard his name he would know what he wanted. He would know another "deal" was in the offing. He would also know the project couldn't be discussed over his business line.

"Yes, sir, I understand you're busy. Yes sir, I'm at my usual number. Thank you, I'll be looking forward to your call."

Ward thumbed the off button and waited. When the phone rang, Ward looked at his watch. It had taken the German industrialist less than a minute to return a trans-Atlantic call. Steitz knew the importance of responding quickly. If he didn't, he could well miss out on something. He didn't know what that something might be, but it would be of immense interest to him, or his American politician friend wouldn't be calling.

"Herr Steitz, what I have for you may be so important you may well consider offering me a partnership in your company, when I retire from politics." It was an opening gambit. It helped set the magnitude of the offer.

Ward explained the nature of the deal and the wonderful possibilities to be had with the apparatus he was offering for sale. He continued to poke the fire. Ward hated cold weather and the money from this project would be converted into a villa where it was warm and balmy three-hundred-sixty-five days a year.

When he finished the call, he yawned and put another log on the fire.

Ward listened to yet another call going through. He was already bored with the auction process, and this was only the fourth call of the afternoon.

He had told each interested party he couldn't ship Cobalt Blue for another two weeks. He was in no hurry to strike a final deal. He just set a minimum price so everyone knew whether they were in or out and waited for their offers. Only one had declined the offer to be included. The rest were players.

The phone was on its third ring when he decided this would be his final call. He didn't need to make any more.

This time the voice which answered was softly feminine with a touch of Asian accent. Ward smiled as he remembered who she worked for. This should probably have been his first call.

The young woman knew when she saw which line lit up which salutation to use. Each light meant a different line of business. There were no personal telephone lines. Her employer received no personal calls.

"Yamuchi Enterprises," she said softly and distinctly into the receiver. Chances were, the person on the other end knew far better than she the nature of Yamuchi Enterprises. All she knew was the phone might ring any time of the day or night and her employer, and lover, would want to know immediately. She put it right through to Mr. Yamuchi.

Kwan Yamuchi smiled when he heard who it was. It had been a busy few days for unusual business transactions. This was bound to be another.

"Tell him I will call him back later," he said into the intercom. As he spoke he was already dialing the number.

"Mr. Draw, how good to hear from you again." He made his voice sound as if he was smiling, when in fact, his face bore no expression at all.

"It has been some time and may I assume you have come to me with another of your usually fine pieces of merchandise?" Mr. Yamuchi listened as Foster Ward explained the nature of what he had to sell and what it was going to cost.

Yamuchi made notes on the yellow pad laying on his desk. He had just leaned back in his chair when something Ward said caused him to start forward. He quickly scribbled on his pad. The block letters spelled out "Cobalt Blue". He underlined it several times. It rang a bell, but he couldn't identify why.

As Ward spoke, Yamuchi turned and began entering data on his computer. It took perhaps half a minute for the machine to make a firm connection with a federal data base on the east coast of America. The screen was half full, with data still cascading down, when Yamuchi smiled at what he saw.

The information was not new to him. Only the code name, Cobalt Blue, was unfamiliar. It was the second time in a week he had reviewed that same information.

He smiled. Ward was doing his best to convince Kwan that his merchandise was worth ten million dollars. Kwan Yamuchi looked at the screen. He had already made an offer of less than half of that for the same item.

Ward ended his sales pitch. Kwan Yamuchi, known in many circles simply as Mr. Kwan, smiled. Ward had no idea he was walking in the footsteps of another salesman selling the same product.

"Thank you Mr. Draw, and I will be getting back to you." Kwan, had no intention of getting back with the American.

He did however, intend on owning the apparatus known as Cobalt Blue. In his hands such a tool would make him invaluable. If his very special clientele was advised that he had the ability to walk in and simply cause a pinpoint, any pinpoint, on a map to disappear, he could name his price. Any price.

Mr. Ward, AKA Mr. Draw, thought he knew how to deal with the darker forces of the world, but he was naive. Barely an infant, where such things are concerned. Kwan Yamuchi lived in that world. He was one of its leading warriors. And it's richest. He was not naive. He knew the true worth of Cobalt Blue as a tool of his trade.

Her kimono slid noisily to her feet and Kwan's slender, but powerful, hands glided about her smooth skin as she stood before him. She made no move other than a quiet smile of appreciation. A finger moved lightly between her small, firm breasts. The finger barely touched her skin, then circled back to dance gently with her nipples. As he touched her breasts, Kwan saw physical evidence he was achieving the desired effect. Her eyes fluttered closed for seconds at a time, as she began to move every so slightly in a rhythmic, undulating fashion.

When her eyes connected with his, he nodded. Her hands reached out, deftly untying his black silk kimono. It slid in a single motion over his taut, well-defined shoulders. Her own fingers began tracing the outlines of large, bizarre tattoos. They completely covered the upper part of his tightly-muscled torso like a dark blue, form-fitting shirt. As his kimono slid to the floor, it uncovered the indelible uniform of the Yakuza, Japan's cultural version of the Mafia.

In his youth, the Yakuza had been the family which had taken him off the street. They made him one of them. But Kwan had seen past the Asian Mafioso to something grander. Something with more edge and more personal satisfaction. And infinitely more personal gain. The Yakuza and their crude methods were a springboard. A place to start.

He had quickly trained himself in the skills necessary to became a black samurai for the dark side of society's upper crust. He became a highly-paid "specialist." His clients sat in boardrooms and parliaments and hired him to do the un-doable. In some cases, to do the unthinkable.

He stood and looked down at her head moving in a sensual rhythm back and forth below his waist. He smiled for many reasons. Ward's call had caught him just in time. A few hours later and he would have been on his way to Arizona not knowing exactly what it was he was looking for.

Ward's call confirmed the existence and possible usefulness of an item named Cobalt Blue. That was a reason to smile. That and the fact one of the finest concubines in all of Japan was building him to a climax that would be an erotic masterpiece.

He had many things to smile about.

Fourteen

The pony wasn't really wild, but it didn't want the three giggling children to gain a position on its back. It fidgeted and stomped, its eyes flickering from side to side. Its ears lay back. One child, a young Chiricahua Apache girl, her glistening black hair flowing halfway to her waist, sensed its fear. Gently, she cradled its nose in her arms and softly began singing.

"Hey, hey, hey little horse," she sang in her own tongue. "We want only to play, to make you our friend. Please don't be afraid."

The words flowed smoothly together, as if syllables in a long, pleasant sounding word.

The fire in the painted pony's eyes flickered out and his ears slowly rose to an erect position.

"Hey, hey, little horse."

Young Sam Tipton held the bridle for her. He glanced past the young girl at a tall young Apache barely into his teens. He sat astride the horse with confidence. His black hair was almost as long as his sister's and his jean-clad legs wrapped around the horse's bare belly. His hands were wrapped in its flowing mane.

Tipton nodded, "Okay, but be easy. He's scared."

The scene faded and became one of a pony running in circles, its world defined by the split-rail corral fence. Dust rose from the pony's flashing hoofs. Its eyes were dancing. It was having as much fun as the whooping, long-haired Chiricahua youth on its back and the other two chasing noisily behind.

The girl's voice rose above the boys' shouting, "Wait! Wait, you guys, come on! Wait!"

The smell of the corral's damp earth mixed with the musty odor of a well-groomed horse. Sam Tipton inhaled deeply and the aroma became laced with the fragrance of pine trees. Of the high mountains. Of the clean air and clean life enjoyed by few. It was the smell of home, and of belonging.

Then another smell intruded. It too was familiar. It was of coal black coffee standing deep in a sturdy mug which took two hands to hold. In his mind it sat on a clean, handmade pine table, the wood's natural white color fading towards a pleasing yellow, the result of many years and many meals.

The coffee smell flowed into his nostrils and flooded his mind causing the trio and their pony to vanish. The dream faded, Tipton moved his arm and became conscious of his body. It ached. As the sensations accompanying wakefulness touched the outer reaches of his body, he became aware of something laying over him, its edge riding lightly on his neck. Everything above it was cool and everything below was fuzzy warm. It felt good, even if his body didn't.

He recognized it as a blanket. He realized the smell of coffee had ignited enough of his senses to drag him out of a deep, ragged sleep. It had been full of images. Of fragmented memories, good and bad. It hadn't been a restful sleep.

Then another image stabbed him in his mind's eye: Charley Yee! The image was strong but unclear. Charley was being hurt. He could see that in his image. But, was it real?

His eyes were barely open and tried to focus on the peeled-pine rafters which formed a series of converging triangles over his head. He could see that the poles were all aimed towards a central point somewhere out of sight. Spaces between the poles were spanned by natural pine planking. His sleep-drugged mind hurt as it tried to remember. He knew the patterns.

He knew the patterns because he'd awakened to the same sight hundreds of times. But that had been in another life, when he was barely into his teens. At that time, watching the low morning light play with the ceiling patterns would have been part of a special privilege. His father had awarded him a special privilege and he had been allowed to sleep over at the Longfeathers' house.

The walls of the Longfeather home were large peeled-pine logs with a natural finish. The huge windows opened out over the edge of a wide canyon. The Longfeathers' back yard was the high desert and the pines and cedar which spilled up out of the canyon formed their front yard.

To young Sam Tipton, the Longfeathers' modernistic hogan had seemed very exotic. To him, each time he went to visit, it was if he was traveling across time to another planet. The fact it was within sight of his own house on his father's ranch which bordered the Reservation did nothing to dim the image.

His father, John, was a widower. Mrs. Longfeather's name literally translated as "Tall Woman" but the elder Tipton always called her Woman. She had lost her husband in a lumbering accident. Both had kids who eventually blended together until it was difficult to tell where one family left off and the other began. They had grown up as a single family with two names, Tipton and Longfeather. Sam had always known Tall Woman as Mom Longfeather. Her above-average height for her tribe was the legacy of a cavalry Captain so long ago. Both of her children were tall for Chiricahua Apaches.

Sam sat up in bed, his back against the log wall. It was cool and he pulled the blanket up around him. Remembering didn't come easy. In this case, the most recent memories, the last twenty-four hours, didn't come at all.

How, he asked himself, had he come to be in the Longfeathers' hogan? It was at least an hour's drive from Pitacho and that was when taking the shortcut which was a major adventure in the dark.

What about Charley Yee? Only fragments of images in which Charley was being hurt returned to him. The shame and the guilt, however, were crystal clear.

A single knock at the door, broke his chain of thought.

"Yeah!" Tipton's voice came out a twisted croak. It surprised even him. Joseph Longfeather's smiling face appeared through the barely-opened door.

"How about it Cowboy, you still alive?" He stepped through the door, his boots making a tight, hard sound against the bare wood floor. He thrust a steaming mug into Sam's hand. He then backed up and dropped into the lodge-pole chair in the corner. Sam's hand was shaking as he reached for the mug. He hoped Longfeather hadn't noticed.

Mug in hand, he pushed further back against the wall so he wouldn't spill what was obviously hot coffee. He then realized he was naked under the blankets.

"Jesus! Who put me to bed?"

Longfeather grinned, "I brought you in, but Mom put you to bed. What's a'matter? She powdered your bottom enough times when you were a baby. Gotten too good for her?"

Sam blushed and he ran a hand through his hair. It was clean. "Damn! She even gave me a bath. This is embarrassing!"

Longfeather laughed and said nothing. A silence settled between the two old friends.

For several long minutes, they drank their coffee, then Longfeather spoke.

"We have to talk. I mean really talk." His blue eyes looked

out at Sam from under deeply furrowed brows. Sam had seldom seen his friend's normally smiling face so serious. He knew where Longfeather was going. Sam interrupted.

"Yeah, I know. The drinking. I know." His voice was quiet.

Longfeather said, "Sam, I'm not the one to talk. We've tied it on together a lot of times, but..."

Sam held one hand up, cutting him off mid-sentence. He pivoted into a sitting position on the edge of the bed, the blankets twisted around him. "Yeah, I've said it to myself a dozen times. No! A thousand times. I'm a drunk. I don't just drink. I'm a drunk. In fact I'm the town drunk."

Hearing his own voice say it out loud in the sanctity of what was, in effect, his childhood home, made the words seem louder. And more damning.

"Yeah, I'm the resident drunk in a town where practically everyone is an alcoholic to one degree or another." The words gave the problem tangible form. They made it a living entity to be dealt with in any way necessary.

Reality became even more real when Longfeather said, "Yeah, you're a drunk. An alcoholic. And I wouldn't be doing you any favors if I didn't say something."

Longfeather stopped talking abruptly and dragged the heavy chair forward to cut the distance between the two.

"You're scaring the living hell out of me," Longfeather said. "I know you had a hard blow. We all loved Marilyn and Melissa. But Sam...that was nearly ten years ago. What would Marilyn say if she could see you? What would Melissa say if she saw you looking like this?"

Longfeather's face was only inches from Sam's. Sam could feel the words knife into a part of him he thought had died. His eyes misted over and he couldn't say anything.

Longfeather reached around and grabbed the long hair on the back of Sam's head, gently bringing him forward until their foreheads touched. "You can do this. Don't let yourself down."

Message delivered, Longfeather gave Tipton a loving tap on the top of his head with a closed fist and stood up. Sam was still looking down as Longfeather turned to leave.

Slowly he raised his head and said, "Thanks, brother."

Abruptly, Longfeather broke into a wide grin, "Shake a leg, now. Mom's got breakfast ready to go and she's dying to see you. She did, however, say something about you looking pretty ratty when I dragged you through the door."

He tossed a bundle of clean clothes at Sam and said, "Get a move on, I want to eat."

Stepping into the airy openness of the huge hogan's greatroom, Tipton smiled. Even though it wasn't his actual home, it had the same warm, homecoming effect on him. The house was octagonal like the traditional hogan of the Navajos, the Apaches' distant cousins. The octagonal floor plan had been retained, but when his father had helped Tall Woman build the house, they had expanded it many times past the usual dimensions. The rooms partitioned off the back walls barely ate into the open feeling which was so much a part of the concept.

The round roof beams soared upwards to a central point, where they were supported by a single, huge, peeled Douglas fir log extending nearly two stories from the floor. Two of the octagon's walls were sliding glass panels which met at an angle and opened onto a sweeping deck hanging out over the canyon. The morning sun rolled into the room as if walls didn't exist.

Sam stood in the doorway and let his eyes roam. Indian artifacts were freely mixed with works of art bearing the Longfeathers' signature. Tall Woman was a recognized painter, as was her daughter Maggie. Sam hadn't seen Maggie since just after he got married and moved east. She was living in Phoenix the last he'd heard. Joseph Longfeather's contributions were large, flowing wood sculptures in which modern Native American influences melded into contemporary shapes. They all sprang from large trunks of indigenous black wood or massive cedar stumps. All three Longfeathers were held in high regard by the art community.

On the far side of the greatroom, a woman moved gracefully around the kitchen, which was open to the rest of the hogan. Her long black hair had streaks of gray and was pulled back into a broad, relaxed pony tail held in place by a silver and turquoise clip. The clip was probably crafted by Joseph Longfeather, Sam thought. She had a white apron over her dark blue, full-length traditional dress which set off the concho belt circling her still-trim waist. As she moved from counter to stove, she hummed a song Sam recognized and he smiled. It was the song she would sing while trying to get the Longfeather and Tipton boys to stop talking and go to sleep. She hadn't always been successful.

Her face was a striking combination. Apache with a touch of Swede contributed by The Captain many generations before. His contribution to the Longfeather DNA, besides the height and blue eyes, had been a subtle refinement to their features that would age into a timeless beauty. A Scottsdale gallery owner had once commented that the Longfeathers were, themselves, classical art.

Sam looked at the only mother he had ever known and realized how right that comment had been.

The smell of huevos rancheros drifted across the room and opened all the valves in Sam's saliva glands. Then Tall Woman Longfeather glanced up, instantly breaking into a broad smile.

"Sam, Sam, Sam," she cried. She started around the counter but Sam made it across the room before she got her apron untied. She flung her arms around him and buried her head in his chest. She was crying even as she tried to squeeze the breath out of him.

Then abruptly, she stepped back, hands on hips, and fixed him with a glare, "Why, Sam? Why, in all these years, you're so close, but you never let us know. Why?"

Sam suddenly felt very conspicuous in the room, as if his rough appearance clashed with the clean, almost tidy environment. He knew exactly why he hadn't called. He felt as if he were ten years old again and Tall Woman was chastising him for chasing the ground squirrels and scaring them.

He dropped his eyes, "I wanted to. I really did. But..."

She interrupted by again wrapping her arms around him as she mumbled, "We've been so worried." She was crying again.

"Don't blame J.," as Sam referred to his Indian brother while with family, "I made him promise not to tell."

Then Tall Woman's again held him out at an arm's length and she asked, "What about your father? Does he know?"

Without turning his head, Sam knew he could step out on the deck, look to the west and see his father's house several miles in the distance. He had spoken to him only a few times since Marilyn's funeral and not once in the last three or four years. He hadn't called for the same reason he hadn't gone home. John Tipton was a proud man who thought he had a proud son. Sam hadn't wanted him to know the truth.

"No," Sam answered, "I couldn't face him. And I can't now, either."

Sam held his mother without saying anything. Then he said, "I just can't face him while I'm the way I am. Mom, I have to ask you not to tell him until I'm ready. Promise!"

Tall Woman nodded and kissed him gently.

"God, I hate family reunions, they always make me wait too long to eat!" Joseph Longfeather's voice was unexpected and sounded loud against the low background music of Native American flute. He was leaning against the doorway.

"Welcome home." Joseph Longfeather said it as if he meant it. "But, I've got to tell you, you really do look like shit."

Tall Woman Longfeather frowned at her son's language, "Joseph, you know how I hate that word." She hesitated a second then added, "However, in this case it's the right one to use."

Sam touched his hair and made a face, "Yeah, I know. Got any scissors?"

"So, anyway," Joseph Longfeather paused to wash down a mouthful of eggs before continuing, "when I came into town in the morning Roberta collared me and said she'd seen you going up the rim road in the dark but didn't come back down. I started to drive up after you, but decided the L-5 made more sense. I flew around for about a while and finally spotted the Willys on the road leading towards that old mine building you told me about."

Another fork full of eggs disappeared and he said, "You were bad, Sam, really bad! For a while I didn't think I'd get you awake, then I brought you here."

Sam wasn't pleased to be the center of breakfast conversation, especially when it had to do with what appeared to be the low point of his long slide downward.

At least he hoped that was the low point.

"I'm sorry," he said. "I don't remember any of it, but thanks. Things are going to change." He looked at his mother and at his best friend. "Things have to change."

He made the statement sound imperative.

The sound of a vehicle braking to a hurried halt in back of the house carried inside. The sound of crunching gravel hadn't stopped before the report of a slamming truck door merged with the rapid opening of the back door to the house.

"Hey, you wouldn't believe what...!" A tall, trim woman in her mid-thirties burst into the room obviously unaware breakfast was in process. She was caught by surprise. Rough-out cowboy boots protruded from the legs of tight-fitting jeans which disappeared into a fleece-lined leather jacket.

The woman's excitement at what she had to say could be read in her dancing blue eyes and quick body language. Her full lips stopped in mid-word, but then curved upward into a slow, bright smile. Her olive skin and high cheekbones were framed by shoulder-length, straight black hair with a hint of curl at the bottom.

She looked at Sam and a question mixed with the excitement in her eyes.

"Oh, I'm sorry, I didn't realize..." Her even white teeth shone through the unceasing smile and her hair bounced as she spoke. Her full eyebrows curled into gentle question marks as she focused on Sam.

He still had a fork full of chili and eggs suspended in front of his open mouth. He had the I-know-this-person look on his face.

Silence hung in the air for several seconds.

"Margaret Elizabeth...Maggie!" Sam dropped his fork and started around the table. He couldn't believe his eyes. He hadn't seen his quasi-kid sister for nearly fifteen years and what had been a startlingly beautiful twenty-year-old had blossomed into a ravishing young woman.

Maggie's hand went to her still-open mouth and her eyes spread wide in surprise.

"Oh, my God! Sam! Oh, my God!" Tears leapt into the corners of her eyes and her arms spread wide to accept the shaggy Sam Tipton. He swept her off her feet and whirled her around. They both laughed as he deposited her back on the floor. Maggie unzipped her jacket, put her hands on her hips, and stared at Sam like a frustrated banty hen.

"Just where in the hell have you been?" she barked.

Then grabbing Sam Tipton by his beard, she said, "You've had this family scared half to death for ten years! Damn you, Sam Tipton!"

Then she hugged him again.

"By the way," Maggie laughed, "Has anyone told you you look like shit?"

Fifteen

Roberta Rodreguez frowned as he studied her face in the cracked mirror over the dingy sink in the dingy bathroom of her small dingy apartment.

"Great! More damn wrinkles!" There was no one to listen, but that was nothing new. No one in the bar out front could hear her. Besides, she had always been her own best audience. She turned her head from side to side, letting the light play with her new discoveries. She knew exactly what the wrinkles meant. They meant she was burning up what was left of her youth trying to ride herd on a bunch of dust-covered psychopaths.

Charley Yee groaned in his sleep as he changed position on the cot. She leaned out of the bathroom door to check him. When she had cleaned him up and applied the bandages, she was shocked to see how quickly the angry purple bruises had developed on his arms and chest. His tightly wrinkled skin, the color and texture of dark, aged parchment, looked ready to burst, as if it could barely contain the runaway blood beneath the bruises.

The two Hispanics had done damage, but none of it looked serious. He would be sore, but whole. When Tipton had called earlier it was obvious he was relieved to find his friend wasn't seriously hurt. The guilt in his voice had also been obvious.

Tipton. That was another one she had to watch out for.

Leaning against the sink, she surveyed the eroding landscape of her face and said, "Always the goddamn caretaker, Rodreguez. Always looking out for the other guy!"

She frowned in the mirror and shrugged her shoulders. What else could she do? No one else would have taken Charley in. And everyone seemed to turn their back on Tipton. Someone had to help. That was, she realized, a habit she had to break.

A cat sat on the edge of the chipped and yellowed, claw-foot bathtub. Its tail swished back and forth against the plastic shower curtain. A long feline yawn punctuated Roberta's thoughts. The white of the bandages and splint on its right front leg stood out in sharp contrast to its dark tabby fur.

Roberta smiled, "Yeah, that's right, Biker, I've got to stop taking you strays in."

The cat leapt carefully off the tub to the floor, managing nicely considering its peg-leg configuration. It nuzzled up against one of the saloon-keeper's boots. As the sound of her easy purring found its way into Roberta's heart she remembered why she did what she did. She scooped the furry bundle off the floor and held it tight, stroking its fur. She held its face next to hers as it purred. She doubted if Charley Yee purred.

She glanced at the two faces in the mirror and addressed the fur-covered one, "What about it Biker? Think anyone's going to take me in when I show up as a stray?"

Sixteen

Frank Frederick lay on his back on the shredded foam cushions and watched the afternoon sun play with the sagging headliner of the RV. For the millionth time he noticed the motorhome's skylight was cracked. The plastic dome sat crooked on the surrounding metal work in the roof. Just another place to let rain in. His mind wasn't thinking about skylights. And he didn't notice the odor of mildew rising from the cushions. He was visualizing nuclear assemblies and mysterious gods. And dried up old Indians.

Where in the hell were Charley Yee's gods hiding because wherever that was, Cobalt Blue wasn't far away. For all Frank Frederick knew, that crazy Indian idolized the box and traded the contents for a bottle of rot gut. Or a bottle of horse liniment. Charley Yee wasn't too particular about what he drank.

He was, however, very particular about whom he drank with. Frederick let a finger explore the swelling around his nose and eyes. The purple color, courtesy of the two Hispanic kids, was so vivid, he could almost feel it. The puffy skin around his eyes flowed smoothly into the nose where it disappeared under a layer of crude bandages. The nose was broken. It had to be.

Maybe his obvious sacrifice to help Charley would buy him drinking rights with the old Indian. If he got him drunk, the old Indian might lead him to his gods. Frederick then had another thought. If Yee didn't lead him to the hiding place, he would simply kidnap him and starve him until he revealed the hiding place.

"What the hell are we going to do tonight? We're not going back to that goddamn bar again!"

Like a dull chainsaw, May Frederick's voice ripped bits and pieces out of his peace of mind. Up to that point he had successfully ignored her sitting in the passenger's seat at the other end of the RV. She was sucking on her seventeenth cigarette of the day while she browsed through a magazine. Her lips were moving as her eyes traveled across the pages.

"Shut up! I'm thinking!" Frederick forced himself into a sitting position.

"Yeah, right!" she snorted.

"Goddammit!" Frederick needed to shut her out for a few more seconds. Just a few more seconds.

"Frank, what the hel..." Frank cut her off.

"Okay, this is the plan," he snapped. "You're going to spend the night at Luigi's, or whatever that wop's name is. You can watch your goddamn TV and leave me the hell alone!"

The plan was set. He'd befriend Charley Yee and, if that failed, he'd tie him up and starve him until he talked. Judging from the Indian's frail-looking body, that wouldn't be long.

Frederick knew it wasn't much of a plan. In fact, even to him, it sounded a little stupid. But he had to do something fast. He had to call Kwan in twenty-four hours. That might be his last chance to back out. He had to know whether Cobalt Blue was still out there and whether he had something to sell. If he didn't, the last thing he wanted was to have Kwan find out he was lying.

He needed proof Cobalt Blue existed. He needed it for himself, if no one else.

Glancing around he located May's camera laying behind the jumbled pile of pots and pans on the small, grimy stove. He knew it was freshly loaded. They'd had a major battle over the cost of the film. What could she possibly take a picture of that even her dim-witted sister in Peoria could find interesting?

That would be his proof. A photo of the assembly. He snatched up the camera and dropped it in his shirt pocket.

"It's getting dark," May Frederick's voice was so shrill, it was painful. And demanding, "Take me over to the store right now! I'm going to miss part of my show."

"You want to go? You walk!" Frank made no effort at being civil. He just wanted her out of his immediate life.

"You're an asshole. You know that?" She huffed out of the door.

Frederick grunted agreement and leaned towards the window to stare out at Charley Yee, rocking slowly as the sun went down. Time to put the plan into action.

Frederick grabbed a nearly-full bottle of whisky on the way out the door. He glanced at the label. He remembered the liquor clerk opining as to how this was one of the finer "inexpensive" bourbons available. It was cheap, Frederick observed. Not inexpensive. There's a difference.

Neither he nor Charley Yee, however, knew nor cared about the difference. Cheap was just fine with them.

The evening sun was still warm and Frank Frederick was close enough to touch him before Charley Yee acknowledged his presence. Even then, it was just a slow turn of the head towards the ex-agent. Their eyes met for a brief second before the meditating Indian returned to gaze at the setting sun. In that instant, Frederick could see that Yee's face was a match for his own. Purple was the dominant color.

Frederick said nothing as he sat down on the rock next to Yee. After a few minutes he silently reached out his hand holding the uncapped bottle. Equally as silently and without taking his eyes off the rapidly-sinking sun, Charley took the bottle by its neck. In a single motion, he brought it to his lips. One long pull and it was back in Frederick's waiting hand. He never took his eyes off the horizon.

Neither said a word for perhaps a half an hour. The bottle passed from hand to hand. Finally, Charley Yee looked over at his gray-haired drinking partner.

"Thank you for helping me." That said, Yee's eyes returned to catch the last ray of direct light. The edge of the sun gave off a diamond-shaped flash before disappearing completely. Just that quickly, the far mountains turned into hard silhouettes.

There are no sunsets as distinct as those in the mountains of the west.

"Does it hurt?" Charley turned, his eyes searching Frederick's face.

"Only a little. And yours?" Frederick passed him the bottle.

"Only when I cough. My chest." Yee took a drink and passed it back. Frederick took a drink. Then Yee took one.

"Hey, Charley, m' man! Ya don' think your Gods are gonna to be pissed, us droppin' in like this unannounced? Oops!" Frank Frederick rolled drunkenly and jerked the wheel to keep from running off the narrow, eroded road. It was rimmed in blackness that could go down for a thousand feet.

"No, I..." Charley Yee was trying to speak, but his mouth refused to cooperate. His head lolled on a limp neck mimicking the motions of the lumbering RV. The old vehicle rolled from side to side like a barge in heavy seas.

"My Gods and I are ver' close. They're glad t' see me. Always." Yee's thoughts came out as a slurred, multi-syllabic word. He nodded his head vigorously to emphasize the correctness of his statement.

The road had never actually been a road. Most of its travelers had been cattle followed by the occasional horse or jeep. It wound along the rim and around a mountain which was invisible in the dark. The two travelers knew of its existence only by the occasional flashes of sage and sand in the headlights. There were scraping sounds as the Mogollon Rim tore yet another piece off the bottom of the old RV.

The bottle had long since been emptied. It was replaced by another of even lesser quality but higher quantity. It too would soon be emptied. It crossed repeatedly back and forth from drunken driver to drunken passenger.

Soon, the silence of the high desert was split by an old Native American voice doing its best to launch a war cry off the edge of the rim. It was followed by the croaking imitation of a very non-Indian voice attempting the same. Frank Frederick would never be inducted as an honorary Indian based on his ability to do war cries.

"Stop!!" Charley Yee announced. "Stop here!"

The old Indian braced himself to keep from bouncing off the dash as Frederick smashed the brake pedal down.

"This is where we go to meet my Gods," Charley slurred.

"Well...it's about...goddamn time!" Frederick slurred. "Thought we were goin' to be in Omaha inna few minutes."

Frederick opened the door and more fell, than climbed, out. He staggered through the headlights to the passenger-side door.

"Come on, old Charley. Let's go meet your gods. Say, you don't supposed they'd have anything to drink, do you?"

"Frank, you sonuvabitch! Where in the hell have you been? It's after midnight. I been sitting on this goddamn curb for...."

May Frederick stopped talking when she leaned into the RV's open window. Her husband's head lay on the steering wheel. He'd passed out the instant the RV made a controlled crash into the tall curb in front of the run-down convenience store.

"You drunken slob!" She jerked the door open, propping Frank Frederick up as he tried to fall out. She started to wrestle him into the space between the two seats when she saw a dark shape huddled in the seat on the other side.

"No, goddamn it! No! Not even in this piece of shit truck!"

she screamed.

When she slammed the door, it pounded Frederick's head back inside with the door frame. She stomped around in front of the still-running RV to the passenger side.

"Out, you drunken Indian!" She yanked the door open and made no attempt to break Charley Yee's fall. He tumbled out like a corpse and landed hard on his side. May Frederick's only humanitarian move was to kick his foot out of the way so she wouldn't back over it.

She forced the limp form of Frank Frederick over the RV's motor cover so he landed on the floor between the cabinets. She yanked the RV into reverse and roared down the still, dark street of Pitacho.

The cloud of dust announcing the RV's arrival at their accustomed parking place hadn't settled before she climbed past Frank Frederick's inert form and fell into the bed in the rear. Frederick belched as she passed and made a clumsy attempt to straighten out his kinked body where he lay on the moldy rug. Then he was again breathing deeply and out cold.

The rising morning sun hammered directly through the windshield of the RV. Its full intensity was focused on Frank Frederick's pale face where he lay on the RV's narrow floor between the cabinets.

The sun was determined to awaken everything and everyone it touched. This included one very hung-over ex-FBI agent.

Frank fought waking up, but the sun wouldn't give up. It bored right through his eyelids into his brain. He rolled sideways as he brought his arm up to shield his eyes. The damage had been done. Enough of his brain was awake that it began to think. The first thought to cross his mind was of Charley Yee. Something which had happened. Something that had happened prodded at him until he suddenly remembered.

Cobalt Blue! Last night! Scattered images struggled to form themselves into coherent pictures. He remembered Charley agreeing to introduce him to his gods. But, then what? Snippets of images flashed through his memory. They were of dark roads. And Charley peeing off the edge of a canyon. Past that, there was nothing.

His head pounded. His mouth tasted as bad as the RV's carpet smelled. Frederick dragged himself into a sitting position against the cracked fiberglass engine cover. Where had they gone? What had they done?

Frederick started to drop his face into his hands. Then he realized one hand was full. It was wrapped tightly around May's cheap little camera. He remembered. He had taken that with him to get proof of Cobalt Blue. Had they found it?.

The light made his eyes throb, but he forced them to focus on the camera. Without reading glasses he had to hold it out at an arm's length. Even then it was too close. Holding it up in the sunlight, he squinted and tried to make out the numbers in the exposure window.

It was a five. Or possibly an eight. His heart began racing. He forgot the pounding in his head. He had taken pictures of something last night! What, he couldn't remember. But it was on the film and the camera wouldn't suffer from hangover amnesia.

He looked at his watch as he held the camera up. He still had time. He glanced at the camera again as he struggled into the driver's seat. Something was on that film which would tell him what had happened last night.

May Frederick didn't even change position on the sagging bed as the RV careened onto the road out of town. There had to be a photo shop in Flagstaff.

Seventeen

Richard Yardley, late thirties, crew cut, slight tan, built like a junior college running back, stood at Baltimore-Washington International's curbside check-in. He did his best not to look nervous. Gray-blue eyes flicked back and forth. The unlit cigarillo never stopped twitching. As many times as he had done this, he had never gotten past the fear of being caught before the project was even underway. He handed the skycap his bag and pocketed the yellow stub. He wondered what the old Black man would have said if he knew he had just tossed two Heckler and Koch submachine guns, four Sig-Sauer high-capacity nine-millimeter pistols, along with assorted stilettos, garrotes and enough ammo to wage a good-sized war, up on the conveyor belt.

Yardley knew this airline didn't X-ray baggage, that's why they always used it. It was scary nonetheless.

He glanced around. The rest of his team was on the other side checking in their baggage. Some of it actually contained clothing. He'd worked with two of them many times before. The kid, he didn't know. And he didn't like him. Something about his Bronx attitude bothered Yardley.

"Yeah, so where is this Arizona?" It was the kid speaking. The way his accent flattened the consonants was already irritating Yardley. "I read it was somewhere over around Nebraska. Hey, Yardley, is that right?"

"Yeah, Hornslee, that's right." Yardley hoped the answer would keep him quiet for a while. The kid was supposedly an ex-green beret with combat time in the Gulf.

Yardley watched the kid gawking at every woman walking past. Combat experience! He snorted out loud. Combat time in the Gulf wasn't combat time. It was a live-fire exercise. Yardley briefly remembered his war. A Shau and Pleiku. Now that was combat time.

He ignored the kid and studied the other two. Estavez looked to be thirty. Maybe thirty three. It was hard to tell. Ladilow was older. Yardley had recruited both out of the New York drug trade. He kept meaning to ask Ladilow, a round-faced, shorter-than-average Hispanic with a failed mustache and full, drooping cheeks, how he came by his Anglo last name, but it never came up.

Estavez's given name was Jesus, but Ladilow always called him Blade. He couldn't have been skinnier if all the muscle and body-fat had been sucked from his body. Bones were clearly visible. Well over six feet, he ratcheted from place to place, his movements jerky, as if his joints lacked enough fat to keep them lubricated. He was the tin man in need of an oil can.

Estavez's coal-black eyes hid deep within his face and flickered around constantly. They too were jerky. Nothing moved smoothly. His bony eye sockets were craters surrounded by pockmarked olive skin so oily it shined. When a teenager, Yardley was thinking, Estavez must have been a real zit-monster.

Estavez always carried a handful of black, triangular, space age, plastic spikes. He said they were carbon fiber and he kept them hidden in his clothing, even on the airplane. Being plastic, they didn't cause so much as a shadow on the x-ray machine.

Yardley had seen Estavez slam a spike up to its hilt in a woman's eyeball to silence her screaming. As he yanked the spike back out, he wiped the blood off on her dress while she was still falling. His facial expression didn't change a bit. It was as if nothing had happened.

Very cold. Very cool. Very dependable. And no questions except how much and when. They were his kind of people. Excellent assets for his current line of work.

As they filed inside the terminal headed for concourse "B," Yardley handed each their ticket packet. None of them noticed his seat assignment put him at the opposite end of the cabin from theirs. Yardley always arranged it that way. Just because he'd work with them, didn't mean he had to spend any more time with them than necessary.

"Hey, Yardley! What is it with this place? All the fuckin' people'r smiling." Hornslee's thin, grating voice carried half the length of the crowded jetway. The flight to Phoenix had been a long one for Yardley. Hornslee had been a truly awful traveling companion. Heads turned, as people filed out of the airplane. The woman directly in front turned and glared. She wasn't smiling.

Barely clear of the jetway, Yardley grabbed his short associate by the back of his collar and dragged him sideways away from the jetway. Passengers glanced over as they passed.

Yardley stood close and hissed at the back of the kid's close-cropped head through clinched teeth. His eyes watched people pour out of the crowded jetway.

"Shut the fuck up! You hear me? I don't want to hear another goddamn word out of you until we're out of the terminal and away from normal people. Not one goddamn word!"

"Now, go!" He gave Hornslee a gentle shove and shouldered his own clothes bag.

He followed the kid towards baggage claim. Hornslee was leering at every pretty girl he passed. Yardley suddenly realized how much the kid stuck out once he was off the East Coast. Hornslee was, he decided, the kind of individual who gave the East Coast an undeserved bad name.

Ladilow and Estavez were waiting in the middle of the sunlit concourse. Both had light travel bags slung over their shoulders. As the quartet started walking, Yardley began talking.

"Okay, I'll get the rent-a-car. Blade, I'm making you Hornslee's nursemaid. If he says one goddamn word while still inside the terminal I want you to shove one of those plastic toothpicks of yours up his ass."

He glared at Hornslee. The kid tried to return the stare. He shifted his eyes within seconds, conceding defeat. Estavez only grinned. Hornslee knew the emaciated Hispanic would happily do as he had been instructed and never look back.

The four separated into pairs. They didn't want to look like a team and attract attention. Ladilow leaned over to Yardley as they walked down the brightly-carpeted concourse. The sun poured through the glass walls making the interwoven orange carpet glow. Ladilow quietly said, "You know Hornslee's right. Everybody in this place is smiling."

"Yeah, I know," Yardley said. "It's the sun."

"You're right." Ladilow's nose tested the air. "And it doesn't smell like piss like some of our airports do."

Eighteen

"**Is Mr. Kwan in?**" The pay phone receiver was hot where it touched Frank Frederick's ear. The lilting Asiatic voice on the other end said her employer was not in and would he leave a message. Frederick smiled and read her the number off the pay phone. He would wait. His wife's muffled cursing could be heard clear across the abandoned parking lot. Thankfully the RV's windows were closed.

The satellite phone in his pocket vibrated. Kwan glanced around, as he answered it. Out the airport concourse windows Camelback Mountain could be seen as a rocky break in the urban greenery that was suburban Phoenix.

"Yes." He needed say no more. The female voice on the other end repeated a phone number. He instantly committed it to memory by visualizing it being written on a large blackboard. "Thank you."

He stepped towards the wall, his fingers dancing on the phone pad. Without warning, a large white man jostled him. He glanced up as the face passed. It was only a second, but he'd studied the face long enough for an alarm to sound in his mind. He interrupted his dialing for a few seconds.

The face. He had seen it before. And it had not been a casual meeting. He then remembered and he smiled.

As the phone against his ear rang, he remembered the meeting. It was with a well-known and loved U.S. Congressman and his courier. The courier had his hands out-stretched handing Kwan a briefcase full of cash. The courier had been wearing the same face he had just bumped into. He searched for a name. Yardley! That was it. Yardley.

Kwan again smiled at the game in which he was involved. It appeared that his long-ago trading partner, who was now a member of the U.S. cabinet, was walking the same path as he. The path to Cobalt Blue was becoming crowded.

Frederick picked up the phone on the fourth ring. His answer was a monosyllabic grunt. Even the tone was offensive to Kwan, but he could easily ignore it.

"Yes, Mister Frederick. So good to hear from you. Have you reconsidered my offer?"

As Kwan spoke into the muffled portable phone, he saw Yardley disappearing down the escalator towards the rental car area. He had another man with him. Obviously another operative. Kwan also recognized a second pair approaching the escalators. They tried to move like tourists. They didn't want to stand out. They failed because they were trying too hard. Their tourist-like floral-pattern shirts and varying shades of khaki trousers were like uniforms. They had been assigned their "casual dress" camouflage and it hadn't worked.

"Mr. Frederick I'm glad to see you think my offer generous. Yes, we can do business...Yes, it will take me several days to get the money together. That much in small bills is not easy to come by...Yes, please call me at my office at exactly 2 PM the day after tomorrow. Thank, you, I am looking forward to hearing from you."

Kwan silenced the telephone and faded into the flow of people. He laughed to himself. Frederick thought he was being cute by requesting the entire amount paid in used twenty and fifty-dollar bills. Didn't he realize four million dollars in small bills would fill a dump truck? Maybe he did know and just wanted to feel wealthy.

Cash is bulkier, but so much more soul-satisfying than the simple knowledge the money is in a numbered Swiss account. Kwan would never do the same himself, but he understood the emotion.

He passed through the downstairs terminal doors next to the rental car agencies. He glanced over at the familiar face he'd seen earlier. He and the others were renting a car. Kwan walked briskly towards the rental car storage area to stand in the shadows. He wanted to see what kind of vehicle they would be driving.

Frank Frederick didn't walk back to the RV. He skipped like a school girl. Then the sudden realization hit him that he had just made a promise to one of the most ruthless men in the world that he might not be able to keep. He had told Kwan he would deliver the apparatus known as Cobalt Blue. Yet, he didn't know where it was. Or if it even existed.

If Kwan found out Frederick had lied, he'd be dead. Or, within seconds of Kwan's finding out the truth, he'd wish he were dead. Frank Frederick sagged up the two steps into the RV and settled behind the wheel. It was time to take the gloves off. It was time to make Charley Yee talk.

Nineteen

"**I'm sorry, so sorry,**" Maggie's words were as soft as the mountain evening just then descending upon the trio. The lonely voice of a great horned owl in the trees below the Longfeathers' porch punctuated the silence. A whisper-like breeze moved through the cedars and pines on the canyon's rim.

"I only knew her for the two years before you moved east, but I really loved her. I'm sorry." She knew she was repeating herself and settled back against the lodge-pole lounge in silence. She didn't know what else to say.

Sam sat on the other end of the rustic piece of outdoor furniture and smiled. "Thanks, I know it seems like a long time ago to everyone else. Sometimes it seems that way to me too, like it happened in another life. Then, the image of Daniel Guy standing at the hotel room door will flash into my head and I re-live it all. Every second of it. Maybe that's when I start drinking. I just don't know." Unconsciously he slowly shook his head.

"I've tried to stop a bunch of times, but never make it past the next time I see a bottle. For a while I even tried to stay away from Roberta's, but that's not the answer."

Maggie and her brother listened in silence.

"I think I actually have two problems. I'm smart enough to realize I can't live the rest of my life letting Marilyn and Melissa hang over me like a dark cloud. I hate to admit it, but I think I've been using their deaths as a reason to keep drinking.

"Jesus," he looked over at the young woman whom he now had trouble seeing as his kid sister, "maybe I don't want to quit!"

"Yeah, you do." Longfeather's deep voice rumbled out of the gathering darkness. The gentle sounds of his fingers running up and down a Martin guitar's fingerboard formed a subtle background. "I've seen you look at yourself, when you're sober and you want out. You can't kid me."

"Yeah, but it's just not that easy," Sam answered. "Hell, we're sitting here talking about me being a drunk and part of me wants a drink. Right now! I've got a real problem and it isn't going to be easy."

"The question, Cowboy, is whether you're willing to try."

Maggie's words cut right to the heart of the matter. The trio listened to the night while Sam thought of his answer. Longfeather's fingers moved smoothly, adding an almost inaudible, languid blues beat to the evening sounds.

"I don't see that I have a choice. Things have to change." Sam wasn't surprised at the conviction in his voice. He wasn't certain he believed it, or whether he could live up to what he said.

He sat silently, then a thought came to mind. It may not be the answer, but it had worked for many civilizations before the current one came on the scene. Maybe it would work for him.

"I think I need a vision quest of my own," Sam finally said, "and I know where to do it. I saw it from the Stinson." Looking in Longfeather's direction, Sam's voice brightened. "If you have the time, I'd like to retrieve my truck first thing in the morning. And let's take a chain saw. We're going to need it."

"How about it kid," his words were directed at Maggie, "You want to come play with the big kids tomorrow?"

Her answer was a quiet, sleepy mumble. "Yeah, I guess so." The words barely made it between her lips as they tried to move. "The school's closed tomorrow," she half-whispered.

Sam then remembered she had a real job, unlike most of the people he knew. She ran the computer literacy section of a high school in Payson and did leather work in a studio near the school.

"Okay, we'll..." Sam stopped himself as Maggie burrowed deeper into the comforter one of her brothers had tossed over her. She was past listening.

The tree was too big to simply cut in half and push aside. The chainsaw converted the middle of it into short firewood pieces, clearing a space for the Willys to pass through. Longfeather stacked the pieces neatly by the side of the road as Tipton whacked them off. The bleating mechanical voice of the chainsaw was clearly out of place in the crisp early morning air.

Tipton pulled the gloves off and beat them against his jeans. "Okay, let's go, pathfinders. It's time to go exploring." The Willys rumbled into life, as Maggie scrambled through the open door. Longfeather fell into the sagging seat. He looked over at his sister sandwiched between the two men and grinned. Her disdain for their disheveled mechanical surroundings was obvious.

"Jesus, Sam, I know you love this thing and J. says it'll climb a tree, but I'm afraid I'll catch a disease just riding in it! "She coughed. The bouncing road levitated the layer of dust on the floor to nostril level.

"Are you certain this goes through?" Longfeather asked. "What the hell's up here anyway?" His words bounced as much as he did. He closed his mouth to keep from accidentally biting his tongue.

In desperation, Maggie wrapped herself around Longfeather's left arm and tried not to ricochet off the roof.

Sam Tipton looked across at this friends. They looked as if they were caught in a fluff-dry cycle. He laughed. "If I knew what was up there, we wouldn't have to go exploring would we?"

As he wrestled the violently dancing steering wheel, he caught Maggie's eye. He gave her his famous, and often used, crazy-as-as-a-loon grin.

"Just watch the damn road, Tipton," she snapped.

Longfeather hung on with one hand while the other fished under the seat looking for the other half of his rotting seat belt.

"Damn, this is absolutely beautiful!" Longfeather said. "No it's—and if you tell anyone I used this word—I'll deny it, it's awesome. Absolutely awesome!"

Tipton stepped out of the Willys and stood next to the smiling Longfeather and his sister.

"What do you suppose it was?" Maggie asked the question on all their minds.

"A mine," Sam stated. "It was a mine and a mill of some sort, but not like any I've seen around this area."

They leaned silently against the truck to soak it in.

The tall, quarried-stone building looked down as if ignoring them. Its empty windows showed no expression as they stared. The narrow end of the building had a line of weathered, gray wooden freight doors lined vertically on top one another. One for each floor. There were four. The door on what appeared to be the main floor, the third from the bottom, was flanked by two large windows. They were covered by rusting, iron shutters. It was as if the building's eyelids were closed. It had been sleeping a very long time.

The door at the very top, under the overhang of the roof was smaller. A rusted hoist hung from an iron rail jutting from the wall above it. The door itself was reduced to a single, narrow board. The darkness within looked complete.

Staring into that small patch of black, Sam felt a sudden, uncontrollable shiver flash up the muscles of his arms and down his back. It was gone as quickly as it came.

The morning sun converted the building into bullion and outlined it against the flawless blue sky and red canyon walls. It could have been an Egyptian temple, lost to memory for generations. Sam Tipton couldn't keep a grin off his face. Longfeather was grinning too. They were born explorers.

It was hard to tell where the old building started. It either started at the bottom of the stone shelf jutting from the canyon walls and worked its way up, or it started at the flat top of the stone plateau and worked its way down. Either way, its tall, relatively narrow structure had four stories at the front but only two at the back, where it sat on the elevated flat surface.

Longfeather tentatively pushed on an old plank door. He glanced over his shoulder at the line of sagging, but sturdy-looking sheds lining the base of the canyon wall behind the building. There was a lot to look at.

"Here," Tipton said. He stood on the edge of a rusting ore car and caught one leg on an empty window sill. He pulled himself up and instantly disappeared from sight. Maggie Longfeather laughed uproariously when she heard him swearing after falling onto the floor.

"You okay?" she laughed. If Tipton hadn't been swearing, she might have been concerned. But, he was swearing, so....

Then there was a long pause and Maggie quit laughing. A worried frown had just begun to form when Tipton's wildly grinning face reappeared out of the window. "Yeah, I'm okay. I'm better than okay! Wait'll you see this! We're into world-class neat shit here!"

The interior of the building was a tapestry of light and dark. The sun pouring through the glassless side windows hung in the dusty air as tangible, unmoving shafts of light. They were spotlights casting hard, white rectangular squares on the debris-strewn floor. The light made the shadows seem darker. And more mysterious. Therefore, more inviting.

The huge, open space around them soared up two stories and was cross-laced with large, solid-looking overhead beams. The effect was that of a long abandoned cathedral. It didn't seem right to speak in loud voices.

Longfeather studied the floor, as he stepped around piles of junk. "It looks like the inside of the Willys," Longfeather said, his voice low and restrained.

"Yeah, I know. I love it!" Sam pivoted, his hand in front of his eyes blocking out light so he could see into the shadows.

"Yo, look back here!" Tipton walked quickly towards the rear of the building, carefully working his way around broken crates and long-abandoned workbenches laying on their sides. Rusting machinery was everywhere, with pipes and gears, cables and pulleys still hanging where they were last stowed.

"Look at this! No one made an attempt to salvage most of this stuff. They yanked out the heavy equipment, but didn't even bother to pick up behind themselves." He hefted a huge spanner. A carpenter's hammer lay next to a pile of nails rusted into a dung-like clump. They were exactly where the worker had left them when he finished his job. Everything was covered with an inch of fine Arizona real estate. It had been a very long time since anyone had disturbed that dust.

As Sam came to the rear of the building, he wrestled with one of the iron window shutter-locks for a second. The hinges protested with a whining screech. With little more than a hard push, the shutters edged open sending a strong beam of light ahead of him. He's eyes tried to follow the light into the darkness.

"Damn! It opens right into the mine! Look at this!" He had to restrain himself to keep from running, which would have invited a broken leg, or worse.

He walked as far as the beam of light would let him and stopped. The Longfeathers joined him.

"I don't know what this place was," Tipton said, "but the excavations are gigantic!"

He was staring into the darkness. The huge cavern absorbed the sunlight. There were no reflections. It was as if they were looking deep into the mountain's mind and it was hiding its thoughts. A continuous cool wave of air wafted out over the trio standing at the edge of the darkness.

"Great place to raise spiders," Tipton quipped.

"And scorpions. And snakes. And bats. And...." Maggie stopped talking when she realized the other two had reversed course and were headed back towards the front of the building. She scampered after them.

Halfway between the yawning mouth of the mine and the front of the large, open building, a heavy, dust-covered wooden stairway beckoned them upwards. It led to an elevated platform framed entirely in square-hewn timbers as broad as Longfeather's shoulders.

"Whatever they had up here was big. And heavy!" Tipton stomped on the floor with the heel of his boot. The dust cloud made them cough and back away. The sound was that of kicking solid rock. The floor boards of the platform, like the rest of the elevated structure, were massive.

"Look up," Sam said, "What don't you see?"

Maggie and Longfeather matched his upward stare and both uttered a single word in unison, "Nothing."

"You're right. Look at that roof. There isn't a single bit of light showing." Sam's voice showed his admiration for the original craftsmen. "And I'll tell you why. The roof is slate. Split blue slate shingles, probably held in place with brass or galvanized spikes. They expected this place to last for centuries."

"Looks like it already has," Maggie answered.

The windows on either side of the large freight door at the front of the building were twice as large as the rest. The shutters covering them were built in four sections, each hinged in the middle. Picking up a short section of pipe, Sam coaxed two of the locks to release their hold. The hinges screeched.

The oxide-red shutters slowly opened and the front half of the big old building yielded to the light. Sam knew for a fact the old iron coverings still had several centuries of life left in them. The dry mountain air was kind to old iron. It, like everything else in the mountains, could be counted on to last for centuries.

Longfeather leaned over and picked up a white object.

"Looks like some of the inhabitants decided to stay." The sun turned the animal skull a fiery white. As he turned it in the light, he held it up for Sam to admire, "Check it out! Could be a wolf, but it sure didn't die of old age."

As he spoke, he inserted a finger in the bullet hole in the top of the skull.

"Ouch, bet that hurt," Tipton responded.

Maggie bent over, her hand coming up with a similar object. "Looks like we have bookends! This one has a bullet hole too."

Longfeather was suddenly scuffling around in the lighted

area. Each time he spotted what he was looking for, he shouted, "Here's another one. There's one."

Sam focused on the floor. There was a layer of scattered bones under the dust. They had been there too long to be intact skeletons. Other animals had seen to that.

"I count nine wolves. Every one died from an acute case of bullet on the brain," Longfeather announced, after completing his survey of the area.

"Kind of a weird place to be hunting big dogs, wouldn't you say?" As he spoke, Sam was walking slowly in circles in the middle of the floor. His eyes were searching, although he didn't know what for. "Ah, hah, here's part of the answer."

He stooped quickly and his fingers came up with a small, oblong object. Holding it up for Longfeather to see, the Native American immediately recognized it.

"Rifle casing, thirty-thirty?" He was guessing the caliber although he was too far away to see the casing clearly.

"Wrong!" Sam made a honking sound indicating the error of the answer, "It's a rimmed case that I don't think I recognize."

Sam prided himself on his knowledge of firearms, especially old ones. A childhood passion, it still burned in his brain. He walked towards the light, rubbing the broad bottom of the case against his jeans as he did.

"Hey, look at this! " he said. "First of all, the bottom of the case isn't flat, it's slightly rounded. Second, check out the headstamp. What the hell are those letters?"

Longfeather took it and held it so the light bounced off at an angle "Egyptian? Nah! Looks like the symbol for Pi…something something. Greek? Then there's a T, a funny Y, backwards R.. Oh wait, it's Cyrillic. That's what it is Sam, it's Russian!"

Sam snatched the casing out of his hand and looked at it again, the markings were now clear, Russian letters on one side with 92 on the other. Sam suddenly recognized the round.

"This goddamn thing is a Russian 7.62 x 54 rimmed." Sam announced.

"So what?" asked Maggie.

Sam dropped the spent casing into her outstretched hand. She knew firearms and was as good a shot as the other two. Sam's father had brought the three up with no differentiation between boys and girls. He made certain she could do anything the boys could do. Her curiosity concerning all things, especially mysteries, was even stronger than the boys'. She eyed the casing while Sam continued to explain.

"The Russians have used this round for more than a century, since 1891, to be exact. It is still one of the most powerful, accurate rifle rounds in the world, but I'm willing to bet there aren't many in the country like this one. It was made in 1892. That's what the numbers mean."

Suddenly, Sam was down on his haunches sifting through the dust with a stick like a badger after gophers.

"Here's another one!" He whipped it up out of the dust next to a fallen ladder, then Longfeather echoed his find.

"There's one here too!" said Maggie.

"What the hell! Look at the pattern of the casings!" Tipton said.

Longfeather replied, "It looks like someone fought a hell of a battle or something here."

Maggie was watching the two from a short distance and saw the patterns the same as Sam, but she had an inspiration. She stepped over the ladder and walked to the furthest wall.

Turning, she shielded her eyes to study the catwalk leading to the open overhead freight door.

"Sam. Longfeather." Her words were solemn and spoken slowly. "Come over here. Someone fought a hell of a battle all right, but it looks like they lost the war."

She pointed up towards the catwalk. The sun clearly illuminated a makeshift chair of crates. A withered human form sat on the crates and stared out the peak door at the western horizon. The dried, sightless eyes had been staring for a very long time.

Twenty

Tipton squinted in the darkness near the roof of the old mine building and focused on the dim outline of the catwalk. It had no railing and he had never been any good at walking tightropes. He hated high places. Hated them! Acrophobia. A common aviator's malady. Sunlight pouring through the few open windows below died long before it made it up to Tipton's level. It revealed little of the catwalk. He felt trapped. Stranded with his nervousness.

Longfeather was inching along in his footsteps and said, "Who's silly idea was this? We could break our necks up here."

Tipton's silence was answer enough. Each time Longfeather took a step, Tipton felt it. He imagined the catwalk swaying and had the urge to drop to his knees and crawl, but couldn't. He had to maintain some level of dignity.

Sam glanced back over his shoulder. Maggie stood behind Longfeather. Arms impatiently crossed. They were blocking her way. She walked along the catwalk as if it was ten feet wide.

"Come on, you guys. Get moving." She said.

Sam remembered her as a teenager. She had taken great delight in routinely humbling the two older boys with her cat-like abilities and she was doing it again.

She had lorded it over both Longfeather and Sam, when she soloed his father's Super Cub before they did. As teenagers, all three learned to fly. But she learned faster. And better. And never let them forget it.

"Hey, what's the hold up, Tipton?" Not for a second did she let them forget. She was giggling.

Tipton ignored her. He moved at his own pace. Slowly.

The narrow walkway snaked through the near-dark to the peak door where someone appeared to have been sunbathing for a very long time. They had probably used the ladder laying on the floor to climb up. Tipton and Longfeather had inspected the ladder closely. Dry and loose. The rungs were collections of long, dried splits. They decided on another route and used scrap lumber to bridge from the two-story platform in the middle of the building to the catwalk. At that moment, Tipton was regretting their decision.

Sunlight spilled through the peak door, surrounding the building's last inhabitant with a dusty aura. Tipton shivered. He didn't think it was because of the heights. As he closed the distance, he eyed the form in the light ahead.

He or she was sitting on a packing crate. A larger crate stood on end behind it forming the back for a crude chair. The chair would last for eternity in the dry air of the Mogollon Rim. So would the person sitting on it.

The excitement of discovery raced through Sam Tipton, but while on the catwalk, he was having trouble enjoying the thrill. One broken board and he'd be just as dead as the ex-person they were sneaking up on.

The catwalk ended on a platform which was littered with industrial debris. The outlines of long-abandoned buckets and crates were softened by a snow-like layer of dust. The makeshift throne rose out of the debris directly in front of the open door and a half dozen feet inside it.

"I don't believe this," Tipton breathed quietly. As he moved past the seated figure, his eyes tried to analyze every detail. They barely understood what they were seeing.

Longfeather was silent. Maggie was unable to stop staring at the withered face. As she carefully stepped around the junk, she was feeling the face with her eyes. It was clearly not as she had expected. Its tranquil expression hadn't died with death. It wasn't a corpse, but a person who was simply no longer living. She could still see the person clearly.

"Wow!" She breathed quietly.

When they had first sighted the figure from the floor, Sam expected to find a skeleton held together by shreds of rotting cloth. He had underestimated the Mogollon Rim and its low humidity. And freezing winters.

"It happened during the winter, didn't it?" It was more a question for the withered visage in front of him than a statement for his friends.

The figure sat head slightly down, as if in the process of falling asleep. Its hands were folded calmly in its lap. Their position was still graceful in death. The sun-dried face was almost hidden within a sagging fur hat. The flaps were pulled down over the ears and tied under the chin. A plaid, woven muffler, its yarn losing much of its color but none of its shape, wrapped around the neck. the muffler had covered the lower part of the face, but over the decades it had slowly loosened and drooped down. A dust-covered beard and mustache encircled stiff lips. The drying process had pulled the lips back slightly exposing even, white teeth. It was a gentle smile.

A frosty mantle of dust clung to eyebrows and eyelashes. The leather-like skin was tight and smooth, the facial bones clearly visible. But the man's features were unaltered. He was as his friends had known him.

Tipton snatched a piece of aged burlap off the deck and beat it against the platform to shake off the dust. He used it to clean dust from the face.

Maggie had moved around to lean over Sam's shoulder. Her eyes moved from feature to feature as if trying to recognize him, as if she had known him in passing and was trying to place him. She reached out and lightly touched the cheek. As Sam dusted, she quietly said, "Red hair. He had red hair."

Just knowing the color of his hair gave a hint to his personality. This they could understand.

"What do you guess? Thirty-five? Maybe forty years old?" Maggie whispered.

Tipton nodded, as he dusted, "Yeah, no more than that."

Maggie hovered over the cleaning process, missing nothing. "How long ago," she asked.

"Dunno," Sam replied. "A long time. His clothes are pioneer Arizona. Maybe the turn of the century. Maybe the twenties."

A long, heavy leather coat, the fleece lining showing through several rips, encased most of the corpse. The heavy dust gave it a soft, woolen appearance. Only the dried hands and the trousers from the knees down were exposed. The legs were crossed as if he had been engaged in casual conversation when he dozed off. Tipton rapidly, but gently, whipped at the top leg with the burlap.

"And here's the reason he's here," Tipton announced. He carefully pulled back some the shredded trouser fabric. It had been crudely wrapped in cloth as if bandaged. Peering inside, Sam nodded, "The leg is torn all to hell. It looks as if it was chewed on long before he died."

Longfeather finished the thought, "I'd bet money he was hunting or something and the wolves or whatever they were, cornered him. They mauled his leg. He scrambled up here and shot as many as he could."

"Look at this!" Sam dusted around the back where a long

strip of canvas was visible. It encircled the crate and into the mummy's lap, where it was neatly knotted.

"He knew he was going to die and didn't want his body to fall off and be eaten by the animals. Damn! He tied the canvas around himself like a seat belt and watched sunsets until he died."

"Oh, God!" The quiet words escaped Maggie's lips without her meaning to. Sam looked back up at her. A tear was leaving a damp trace down a dusty cheek. Sam instantly remembered the same face with other tears. She couldn't stand another's pain. She was imagining the man's hopeless last hours.

"The old guy bled to death and then was probably frozen solid," Sam said. "By the time spring showed up, he was already dried out. The sun did the rest."

Glancing over the railing at the floor, Longfeather could see several animal skulls. He studied them and said, "So what did he shoot them with? I don't see a rifle around here."

Tipton scanned the area. "Yes, you do. It's right here."

He whipped at a long, slim shape laying in the shallow crate next to the mummy's throne. "What the hell?"

Sam whipped harder and dropped to his knees. Longfeather asked, "What's wrong?"

"There's a rifle here, but it's covered with something." The words came through gritted teeth. He worked his fingers under the shape, prying it from the bottom of the crate.

"What the hell is this?" It was obviously a rifle, but was overly long and wrapped in dry, crinkly burlap. The wrapping made it look more like an mummy than its former owner did.

Sam "Cowboy" Tipton attempted to unwrap it, but the burlap was brittle and stuck to a hard layer of something underneath. Finally, one end let go. Small pieces tore away to reveal a still-glistening layer of something soft and gooey.

"This goddamn rifle is completely covered in grease." He glanced at the pail next to the crate and dusted off the fading label, "Axle grease, that's what this stuff is. Dried axle grease! Our man here spent his dying hours mummifying his rifle!"

"Look at his hands," Tipton whipped the dust off one hand as he spoke, "They're covered with the same grease. He shoveled the stuff out of the bucket bare-handed and lathered up his rifle. He must have really loved this thing, whatever it is."

The long shape was impossible to identify. Removing the wrapping was going to be a long, messy process.

Sam looked closer at the mummy's withered, grease-caked hands. One was wrapped loosely around a small, canvas package. Carefully lifting it from under the hand, Tipton peeled the canvas aside, revealing several items covered in grease and burlap.

Sam immediately recognized the first. He burnished the grease from its surface and held it up in the morning light for Longfeather to admire.

He said, "This one of the finest old long-range tangent sights I've ever seen and it's graduated out to twelve hundred yards. This is a serious rifle we have here!"

He then turned his attention to the other small package. As its contents fell out into his hand, sunlight reflected off the gold surfaces of a pocket watch with a locket for a fob. Tipton inserted a fingernail into the crack. The locket popped open as if it had been closed only the day before.

Looking over his shoulder, Maggie Longfeather let out a single, soft syllable, "Oh!"

For the first time in generations, the sepia-toned photo of a young woman saw sunlight. She wore a turn-of-the-century, high-necked blouse, her long dark hair pulled over one shoulder. She stared into the camera with gentle eyes. Sam felt what the man sitting on the crate must have felt in his final moments. He could see the man's thoughts in the eyes of the young woman. She loved him, that much was clear. And he loved her. That was made clear by the effort he had put into preserving her picture.

Sam yanked a clean handkerchief out and carefully wrapped the watch and locket. Adding a layer of dusty burlap to the outside, he dipped his fingers into the still-soft bottom layers in the bucket and covered the small bundle with grease.

As he gently placed the packet back into the withered hand, he glanced up into the face. He said, "Sorry. Didn't mean to pry."

"Are you sure you want to do this?" Longfeather leaned against the side of the Willys, Maggie beside him. Both watched Sam stack his gear beside the mine building.

Sam Tipton set the bedroll up on a rock and answered, "Yeah, I want to do it. More than that, I need to do it. I have to do it!"

"How long do you figure?" Joseph Longfeather asked.

"Four days, Tipton answered. "Come back for me Thursday morning. I've got water for that long and that's all I need."

"Sam," Maggie sounded worried, "Are you sure you don't

want us to leave some food?"

"Nah, Charley says the peyote takes care of that." He dangled a small leather pouch out where the Longfeathers could see it.

Longfeather frowned and then smiled, "You know the Apache don't use that stuff. But it may help. I've heard all it does is make you nauseous and leave a hell of a headache. Be careful though, they say it can give you some really bad dreams."

Tipton smiled. It was a rueful smile. He said, "I'm already an old hand at bad dreams. Besides, I thought that's what a vision quest was all about. Facing up to your bad dreams and making them into good ones. Besides, I doubt if I've gone for four days without a drink for ten years. I ought to stay up here a full week."

Longfeather snorted, as he kicked the Willys into life and said, "No way. Four days. That's it."

Maggie echoed his sentiments from the other seat.

The sounds of the Willys bouncing back down the road faded and the late afternoon sun edged towards the horizon. Cowboy Tipton felt the first hint of an evening chill and buttoned his denim jacket. Grabbing his bedroll, he walked straight through the meadow's grass towards the stream where it fell off the edge of the mesa. His gear had barely hit the ground when he dropped down to lean back against it. He breathed deeply. The air had a near-narcotic freshness to it and evening shadows sculpted and re-sculpted the red stone of the canyon's walls. A doe stepped out of the pines. Its nose had found him. Its eyes were searching.

Four days, Tipton was thinking, as he looked around. This, he realized, was where he'd find himself, if indeed he could be found. The doe ambled slowly forward, its nose in the grass. She sensed Tipton was no threat.

Sam once again felt the old building staring down on him and he returned the stare. The darkness within the peak door high on the wall revealed nothing. He knew he was being watched from within. He felt as if he was being judged and that was okay. That was another part of a vision quest. To be judged by parts of the mind which have remained silent for too long.

Sam looked into the dark of the peak door. He welcomed the all-knowing gaze he knew was being returned. He was ready to be judged. He was ready to have his faults pointed out and dissected. He was ready to start over.

Twenty-one

"Sam! Exactly what the hell to do you think you're doing? Look at yourself! You're disgusting!"

The words stung. They knocked him even further off balance than the peyote had. Marilyn Tipton had never used that tone on him before. In fact, in their nearly ten years of marriage Sam wasn't certain he'd ever heard words come out of her with such vehemence. He huddled in his blanket protecting himself against the night cold and the awful truth of her words. Each syllable was an icy stiletto and left nasty, jagged wounds.

"How could you do this to us? I loved you so much, but not enough to make you do this!" Marilyn Tipton said.

She floated in Sam's vision. She was a fierce, gossamer phantom that foiled his attempts at focusing on her. Feet apart, hands on hips. She scolded him as he had never been scolded.

"Don't try to blame me or Melissa for this! Dammit, Sam Tipton, I'm not certain I even know who you are anymore."

Sam opened his mouth to speak but the words weren't there. After three days, he was too weak. Then, his words came as a quiet moan.

"Oh, God, Marilyn! Please!" Only the deteriorating strength of his body and the confusion of the peyote kept him from chasing her across the meadow. Or off the edge of the rim.

"Please! Please, don't hate me! Please, God I miss you so much!" His voice had become a soft wail.

"I miss you so, goddamn much! God, I...I...." The words struggled out between building sobs.

They fell on deaf ears.

"Sam Tipton, don't you try that shit with me!" A fiery glow danced around Marilyn Tipton. She wouldn't accept excuses.

"That's a crock and I don't want to hear any more of it!" she barked. "You're stronger than this! What the hell possessed you to think that losing your wife and child is an excuse for becoming a drunk?

"A drunk, Sam Tipton! That's what I said, a gutter-crawling drunk!" Her words were hard. Their barbs focused on the softest, most vulnerable parts of Sam's emotions.

"You'll never know how much I love you," she said. "You're not the first person this has happened to. If you had been killed while flying, what would you say to me, if I went out and became a drunk? Jesus, I'm disappointed in you!"

She continued without taking a breath, "Yes, that's the right word. I'm disappointed in you. And that's something I never thought I'd ever say about you. Or about any Tipton. You've let me down. You've let your father down. You've let the Longfeathers down. The other night you even let poor Charley Yee down. Most of all, you've let yourself down. Now, get up off your alcohol-soaked butt and be what you and I both know you can be. Now do it, dammit!"

All Sam could manage was a weak nod. When he looked up, she was gone, replaced by the dark nothingness of a fitful sleep.

"Daddy?" The voice was quiet and soft. The words tentative. The speaker wasn't certain it was okay to speak.

Sam looked up to find a sandy-haired young girl barely into her teens. She looked at him with questioning eyes.

"Daddy, it's me, Melissa. What's wrong daddy? What's happening to you?"

Sam blinked his eyes. He tried to focus on his daughter grown up. She was wearing one of his old Marine Corps sweatshirts. Her glistening, sandy hair flowed well past her shoulders. She wore cut-off jeans and bright blue sneakers. Sam took a quick breath of disbelief.

"Oh, God, Missy, you look so much like your mother!" His hand moved out to touch her. She was out of reach and he couldn't bring himself to stand. The shock of seeing her grown up overcame the shock of seeing her at all.

"Turn around, baby. Please! Turn around, I want to look at you." As she obeyed, he fell back to a sitting position and beamed. "Sweety, you're beautiful! You're absolutely beautiful!"

Tears welled in both of their eyes.

"Oh, daddy, do you really think so? Really?" Melissa Tipton said brightly.

"Oh, baby, how could you doubt it?" Sam replied.

"I miss you, daddy, and mommy does too. But, she's really mad at you right now. Really mad! She says you're blaming us for something we didn't do. I'm not sure I understand what, but you look awful, Daddy. I don't want to think we did this to you.

Please tell me we didn't do this to you."

Sam was quiet for a moment. Then he answered.

"You didn't, baby. I did it to myself. And...I'm sorry. I'm sorry and I'm going to get better I promise." As he spoke, he felt a thousand pieces of his soul fall into place as if a gust of wind had passed and autumn leaves were settling back to the ground. He suddenly felt tranquil. The storm was past.

"I hope so, Daddy, because it hurts us to know you're hurting. Please get better." She spoke as she walked towards the rim. Then off the edge. She stood in mid-air and looked at her father.

"Daddy, we love you and we just want you to be happy. You'll never know how much we want you to be happy." Her sad face brightened momentarily with a smile.

"Oh, yeah, one other thing, Daddy. His name is Ivan! We call him Ivan P. up here."

"Who, baby?" Tipton asked.

The only answer was the low whistling of the Mogollon wind through the pines below where he sat.

He repeated to himself, "Ivan who?" and fell into a deep, undisturbed sleep.

The sun was well up and Sam wasn't certain what woke him first. Blazing sun-light was trying to weasel its way into the sleeping bag which was securely zipped over his head and the sounds of something mechanical intruded on the early morning sounds of a canyon coming awake. A truck was coming.

 He gave up and surrendered to the morning. He wormed his way out of the bag and struggled into a sitting position. Only then did he realize he felt wonderful. His body felt like Raggedy Ann, floppy and weak, but overall, he felt wonderful.

Then a realization hit him which was so tangible, it was as though he could reach out and touch it. His mind was clear and no longer flitting from vague subject to vague subject. The fog of confusion was gone. He was focusing on one idea at a time. More important, the thoughts appeared to be leading somewhere as if they were part of a plan. It had been years since he had awakened to find his mind in gear and functioning. A smile tugged at the corners of his mouth.

He twisted around as Longfeather's big Jimmy crew cab four by four rumbled into the valley. He struggled out of the sleeping bag and stood unsteadily by the still smoldering remains of the campfire. The truck pulled alongside and each door opened to let a Longfeather exit. Maggie made it to him first.

"Sam...?" She stopped short and looked into his eyes. Her words were uncharacteristically timid, "...Are you...okay? How are you?"

Sam did his crazy Jack Nicholson imitation again and laughed loudly. Two hawks fluttered out of a pine a hundred yards down the valley. He grabbed Maggie, pulling her in to squeeze the life out of her. Longfeather stepped up beside them. He knew something was different.

Sam grinned, "How am I? I wish I knew. I wish I could tell you where I've been. It was a hell of a trip. A helluva trip! All I know is that I feel so wonderful I'm afraid to talk about it out loud. I might find I'm still dreaming."

He staggered slightly and Longfeather stepped forward to grab one arm.

"I feel wonderful and so goddamn hungry I'm going to eat a tree, if you don't get me off this mountain," Sam said.

"Let's hit Roberta's. I'm buying. Enchiladas all around." He stooped for his bedroll, being careful not to land on his head.

Just before climbing in the truck, he turned and stared into the small door on the top of the old building's front wall. He grinned. He and the building's long-time inhabitant shared a secret neither understood.

Twenty-two

Tipton should have been tired. He hadn't slept since Maggie and Longfeather had brought him home from the valley and he was still weak from trying to make sense out of his life. Introspection can be tiring. As his fingers pried at the dried, brittle, grease-soaked burlap, however, he was anything but tired. The fire generated by the enchiladas resting in his belly, washed down with a gallon of iced tea, had stoked his body's furnace. He kept asking himself, what was inside the over-sized bundle the mine's long-dead resident had cared so much about? The thought kept Sam wide awake.

The adobe's barn-like work area was a dark, dimensionless tomb. The reading lamp pulled low over the extra-long ancient bundle on the workbench created a small, indistinct ball of illumination that seemed lost in the building's expanse.

Sam started peeling at the skinny end of the bundle, cracking and pulling the covering until the brittle burlap grudgingly gave way. The first thing to appear was the end of a heavy, octagonal barrel. The dried matrix broke free and the front sight appeared as a glistening blob of still-fresh grease. A rag quickly rubbed it clean. Sam grinned at what he saw.

A short, protective metal tube hid the sight blade. Tipton turned the knurled knob on its side and felt it click. The sight had moved an unseen increment to one side. A final swipe of the rag revealed the small, liquid-filled tube mounted to the back of the sight. A tiny ball rolled lazily back and forth in the tube. It lined up with an index mark only when he held the rifle perfectly level.

"Well, old fella, you were one very serious shooter, that's for damn sure!" He knew spirit level front sights were seen only on the very finest target rifles at the turn of the century.

"I think I'm beginning to see why you loved your weapon so much. Let's see what else you have hidden in here."

He carefully inserted a knife between the barrel and the wrapping. He split the covering lengthwise as though removing an athlete's cast.

His fingers worked deep into the grease of the burlap mummy case. He forced the knife-cut open and freed the rifle from its grimy funeral wrappings. Even freed of the covering, it had so much grease globbed onto it, it was difficult to make out the shape within.

Tipton elbowed the empty husk aside and set about removing the bulk of the grease. First, wads of old newspaper. Then rags. Lots of rags. The grease began to thin.

"You've got good taste, old man. Good taste! Remington rolling block. Nice!" Sam wiped as much of the action clean as he could, "Yessir, you were a very serious shooter."

He pulled the massive hammer back and thumbed the receiver block open, exposing the chamber. It was also full of grease, "Boy, you didn't want this thing rusting did you?" Sam laughed.

The more he wiped, the greasier it became, it seemed.

As the fancy crotch grain of the claro walnut stock came to light, so did the silver sheen of a carefully inlaid silver plate. The engraved lettering was upside down and he flipped the rifle around to read it. A fresh rag wiped and the letters came into focus. He read them out loud. "First Place, 600 yards, Ivan Petrovitch, Sept. 17, 1902."

Sam didn't even hear himself, as he repeated, "Ivan Petrovitch. Ivan P.!"

He went limp as his mind re-lived his peyote dreams. He wanted to say something but didn't know what. She had said it. Melissa had said Ivan P.!

"Missy, you knew all along!" He barely breathed the words. His eyes roamed slowly the length of the exquisite long-range target rifle. "Well, Ivan P., not only do you have great taste in firearms, but you know how to pick your friends, as well. I envy you. Tell her 'Hi!' for me."

Sam Tipton slept soundly that night.

Twenty-three

Ted Fowler hated coming to a stop at the crumbling curb. The dust cloud following would settle on his BMW, then he'd have to risk washing it, which meant risking rag scratches, which meant having it compounded, which led to thinner paint, which....

Ted Fowler's BMW was his image machine. He reserved it for Kiwanis meetings or going to the bank. Real estate prospecting was done in his hulking Ford station wagon. That also kept him from sticking out as being an outsider and outsiders have more money than brains. Most Pitacho regulars knew that.

He did a toupee check in the rearview mirror before stepping onto the gravel-strewn concrete in front of Roberta's open door. For the same reason he called it his Kiwanis Kar. He needed an image boost.

That time of the day the streets were even more deserted than usual, with not a person or a car in sight other than his own. Mid-morning in Pitacho didn't really exist to the locals.

As Fowler stepped through the door, he hesitated, to let his eyes adjust to the darkness. It was as he expected. He had the bar to himself.

Making his way through the tables, he was suddenly aware of the primitive nature of the saloon. He hadn't noticed it before. Dark nights, low lights and a lot of beer gave it a certain rustic quality. The cold light of day stripped away any hint of ambiance. By day, it was a miserable, empty old building. The only sounds were the subtle clinking of glasses being washed to the accompaniment of generic country music coming from an old portable radio with a badly-cracked speaker cone.

The saloon's busty matron was washing glassware from the night before. Roberta looked over her shoulder at the sounds of peanut shells being crushed underfoot.

"Hey, real estate man!" She always assumed a friendly encounter unless proven otherwise. "Otherwise" could be taken care of by the .45.

"Hi! It's Roberta isn't it?" Fowler's voice had slid up in pitch until it was only marginally lower than Roberta's.

"Ted Fowler." He offered his hand over the bar.

Roberta held up both suds-covered hands and smiled, "Sorry."

Fowler smiled and nodded.

"What can I do for you ?" Roberta asked. "I haven't started lunch yet. How about a beer?" She wiped her hands on the towel hanging over one shoulder.

"Yes, that would be fine." Fowler stretched slightly to watch her lean over to get the beer out of the depths of the cooler.

Her usual leather vest had been discarded in favor of a tight fitting, sleeveless tee-shirt for work around the bar. Fowler could see she wore no bra. Her breasts moved independently, as she leaned over. They appeared soft beneath the thin layer of cotton. Ted Fowler licked his lips and looked away as she handed him the beer.

"Yeah, just drove up for the day," he said awkwardly and motioned even more awkwardly towards the dust-covered, but still-gleaming Beemer visible through the door.

Roberta glanced at it, "Nice car."

"Thank you," Fowler said as he tried to engage Roberta's eyes. He failed.

"Say, don't you have anyone helping you here?" He asked.

"Nope, just me. That's all I need. All I want." Roberta kept her head down, back to him, washing glasses.

"Ah, come now, everyone needs someone," Fowler's voice lost some of its shaky tone, as his nerves calmed down.

Roberta lifted her head for a second and pushed the hair out of her eyes with the heel of one hand. She glanced in the mirror at the real estate man behind her. He was licking his lips and hadn't touched his beer. Jesus! Here we go again, she thought.

"No, Fowler, I need no one. I want no one and I mean it." She continued scrubbing glasses.

"Well, you know," Fowler's reflection in the mirrored showed him reaching in his pocket, "Someone like me could make it a lot easier for you."

He punctuated the sentence by slapping something onto the bar. Roberta turned to look. It was a wad of bills as big as her wrist. The bill on the outside was a hundred.

"Exactly what are you saying?"

Fowler slipped down off his stool. He pushed the money towards her and walked quickly around the bar. Roberta subtly nudged the exposed barrel of the .45 with the inside of her forearm. She wanted it loose in the abbreviated holster.

He walked up to her, his chin barely over Roberta's softly moving breasts. He held the wad of bills up and said, "What I'm saying is, I can be very nice to people who are very nice to me. That's what business is all about."

His eyes traveled slowly up and down the dark barkeep and he said, "You take care of my business and I," he flourished the bills up at eye level, "will take care of yours."

Roberta smiled wickedly, "Why Mr. Fowler!" her voice carried a playful lilt, "If I didn't know any better I would say you were propositioning me."

Fowler moved closer. He could smell her combination of bath oil and soap suds. He licked his lips again.

"Oh, I don't think I'd phrase it that way," Fowler tried to put a lilt into his own voice but failed. "However, if you could find me as attractive as I find you, there's a good possibility this will stay where it is."

A bead of sweat rolled down Fowler's forehead as he placed the wad of bills on the bar.

"Mr. Fowler! That looks like all the money in the world." She sounded like an excited little girl and smiled even more wickedly, if that was possible.

"Five hundred, Miss Roberta, five hundred dollars!" Fowler said the words as if he was announcing the State Lottery winner.

"Oh, my God, Ted, are you saying you would give me all five hundred if I would just let you make love to me?" The coy excitement in her voice was a bit overplayed. Actually, it was a lot overplayed.

"If you want to put it in such blunt terms, Yes, I guess that's what I'm saying," Fowler answered.

"I don't believe it Ted! Five hundred dollars and all I have to do is fuck you?"

Fowler was instantly aroused. The blood which was being diverted to his crotch from his brain slowed his thought processes. He had missed the way Roberta's words had lost their excitement and became hard.

"Ted Fowler, I'd be happy to fuck you for free!" she growled between clenched teeth.

Roberta's booted foot came up between Fowler's legs and lifted him a solid six inches off the floor. Eyes instantly wide and round, he stared at Roberta on the way to the floor. Then, as he twitched into an embryonic position, the pain registered. He clutched his crotch and screamed.

Roberta scooped the cash off the bar and stuffed it into the front of Fowler's pants. Then she dragged him towards the door like a sagging bag of laundry. She gained momentum and used it to launch Ted Fowler, real estate mogul and rejected lover, through the air onto the hood of his own car. The dent he made was shaped like a metal snow angel.

Roberta was already back inside the bar by the time Fowler fell off the hood. He had to crawl into the driver's seat. He never saw her staple his toupee to a beam over the bar next to the one he had lost weeks earlier.

Roberta never heard Fowler hissing quietly as he backed painfully into the street and drove slowly away.

"I'll get you bitch. I'll get you. First Tipton. Then you."

Twenty-four

Kwan was unusual for his race and he knew it. He was unusual for many reasons. Not the least of which was his willingness to shop in a used clothing store. Most in his native Japan would not associate with another's clothing. It was unclean. Kwan, however, had a need to look decidedly unclean.

He studied his face in the mirror while trying on a number of tired-looking cowboy hats. This was one time that another unusual feature, his mixed ancestry, would come to his advantage. An orphan, he never knew for sure which side of his family it came from, but it was likely there was some Filipino in his blood. Or some other western Pacific DNA. It had all but erased the skinfold down the corner of his eyes.

He looked closely at his eyes in the dirty mirror. A single minor cosmetic feature, like the shape of one's eyes, had set race against race for thousands of generations. The willingness to kill because of a cosmetic difference was, he recognized, one of man's many universal failings. It was also one of the foundations for his business. He had made a huge fortune, even by Japanese standards, from the illogical dislike of one group for another.

Though he had his own clear-cut definition of right and wrong, he never applied those standards to his clients. Neither was right. Neither was wrong. There was simply the side with the most money. He'd do the job. Take the money. Then disappear back into his own elegant world which existed in a nearly invisible crack between the other worlds.

He glanced at the mirror again. Eliminate that single fold of skin and it was difficult to tell race from eyes alone. That's how it was with Kwan. His ancestors had given him almond-shaped, dark eyes which could be from anywhere in the Pacific Rim. Or the eyes which stared back at him from under a sagging old cowboy hat could be those of any number of Native American tribes.

The skin color wasn't quite right. And the features were a little too fine. Dressed in a faded denim shirt and five-dollar jeans, however, few would question his ethnic origins. He looked local.

A genuine imitation silver and turquoise belt buckle had cost twice as much as the pants and shirt and his feet felt trapped in the pointy-toed cowboy boots. Like everything else he wore, the boots were scuffed and bruised. Desert dust had worked its way into the crevasses and small drying cracks radiated up from the soles. The boots had worked hard in their lifetime. Kwan now had the same look.

It was all camouflage. Turning his head from side to side in the mirror, he saw the camouflage worked. He would be nearly invisible anywhere in Arizona. He loosened his short pony tail to let the jet black hair hang loose beneath the sweat stained, mottled hat. Yes, he would pass.

As Kwan disappeared through the door carrying his new wardrobe in several bags, the dried up old Mexican woman behind the cash register watched. She judged him to be a nice man. For an Indian, that is.

It took only a few minutes for the cab to pick him up and sun-bleached side streets channeled it north towards downtown Phoenix. He had some more serious shopping to do. Head near the window, Kwan caught as much of the blistering breeze as he could. He again reminded himself why he so hated American transportation systems. Seldom did they include hygiene and maintenance. The stitched welting in the upholstery acted as mini-dams, collecting as much dust as they would hold. Cords showed through carpet with its nap polished flat. Grime and dust. Cracked plastic. Fraying foam rubber. Very crude transportation.

He stared through heat waves at dirt back yards drifting past. Sad little houses. Vacant lots harboring neighborhood refuse. Mummified junk cars, looking like metallic cadavers. Each car attracted a seemingly identical number of brown-skinned kids and skinny dogs. Everything was rooted in dust. It rose into the heat to form a thin haze. It made the heat seem tangible. As if he could reach out and touch it.

Dust didn't exist in his homeland. Not even in the rundown areas. There was too much rain and vegetation. Too much pride.

Here, he'd have to learn to live with dust. And with the monochromatic landscape that was the American West. In some ways, he found the profound nakedness of the landscape comforting, as if it had given up hiding its true form. As if it was allowing him to see its inner-self.

He remembered an American cowboy author who had once said that to make peace with the West, a person had to forget the color green. The west had baked that color out of the spectrum. Kwan could make the adjustment.

"Stop!" Kwan was instantly leaning over the front seat, "Stop right here. I need to buy something in there." He gestured out the window at a Circle K convenience store. "Wait."

He walked quickly inside and emerged a few minutes later. His very Native American-looking eyes were hiding behind a pair of very American-looking wraparound sun glasses. He'd seen something similar in a movie which he liked. The cab driver interrupted his study of a Bulgarian-English dictionary as Kwan returned. He made up his mind to laugh if the Indian said, "I'll...be...back" in a fake Austrian accent. If he laughed, maybe he'd get a decent tip out of this one.

"Take me to this address," Kwan ordered. He handed a slip of paper to the driver. As the cab sped along, Kwan continued to amuse himself by looking at all the unusual cacti. Especially the tall skinny ones they called saguaros. They looked like something only Hollywood would concoct.

The test hadn't been hard. He'd stood in line waiting to take the test longer than the actual testing process had taken. As he stepped out into the sunlight he held the newly-minted drivers license up and studied it. The dead pan picture on it was that of a Native American named Thomas Hogan.

His laptop computer had selected that name after a series of parameters were fed to it for searching the data base. One of the parameters was recent death. The computer said Thomas Hogan's name had become available only yesterday. It would be weeks before the rest of the Nation's computer files knew Mr. Hogan had died and thereby loaned his social security number and life experience to an enterprising Japanese entrepreneur.

Thomas Hogan sounded like a safe name. He didn't want to sound too Indian and not be able to answer questions he should know. He just wanted to look Indian.

He slipped a quarter in the pay phone and called another taxi.

"Yes sir, can I help you? We have a fine selection of premium used vehicles..."

Kwan had barely closed the door to the taxi when the car salesman descended upon him. He was short and fat with horribly pock-marked skin. Kwan found him offensive in every detail.

Kwan tried to stay upwind of the yapping salesman as much as possible and ignored him. Kwan knew exactly what he was looking for. As he cruised the long line of dust-covered vehicles with signs painted in fluorescent yellow on the windshields, however, he didn't see it.

The salesman was at his heels like an obese bull terrier, when Kwan stepped back to the curb. He looked in both directions for another car lot. The salesman intensified his barrage of salesspeak. Kwan raised his psychological defenses another notch.

As he pivoted his head from side to side, he finally saw what he was looking for. It was sequestered at the back corner of the lot. It sat high on its knobby tires, but not so high as to be out of place in the area. It was less than ten years old, but looked older. Its past owner obviously liked racing down dry washes to go vaulting up the sand banks like a three-hundred horsepower skateboarder. He had modified it accordingly. The roll bar was rusting gracefully and two of the four lights on the overhead light bar had broken lenses. The dark maroon paint was oxidized to a dull reddish gray. It had obviously spent its entire life being broiled by the Arizona sun.

Kwan approached and dropped to his haunches to study the underside. It was as he hoped. The mechanical underpinnings were stout and much newer than the truck. The owner had used, but not abused his toy. He had enjoyed taking care of its functioning parts.

"Ah, I'm sorry but that truck ain't for sale. It belongs to my boss." The sales terrier had taken much longer than Kwan to cross the lot. Sweat streaked his forehead from the work-out. "He loves this old thing and spends every weekend puttin' somethin' new on it."

Kwan ignored him. His eyes continued studying the truck, as he spoke, "How much?"

"I'm sorry, I guess you didn't hear m..."

"I said how much?" Kwan still ignored him.

"Now, look Indian, I just said..."

Kwan snapped his head around and stared hard into the salesman's eyes. His voice showed his irritation. "Go find him and tell him I want to buy his truck. Now!"

The salesman's mouth was frozen in mid-word and the sweat on his brow instantly doubled. "Yes sir," was all he could mumble. He stumbled backwards toward the bleached and rust streaked trailer that was the office.

He was back in minutes. A tall, heavily tanned, athletic-looking blond man in his late twenties was on his heels. His dark blue tee-shirt was stretched to its limits and showed the painstakingly sculptured weight-lifter body to its maximum. The effect was exactly what the young man wanted. He looked impressive. He knew he looked impressive, and was used to impressing people.

Kwan was not impressed.

"I want to buy your truck," Kwan said quietly.

"Now look, buddy, my man here told you..."

Kwan ended sales negotiations by pulling a thick wad of bills out of his pocket. The weight-lifter's blue eyes got even wider as Kwan counted off one-hundred-dollar bills. He kept counting until he was certain he had exceeded the value of the truck by a wide margin. He wasn't in the mood to quibble.

"Sir, you have just bought yourself the most reliable, most powerful, most..." the blond bundle of muscle started to say.

Kwan interrupted, "Finish the paperwork now. I want to leave in a few minutes."

"Yessir. Immediately. I'll even have my man wash it for you right now. I spent yesterday in the desert and..."

"Don't wash it. Don't touch it. Don't look at it. Just finish the paperwork and let me get on my way." Kwan had little patience for small people, regardless of their size. Besides, the dirt and mud layered on the truck was all part of the camouflage.

Faded jeans. Scuffed boots. Sweat-stained hat. Dirty four-wheel-drive truck. He looked like a Native American who had never been out of the state. He looked like a Zonie.

The instant Kwan keyed the ignition preparing to launch into traffic, the tape player blared into life. A hard-driving country song stabbed Kwan with a whining twang. He ripped the tape out of the player and flung it out the window at the Mutt and Jeff of used car sales who were still excitedly counting the money.

Kwan would do many things in the interest of camouflage. Listening to American country music, however, wasn't one of them. He had his own dignity to consider. And his sanity.

Twenty-five

The noise still echoed off the surrounding cliffs when Longfeather said, "Six o'clock, two inches low."

His eyes never left an old brass telescope resting on the window ledge.

Another explosion and Longfeather's voice droned into the still air within the adobe, "Touching the last one."

Another explosion, "An inch right of the other two. You have a loose cloverleaf two inches down."

Sam twisted the knurled knob on the tangent rear sight. The aperture disk through which he was sighting crept up few thousands of an inch. A hollow "thunk" echoed down the heavy barrel as a fresh round slid into place. Sam took a deep breath and lined the sights up on the bullseye four hundred yards distant. He pushed the trigger forward to set it. The slightest pressure would now release it. Half of the breath came back out and he held it.

His finger barely touched the trigger. A sharp crack slammed the heavy rifle into his shoulder. Even the shooting muffs couldn't protect him from the muzzle blast as it rolled back over him.

"Bull! Dead on!' Longfeather said.

Many explosions later, Longfeather walked back into the building, target in hand. Tipton was running a cleaning rod down the old single-shot's barrel from the breech end. Longfeather held the target up, "It doesn't come any better than this, partner!"

The center of the target was a confused collection of holes, none of them more than a inch from the center.

"With a scope, that thing would be incredible. If old Ivan hadn't gotten himself cornered by wolves, he would have been in all the record books." Longfeather thumb tacked the target to the window frame over the shooting bench.

A knock on the door drew their attention. Sam "Cowboy" Tipton carefully laid the rifle down and walked to answer it. He opened the door and found two of his own faces staring back at him, reflected in silver sunglasses under a stiffly starched cowboy hat of the style only worn by the Sheriff's deparment.

"Hey, Tipton, you're waking up the neighbors!"

The speaker's hand rested confidently on the butt of a stainless steel Smith and Wesson .357 riding in a thumb-break holster on his hip.

"**Sam, this is Ted Fowler**, the owner of this property. He's asked my office to assist him in evicting you." Sam looked past the tall, slim sheriff at the triumphant eyes of Ted Fowler peering back at him. He was smirking and stood a respectful distance back. Sam only barely recognized him. The poorly-fitting toupee was all that jogged his memory.

The words finally worked their way into Sam's pre-occupied brain and he asked, "Owner? Sheriff, I don't think there is an owner to this dump."

"There is now, Sam," the sheriff's eyes said more than his words. It was obvious Fowler wasn't one of his favorite people. Especially since he was forcing him to serve papers on a friend from his own hell-raising days back in high school.

The Sheriff held up a folded piece of paper and said, "Fowler has legal deed to this property. Bought it at a tax sale a couple of days ago and I'm here to ask you to vacate the premises."

"...vacate the premises..." The legal phrase seemed out of place coming from Wally Rickert's mouth. To Sam, Rickert would always be the same stringy, bespectacled, shy kid who walked down the school halls with his eyes on his feet but became an absolute wild man after only two beers.

"Wait a minute! Don't I have thirty days or something?" Sam asked.

"Oh, come on!" Fowler had finally found enough courage to speak up. With the Sheriff between him and Tipton, he found more courage than was necessary. "You're a squatter, not a goddamn tenant. You're trespassing. Shit, I could have you arrested for that alone. You ought to thank me that I'm only asking you to get the hell off my property."

Then, under his breath, but not quiet enough, Fowler said, "...I'll teach you assholes to mess with me. All of you..."

"Fowler, you miserable little shit, just what the hell..." Sam took a step towards the real estate man. Fowler backed up and the sheriff put an arm in front of Sam.

"He's within his rights," Rickert said. "Technically, you are trespassing and I'm going to have to ask you to get off the property. I'm here representing the law, Sam, you know that. Please, don't cause trouble," the sheriff implored.

Tipton finally found his voice, "Goddammit, Wally, I've been living here nearly eight years and now that sorry little puke wants me to just walk out? Come on! Give me a break!"

"Hey, what's happening?" Eddie "Mad Dog" Mandell sauntered around the corner of the building. A large gear missing several teeth was clutched in one hand. Seeing what was obviously a confrontation, Mandell seized the opportunity. He glanced at Fowler, than back at Tipton. He laughed, "What happened? Did the guy in the cheap sports jacket offer to trade you a drink for a blow job and you refused so he's suing?"

Mandell was just starting to laugh when Fowler barked, "Shut the fuck up, fat man, you're trespassing too. Get the hell off my property."

"Now just a goddamn minute, you little..." Mandell started.

Sheriff Rickert stepped between the two.

"All of you shut the hell up!"

Eddie Mandell's face was the same bright red as his new Cadillac. His pudgy little hands clinched and unclenched at his side. He was pissed. Fowler had not made a friend.

Sam faced the sheriff, "I've got too much stuff. I can't just walk off and leave all of this." His hand gestured towards the immense amount of what appeared to be junk carefully arranged in rows behind the building.

The sheriff turned and looked. He knew nothing about airplanes, although the remains of the Staggerwing Beechcraft biplane were impressive. The fabric cover hung in tatters between the ribs, like flapping skin on a wood and steel skeleton. The other airplanes were too far dismantled to identify. The old cars scattered between the ancient mining equipment were mostly Ford roadsters. Those he could identify and he again remembered high school days. Longfeather and Tipton had been legends for building fast hotrods in Tipton's shop on his father's ranch.

"Tipton, you get your shit off my property, now! Right now! Hell, I'll even help you." Fowler was taking his new role of land owner seriously.

Feeling the weight of the law behind him, the real estate weasel took several quick steps forward. A cigarette lighter flashed in his hand. Instantly a piece of fabric hanging from the Staggerwing burst into flame. The bright yellow tongue licked hungrily up the fabric towards the rest of the airplane.

Without a word, Tipton leaped forward, ripped the fabric

clear and threw it to the ground. Mandell stomped out the flames.

"Jesus, Fowler! How fucking dumb can you be?" Mandell yelled at the real estate man who was still grinning. "You want to start a brush fire here and burn the whole goddam town down? What the hell has Tipton done to you, anyway?"

Fowler's lips were just framing an answer when Sam Tipton flashed past Mandell. His fist caught Fowler squarely in the nose. Blood spurted in all directions. Eyes round and unfocused, Fowler fell backwards into a sitting position on the dirt with Sam right after him.

"Sam!" The strong voice of Joseph Longfeather cut through the commotion. He leaned in the doorway watching the proceedings. Ever the peacemaker.

Tipton stopped in his tracks and looked down at Fowler's round face. A red rivulet ran from both nostrils.

"Sheriff! Jesus Christ! Sheriff, did you see that? Arrest him. Arrest him now!" Fowler was screaming.

Sheriff Rickert didn't make a move.

"Goddammit, Rickert," Fowler screamed. "I pay part of your fucking salary. Now earn it and arrest Tipton. You saw what he did."

The sheriff looked down at Fowler sitting in the dust and frowned. He pushed his hat back with a thumb. It was an exaggerated, theatrical move he'd once seen in a movie.

"Gheez, Mr. Fowler, I'm really sorry. I must have blinked because I didn't see a single thing until after you tripped and fell."

"You piece of..." Fowler caught himself.

"I don't give a shit, get him off my land." Fowler held a handkerchief to his nose and pointed at Tipton.

Wally Rickert looked at Sam, a question in his eyes.

Sam looked at the massive collection of seemingly worthless mechanical contraptions of all descriptions. It represented a decade of desert scrounging. A hopeless look settled into his eyes. Longfeather walked up and put a hand on his shoulder.

"Where to, bro? We can do it!"

"Where to?" Tipton was thinking as he spoke. "Shit! I don't even know how! That's a lot of junk."

"Get it off my goddamn property," Fowler yelled as he walked slowly towards his car, handkerchief wadded to his nose. Sheriff Rickert caught up with him and, out of earshot, had a terse conversation. Rickert appeared to be doing all the talking. Fowler listened with a stone face.

"Okay, goddammit! You have two days!" Fowler yelled at Tipton. "Two goddamn days and I burn everything left. Everything, you got it!" Fowler's screaming was that of an enraged washerwoman. As he slammed his station wagon door, a muffled "Two goddamn days," escaped through the closed windows.

Sheriff Rickert ambled easily back towards Longfeather, Mandell and Tipton. "I could be wrong, but I think Fowler wants you off his land in two days. What do you think?" Rickert was only half smiling. "Can you do it?"

Tipton looked over at Longfeather and suddenly felt weak. "Hell no we can't do it! We'll just take the lightest stuff and let him torch the rest. Shit!"

He looked upwards into the empty sky, "Shit!"

Tipton focused on the sheriff and said, "My two days start tomorrow right? Not right now."

"Yeah, I think we can make that interpretation. Two days starting tomorrow. But, where're you going to put everything? This is a helluva lot of stuff," the Sheriff said.

"I have an idea," Tipton answered, "but I don't have the slightest idea how. We only have the two trucks and one trailer. Worse than that, we have to rig an 'A' frame every time we want to lift something heavy. But..."

He was interrupted by the sound of Mandell's Cadillac scattering gravel as it slewed sideways towards town.

"That's what I've always liked about Mad Dog. You can count on him in a crunch." Looking over at Longfeather, Sam Tipton squared his shoulders and said, "Let's go. We have some packing to do. But first...." He held an index finger in the air, "A trip to Roberta's."

"Damn!" he lamented. "One day sober and I'm already wishing I was still a drinking man."

Twenty-six

"**Okay, Tipton,**" **Longfeather** spoke through gritted teeth, his shoulder hard against an old flat-belt lathe that didn't want to go up on the trailer. "Tell me again whose silly damned idea it was to piss Fowler off."

He paused to wipe the sweat out of his eyes with his sleeve. Longfeather looked across the trailer, "Roberta told me what happened. All of this over a stupid toupee!" He tried to sound angry, but Longfeather had never been good at hiding his grins. He started laughing.

"I thought it was funny at the time, but this is getting to be hard work! Besides, since when does a white man who's a graduate of Penn State take scalps?"

Tipton didn't answer.

"Incidentally, I don't think a toupee counts as a scalp," Longfeather added.

Tipton was breathing hard as he looked at the disheveled pile of mechanical exotica heaped on the trailer. His truck was also full. The Willys bulged with smaller tools and taped-together computer units, its suspension was crushed tight to the axle snubbers by the load.

The sun had begun to crawl out of bed and was driving horizontal gold spikes through everything in sight. Dark shadows lay between the shafts of light. The Tipton/Longfeather junkyard was a jumbled maze of light and dark as the low light found its way through missing windshields and open fuselage trusses.

Sam leaned back against the trailer rail and watched the quickly-changing light-show in progress.

"We're not going to make it," Tipton said. It was a flat statement. "This is our first load and we must have twenty out there." His shoulders slumped a little as he spoke.

"Yeah, I know. But we'll just do the best we can," Longfeather replied.

"But we can't lose the Staggerwing." Tipton was emphatic. "It'll take us the rest of the day to get it apart and loaded, but I don't want that slimeball to burn it. The old girl deserves better."

Longfeather nodded.

The low light was just beginning to outline the Staggerwing's bones. Her sleek windshield was dust covered and spider-webbed with cracks but still flowed over the rotting five-place cabin. Sixty years earlier a wealthy tycoon had luxuriated in his ability to lay back in that cabin and cross the country at the unheard of speed of two hundred miles an hour. Now, her four elliptical-shaped wings were a ragged pattern of torn fabric and exposed wood. Where the big radial engine should hang was a blunt collection of severed wires and bent tubing. Even in the near dark, she was beautiful to Sam Tipton's eyes. He wasn't going to let her die at the hands of a small, spiteful and very bald man.

Tipton smiled a melancholy smile. Much of his precious junk was going to die. He hadn't done much with his life since Marilyn and Melissa, but what he had done was in that old building. Or crowded around it. Now much of it would disappear because of a toupee.

"I don't know, Longfeather. Maybe it's just as well." Tipton was trying to sound philosophical. "We were getting too much junk anyway. Thoreau was right, 'simplify, simplify.' Of course Thoreau wouldn't know neat shit if it bit him in the ass."

He laughed in spite of his feelings. Biting Thoreau in the ass struck him as being funny.

"What the hell is that?" Longfeather cocked his ear at a deep-throated rumble coming from the street-side of the adobe. In unison, the two walked around the building to the street.

As they stepped into the nearly-dark main thoroughfare of Pitacho they were blinded by a endless line of headlights.

The first vehicle rumbled past in a cloud of dust. It was a huge wrecker of the type used to move tractor trailers. That didn't surprise either Tipton or Longfeather. The oversized wreckers were a common sight around mining areas. The men were surprised, however, when the wrecker turned and pulled around behind the adobe. The procession followed its leader. An endless line of trucks and low-boy heavy equipment trailers flowed down the dark street and curled around the adobe.

Sam pounded on the driver's side door of the wrecker with the flat of his hand and shouted up at the face within, "Hey, what's going on? You working for Fowler?"

It would be just like the narrow-necked geek to send a crew to grind all of his rusty treasures into the dirt.

A face leaned out of the truck. Sam recognized it as Larry

Crandall, one of Mandell's machinists. They had worked together on a number of repair jobs.

"I don't know no Fowler," the young machinist yelled above the din of idling diesels, "and we don't work for him. The boss said we work for you today. Actually, what he said was the mine was closed for the day and he wouldn't notice if any of the equipment was missing."

Sam stepped back and focused his eyes on the door of the truck. The sun cast just enough light for him to make out the words, "Mandell Mining, Inc."

Tipton was barely able to overcome his surprise enough to yell, "You mean the old man did this for us?"

"Hell no! He's still in L.A." Crandall yelled. "Eddie gave us the day off and told us about your problem. Said something about not wanting to lose a machinist. So, me and the boys thought we'd stop by and see if you needed a hand."

Sam looked down the line of trucks. There were dozens of empty beds and long spacious trailers. He looked at the big wrecker. It could load the adobe itself on board a trailer. He was glad it was still dark enough no one could see the mist in his eyes.

"So, what about it, Tipton? You've done favors and fixed things for every man in this line. You have anything we can do to help pay you back?"

Sam was speechless. The door on the other side of the truck slammed. The sound of boots crunching through gravel worked its way around the front of the truck until two significantly-shaped female forms stood in the head lights.

"Hey Tipton, you going to stand there and make us do all the work?" Roberta's raucous laugh rang through the gathering light.

"And how about you, Joseph Longfeather?" Maggie's voice taunted her brother, "You going to let us girls show you up?"

As if on signal, men poured from all the trucks and crowded past the still-shocked Joseph Longfeather and Sam Tipton. The two stepped numbly aside as the wrecker backed into the open door of the adobe. It extended its lifting rail to a huge old milling machine the two had written off as being too heavy to move.

Several men moved to the milling machine. They turned and looked expectantly at Sam Tipton. He returned the stare.

"Sam!" Maggie pulled at his sleeve forcing him to refocus on the proceedings.

In an instant, his mind snapped into gear. He scanned the

crowd of men, all of whom were looking at him.

"Longfeather, you take the airplanes. I'll do the machine shop. Then the cars." His words were quick and direct, just short of being orders.

In a matter of minutes he was pointing and talking, rapidly telling men wearing leather gloves and plaid shirts what to do with all of his earthly possessions. In only a few minutes the first truck was loaded and lined up on the road waiting for the rest. The old adobe was a swarm of worker ants working frantically to move the nest to higher ground.

In the middle of it Sam Tipton answered questions and helped pack smaller items into boxes and bags. At one point he looked up and caught Maggie Longfeather staring at him.

She smiled and Sam felt its brightness cut clear to his heart. She was proud of the change she was seeing and he could feel it. He was proud himself. It was a beginning. He started to walk towards her for a hug, but she ducked into the crowd and began to carry another load towards another truck. Sam reminded himself to get that hug later.

Sam Tipton stood in front of the wrecker, now parked on the street with the rest. He looked down the line of trucks stretching most of the way across the small town. The dust-covered chrome stacks and typically red Mandell paint jobs glistened in the late morning sun. He couldn't believe what he was seeing. It hadn't taken even half a day for the mob of men and equipment to load every piece of scrap-iron laying around the adobe.

The Stinson L-5 looked forlorn and lost in the middle of an empty piece of desert behind the adobe. Only a few hours earlier it been a massive, and very unique, junkyard. Longfeather was at that moment climbing into the old aircraft. He was going to fly to a local field to get gas. Then he'd make the short flight to the Stinson's new home. They didn't want to leave the old airplane behind for even a second with Fowler on the loose.

"How 'bout it Cowboy? We're ready to rock and roll!" It was Roberta standing on the running board of the wrecker. The Willys was in front of it, ready to lead the procession.

She held on to the edge of the roof, leaning out like a wagon master. She looked ready to yell "Round 'em up and move 'em out!" expecting Rowdy Yates or some other Eastwood lookalike to jump to her command.

Maggie stood by the Willys waiting for Sam.

Tipton held up a single finger, silently saying he'd be back in a second. He walked quickly around the adobe and through the same old massive door he had opened a thousand times. It hadn't been a palace. But, it had been home. It was there that a part of him had continued to live. The mechanical part had made it home after the emotional part had died.

It was his machines that had kept him sane. And kept him alive. Without them he knew sooner or later he would have been found curled up beneath a greasewood bush frozen to death. Or dead from alcohol poisoning. It had happened to lots of others.

Stripped of its motley collection of machines and assorted junk, the inside of the adobe seemed much larger. It had a hollow loneliness about it. It looked so much different than he remembered when he had found himself out back sleeping in the abandoned Willys. Breathing life back into the Willys had been his first project.

That first morning, the adobe had looked like a mud and stucco version of himself. Warped and leaning. Badly cracked and barely able to stand. Why he had decided to call it home he never knew. And still didn't. Maybe he had recognized himself in the old building. But it had been a home. Now it was a home in the past tense.

He stood momentarily in the middle of the dark, empty cube of ancient space and said, "So long old girl. We'll try to protect you from Fowler."

He walked over to where his cot had stood. He picked the clear plastic bag containing the shined pair of boots off the wide, adobe window sill. The boots went where he went and he was going to a new home. As he stood in the doorway, hand on well-worn wrought iron ring, he looked back inside one last time and he smiled. It was time to move on. He was ready for it. He jogged around the corner and saw Roberta and Maggie standing together at the wrecker. He grinned as he shouted, "Round 'em up and move 'em out."

Dozens of diesels rattled into life as he dropped into the driver's seat of the Willys. Maggie climbed in to ride shotgun. He grinned at his own bright eyes reflected in the rearview mirror. Yes, he was ready to move on.

On impulse, he grabbed Maggie and gave her a strong kiss on the lips. He immediately dropped back behind the wheel. He was coaxing the old Willys into life and missed the surprised look in Maggie's eyes. He also missed the subtle smile on her lips.

The Willys had been the first into the valley. Sam and Maggie stood at the top of the grade and looked down at the long line of heavily-loaded trucks inching their way up the tortuous road. It was wasn't wide enough for a normal truck so the low-boys had one side hanging out into space to keep from rubbing the rock wall. They would make it, but just barely.

Sam hadn't given any thought to what they were going to do with all that stuff when the trucks unloaded. All he knew was the mine and its building was big and empty. And free.

Just then a shadow flashed over them. Maggie instinctively ducked as the Stinson roared over the canyon wall, diving directly at her. Seeing her duck, Longfeather knew he'd achieved the desired result and came around to land. The big tires whispered through the tall grass as the airplane sighed and settled back to Earth. Sam and Maggie walked to the airplane's side and were joined by the wrecker driver, Larry Crandall. A number of the other drivers followed.

"What now? Where do you want your stuff put?" Crandall had asked a logical question.

"I don't have the slightest idea. We don't know much about this place." Tipton replied.

Sam walked slowly down the side of the building. He was eyeing the way the back of the structure fit into the canyon wall.

"Longfeather, the mine's back there, right?" Longfeather looked at him, but remained silent. It was obvious from the look on Sam's face he didn't expect an answer. He was just thinking out loud.

"We saw a huge opening to the mine from the inside. It wasn't a narrow shaft, right? It was a really wide opening. They weren't going after a vein. They were going after an area."

"Okay, so what you're saying," Longfeather was ahead of his logic, "is they had to have another way in for the heavy equipment because the building blocks the mine entrance."

Neither of them said anything as they walked quickly towards the corrugated iron sheds that were still securely attached to the canyon walls behind the building. Each was closed by a series of wide sliding doors. Rust on the overhead tracks was visible where it streaked down the face of the galvanized iron doors like oxidized moss.

Maggie put her shoulder to the door and started pushing. Sam reached over her head and leaned hard with a gloved hand. The door refused to budge. Then Longfeather curled both hands around the edge and put his back into it. For a brief second the door refused them. Then there was a muted screech and scabs of rust showered down. Rollers which hadn't moved in nearly a hundred years broke free.

The door wasn't open a foot before they felt cool air flowing over them from inside. They pushed the door open to its limit, rust raining down, then stood and looked inside at the darkness.

"Larry," Sam yelled. "You have a flashlight with you?"

"We're miners remember? Hell yes we got lights," Crandall replied as he looked inside the shed at the darkness beyond. Feeling the rush of cool air, he said, "Well, well, well. What have we here?"

His electric torch cut deep into the dark prompting a fluttering sound like dry leaves falling on a concrete floor.

"Look out folks," Crandall laughed as he stepped back against the wall.

At that instant, Roberta walked around the corner of the open door. She was just in time to stand in the way of half the starlings in Arizona which were in a hurry to escape. No less than a dozen rats flashed past her feet before she could even jump. An irritated-looking horned owl was the last out and several others could be heard slowly flapping in the dark within the cavern.

"Holy shit!" She screamed. "What the hell is this place?" She shuddered visibly and backed out into the blazing sunlight. Perfectly willing to take on a bunch of bikers bare-handed, Roberta Rodreguez was the first to admit she didn't do bugs or creepy things well.

Larry Crandall and several of the other miners had walked deep into the dark. Their locations were pinpointed precisely by the spears of light shooting out in every direction as they explored. One of the lights worked its way back toward the shed entrance and Larry Crandall slowly materialized out of the dark.

"You've got yourself one hell of a big hole here!" Crandall reported. "It looks like copper overlaid with too much rock to go at it from the surface. The way the canyon was shaped let them come in from the side. What you have here is, in effect, an open pit mine done sideways. There's no telling how far back it goes!"

He flashed his light back into the dark. He directed it to a hewn column of rock extending from the even cavern floor to its rough, curved roof. The roof was at least two stories high. In places it went up three stories.

"They'd cut out as much as they thought they could. Then they'd leave a pillar in place for support and work around it. There're only one set of ore car tracks, so they must have done most of the hauling with wagons or something. Look around in there and I'll bet you find all sorts of stuff for moving ore."

He started laughing uncontrollably and finally coughed to a stop.

"Jesus, Tipton, you not only saved your original junk, but it looks like you found a mother lode of new junk!" He started laughing again.

"Up yours," Tipton snorted. "Let's get this stuff unloaded."

Sam was in the process of hoisting cardboard boxes up into the cab of the wrecker when Larry Crandall walked up behind him. The trucks were all unloaded and queued up for the slow trip back down the mountain.

"What's that?" Crandall asked.

"Call it a gift. A thank you present," Sam replied

"Thanks, but what is it?"

Sam opened the top box, inside was a square metal unit with several arms with cutter bars attached. At its base it was machined with a series of dovetails and threads.

"This is the Sam Tipton Magic Machine, as Longfeather calls it. Just yank the entire tool assembly off your lathe, right down to the ways and lead screw. Everything! Clamp this over the lead screw and you're in business."

Crandall was looking the unit over closely. "To do what?"

Sam opened the box underneath, revealing a small computer monitor and keyboard, both of which obviously came out of someone's garbage before becoming part of Tipton's junkyard treasure throve. "This is a basic CNC unit, you program in the various coordinates of the cuts you want to make and leave the rest up to the unit."

"Are you telling me this gizmo computerizes my old fashioned lathe?"

"Absolutely! I'll stop down and get you started next week. You'll love it."

"Thanks," Crandall's sincerity was real. "What'd this thing cost you to build, anyway?"

"'Bout twenty bucks and some scrap iron," Tipton replied

"This is creepy," Roberta couldn't keep her mind on the wine glass in her hand and kept looking up. "What are you going to do about...about...him?"

She glanced up and curled her lip.

The girls had set up a picnic supper in front of one of the large windows in the front of the building. Maggie and Roberta had commandeered several of the miners to help them. That hadn't been hard considering most had already fallen in love with one or both of the girls.

Roberta had been very much taken by the building. She was enjoying playing industrial housemaid until Maggie introduced her to Ivan Petrovitch. She was setting up the picnic table under the catwalk at the time. Roberta had the cork out of the wine in a matter of seconds.

Her reaction had started with "Are you shitting me?" and went down hill from there. She was not as enamored with Ivan as the rest. She just couldn't handle creepy.

The sun had settled into that last hour of daylight where it decides its purpose in life is to be beautiful, not useful, and this night was no exception.

"Hell of a view, Tipton. I think I'm jealous of your front room." Maggie was sitting on a crate, her feet propped up on the window sill, watching the cirrus clouds floating over the horizon to turn various shades of red, gold and purple.

"Thank you my dear." Sam tipped his wine glass towards her and took a sip. He was surprised how fast he had developed a taste for club soda. But, he still craved a cold beer. He glanced over at Longfeather who leaned against Roberta, his eyes at half mast. Roberta's eyes were big and round. They cycled up periodically to see if Ivan had moved.

All of Sam's treasures were stacked in the dark of the mine. The last truck had rumbled down the narrow road an hour earlier so Sam was surprised when he heard a truck's throaty exhaust working its way through the trees below. By the time he got to his feet and to a side window, the Mandell Red four-by-four had stopped at the side door and its driver was getting out.

"Hey, Tipton you in there?" Eddie Mandell stood by the side

of his truck and yelled. .

"Yeah, hey, in here!" Sam leaned out and motioned at the side door. He returned to his perch by the window.

The rotund shape worked its way through the shadows to where the quartet was sitting around a checkered table cloth. The remains of some of Roberta's best burritos were scattered on three of the paper plates. Roberta's own burrito didn't have a bite out of it.

"Tipton, I've got to hand it to you. If there's a hell-hole to be found, you'll find it!" Mandell turned slowly in a circle while he surveyed the surroundings. Even he liked what he saw. "Christ, this is one hell of a building. Who owns it?"

"Who the hell knows? For all I know Fowler owns it. Wouldn't that just be my luck!" Sam laughed, but suddenly his heart wasn't in it. The possibility of Fowler doing it to him again hadn't occurred to him until just that moment.

"I hope to hell he doesn't know where we've moved. Damn! I hadn't thought about that."

"Relax," Mandell started, "even that bald-headed piece of shit couldn't find this place."

"I hope," Tipton finished.

Sam stood up from where he had been sitting on a window sill and walked towards Mandell. His hand was stretched out in front of him.

"We owe you a lot. A hell of a lot. I just wish I knew how to repay you."

Mandell clasped Sam Tipton's hand, uncomfortably at first. "Yeah, all right. A thanks is good enough. I don't want you kissing me or nothin."

"Eddie, I just want to..." Mandell cut him off and said.

"Oh yeah, there is one thing. Drop the Eddie. Call me Mad Dog.'" It was Eddie Mandell's turn to smile.

Sam Tipton lay still. Listening. The coming day was on its way. First, it was the low song of a single morning bird. It had sensed dawn long before the first rays of light threatened the night sky. It had been Tipton's first night in his new home.

As day came to the valley, other feathered voices joined in. A pair of great horned owls flew in through a glassless window, barely clearing the raised, heavy timber platform Tipton had taken over as his bedroom. Their wings softly sculpted the still air into flight. He imagined he could hear each feather working its aerial magic as the pair disappeared into the mine. The sun was coming. Their hunting time was past.

Tipton rolled into a sitting position on the edge of the cot. Something was different. Something was missing. Then he realized his head didn't hurt. His tongue wasn't coated with something he couldn't identify. He wasn't hung over. As he realized his head was whole, another thought formed, simultaneously. He'd kill for a cold beer.

He doubted if the image of a beer would ever leave him. As good as it looked, however, he had to try to ignore it. It was a good trade-off. Waking up without a headache wasn't all bad. Besides, other images had danced through his dreams. Good images. Melissa and Marilyn were there. For the first time in a long time he smiled at their memory. The pain seemed further away. More manageable.

Ignoring his jeans, he wiggled into a shirt and pulled on his boots. He grabbed the small duffel bag containing his even smaller supply of bath articles. A razor was not yet among them. But soap was. And a toothbrush. He was liking the feeling of being clean. It wasn't a new feeling, but one that hadn't been a large part of his conscious thoughts for quite a few years.

He ambled down the brutish, dusty stairs and across the recently-cleared floor of the huge building. He glanced around at his new home.

"Jesus," he whispered out loud. "Talk about a man's house being his castle!"

His eyes traveled from the huge black hole at the back of the building to the open windows at the front. The high ceiling was still dark and invisible. The morning light was barely strong enough to light the bottoms of the beams.

Looking forward, he remembered he was just a house guest and offered a salutation to his host.

"Hey, Ivan," he whispered hoarsely. "Sleep well? I slept like the dead. Oops, sorry."

Tipton laughed silently. He'd dreamed about Ivan too. They had been laughing together. Ivan said he liked Tipton's sense of humor. Tipton felt an odd sort of kinship to his dried-up friend. He'd felt it even as he brushed the dust away when they discovered him and stared into the eternally-sleeping face.

Ivan Petrovitch and he would have been good friends had

their paths crossed. Now, he was thinking, their paths have crossed. Something told him it wasn't a coincidence. Sam Tipton didn't believe in coincidence. There was an unseen purpose. Something they were meant to do together.

Stepping through the door into the sun-lit meadow, the cool morning air wrapped itself around his bare legs. The air tasted clean, as if it was a fresh supply, just delivered. Everything around him felt and looked fresh and new. As he walked across the small valley and looked back, he could see his path clearly marked as a green slash through the dew-silvered grass. In a few minutes the sun and dry Mogollon air would suck the morning's moisture back into space. But, for the next few minutes, it clung to the green carpet covering the meadow.

The brook was as clear and clean as the air. But about a dozen times colder. As he splashed it onto his face, it felt sharp. Each drop had an edge. Any cells on his skin that might still be sleeping were rudely awakened on contact.

"All right, Tipton, let's see what kind of guts you've got." His own voice challenged him and his clothes and boots fell to the bank next to the deep pool at the rim's edge.

There was no one to hear the splash as he jumped naked into the pool. There was no one but Ivan to hear his shout as the near-freezing water slammed into every pore. He felt his his diaphragm jerked tight from the icy shock. For several seconds it refused to let him take another breath.

It was through sheer willpower he forced himself to use the cold water and soap like icy sandpaper to scrub himself brutally clean. As he cleaned, he realized his genitalia had all but disappeared. They were, he thought, no fools. They had retreated into any warm place they could find.

He was standing on the bank rubbing himself down with a towel donated by Tall Woman Longfeather when he heard an airplane engine. He had barely identified it as the throaty rasp of the Stinson's big Lycoming when the patchwork airplane dropped over the edge of the canyon. It headed straight for him.

Recognizing Longfeather at the controls, Sam made a conscious decision not to duck no matter how low his friend flew. He stood tall, a grin on his face. His towel over his shoulder. His stark naked, glistening white body was a glowing target for Longfeather's fun.

He could clearly see Longfeather laughing, his mouth open as if shouting at him. Tipton grinned back. Then, as the airplane banked away to circle around at low altitude, he saw why Longfeather was laughing.

Maggie was in the back seat. Longfeather had banked around to give her a better view. Even at a distance, Tipton saw her pointing and obviously laughing harder than Longfeather.

Tipton suddenly felt uncharacteristically embarrassed and yanked the towel down to cover himself. He ignored the cold water still dripping down his back and had his shirt and skivvies back on before the Stinson again whispered quietly overhead, throttle back, to land in the grass.

Pulling his shirttails down as much as possible, he walked quickly towards the mine building. The Stinson got there first. The propeller hadn't stopped turning before he heard the laughter roaring out of the cockpit. Longfeather's booming bass couldn't drown out Maggie's soprano laugh.

Satisfied his shirttails were long enough, Tipton turned, hands on hips and faced the two as they fell out of the airplane, still laughing.

"Okay, who invited you two jerks up here?" Tipton was trying to hide his embarrassment, but he wasn't succeeding.

"God, we're sorry..." Maggie couldn't catch her breath, she was laughing so hard.

"Yeah, we're sorry." Longfeather choked his laughing long enough to say, "Boy, I hope my sister knows how to compensate for temperature. Otherwise she'll think very little of you!"

He fell against the airplane, convulsed in laughter. Maggie had to sit down on one of the Stinson's big tires, her arms wrapped around her stomach. Tears streamed down her cheeks.

"Stop!" She gasped. "Stop, please! I'm going to pee my pants!"

She launched off on another gale-force laughing jag.

"Screw the both of you!" Tipton was doing his best not to laugh, and wheeled around to step back into the building.

"No...No, Sam, we're sorry." Maggie was gasping but close to being in control of herself. "Really, we brought breakfast!"

She gagged a laugh and put a hand to her mouth. The smile showed around the hand.

She held up a grocery bag. "Really!" Another gagged laugh.

"Yeah, well, if you don't mind, I think I'll dress for breakfast." Tipton disappeared back inside the building and left the others laughing. He glanced towards the front of the building and said loudly, "Ivan, my friends are assholes. Just ignore them."

"**First, hot water.**" The answer was in response to a question about improvements to his new home. The answer came around a mouthful of scrambled egg sandwich.

"Seems like a good idea, but how?" Maggie asked. She was well past laughing but had giggled occasionally while making breakfast over a fire Longfeather had built in an old forge at the back of the building. A dozen bats fluttered out the top of the chimney when he started a draught with burning newspaper.

"I thought about it a lot last night." Tipton began. "There's a big tank of some sort up against the back wall well up in the roof structure. I'll just rig a huge bank of solar collectors at a lower level on the roof. I might get by without any pumps at all if I use rain water or snow melt. It looks to be about a three-hundred gallon tank. Love it! Hot showers unlimited!

"There's that generator we salvaged from the abandoned power truck and that'll give me electricity. Given enough time, I'll rig up a solar or wind system."

He went silent for a moment as he thought.

"No, better than that! I'll put a water turbine in the falls...yeah, that'll work. Free electricity and no pollutants."

He was obviously satisfied with himself as he worked his way through half the sandwich in a beaver-like sequence of bites.

"What about Ivan?" Maggie asked. "Do we bury him?"

"Hell, no! He's seen a lot of sunsets up there and, as long as I'm here, he'll see a lot more. I'll just put a window in the freight door for him. Besides, it's his house. Didn't your mother ever tell you that burying your host is just plain rude?"

Tipton again grinned his lunatic grin at the serious-faced Maggie Longfeather.

She sneered and didn't bother answering.

Twenty-seven

Kwan adjusted the hotel blinds carefully, angling the slats so the morning sun could find its way in, but early risers walking past couldn't see what was happening inside. Flagstaff was slow that time of the morning anyway.

Finished packing his clothes, he smoothed the fraying motel bedspread as he unloaded the fruits of his shopping trip in Phoenix. He spread the contents of the bags evenly on the bed. He hadn't expected to find so many gun stores in such close proximity. It had made gathering the necessary supplies easy.

His thumbs worked automatically, mindlessly loading .223 cartridges into blunt, rectangular magazines. His mind was south on the Interstate, working out the details of the upcoming phone conversation with Frederick.

Hands continued moving until ten twenty-round magazines were stacked side-by-side on the pillow. Each was held up to the light, making certain loading lips were straight. Kwan wanted no jams because of a faulty magazine. Satisfied, he slammed a magazine into the abbreviated form of the Ruger Mini-14. The rest into army surplus magazine pouches.

The Ruger was a civilian semi-automatic rifle, common on ranches. It lacked a military look. It was, therefore, politically correct. To Kwan, the popular assault rifles were too sinister-looking. They said too many things about the owner. To any curious highway patrolman, the Ruger would say this was just another Indian with his ranch rifle. His deadly ranch rifle.

He carefully arranged the magazines in a faded duffel bag. Another second-hand store purchase. Extra jeans and shirts protected them from pistol magazines already loaded. The Ruger went in next. The H & K automatic went into the back of his belt, hidden under a worn, black leather vest with a single silver concho in front.

One stiletto went in the sheath Velcroed to the inside of his left forearm. The denim shirt sleeve hid it completely. The other went inside the top of the right boot. He didn't expect to need a single weapon on this project. But, if he did, he was ready.

Hat pulled low, the duffel and empty shopping bags were

deposited in the truck. Returning to the room, every exposed surface was rubbed down with a damp towel, wiping away every trace that Thomas Hogan had ever been in the room. He was particularly careful to wipe down the shower cabinet and sink, letting the hot water run for a long time.

A half-bottle of lye from his grocery shopping was poured down each drain so that no hair samples remained. Hair DNA was nearly as positive an identification source as fingerprints.

His eyes swept the room one more time and he pulled the door shut with his elbow. Neither Kwan Yamuchi nor Thomas Hogan could now be connected with the Indian who had rented the room.

As Frank Frederick rushed out of the photo store, the midmorning sun tried to incinerate his eyes. They were bloodshot and every heartbeat made them bulge in their sockets.

He didn't notice the pain.

Squinting against the sun, he opened the envelope as he walked back out. He was anxious. it seemed as if it had taken forever to get the film developed What would the camera tell him about his lost night in the desert? Sunglasses were exchanged for reading glasses. His heart pounded as stubby fingers fumbled the envelope open.

Back to the sun, he turned the small stack of pictures over. There were only eight.

The one on top was an underexposed photo of an elderly Indian, pants unzipped, grin glaring in the feeble flash as he peed into space. The second picture was of an elderly white man, Frank Frederick, doing the same thing.

The next two were of rocks and cactus, as if the camera had gone off unexpectedly. Frederick could feel disappointment rising as he came to the last three prints. The top one was an off-centered shot of an elderly Indian's bare rear end. The phrase "Indian Summer Moon" flashed across Frederick's mind. He didn't feel like laughing.

Flipping to the next picture, his heart skipped a beat. Then two. It was a clear picture of him standing with one hand on top an idol or dummy Charley Yee had apparently fashioned. Frank Frederick had no interest in that.

His eyes focused on the large rectangular metal object under his other hand. The circular pattern of three yellow triangles, the universal symbol for radiation on its surface, glowed fluorescent in the camera's strobe. The rest was a dust-dulled, machined silver. Its sheen untouched by the passing years. Frederick remembered the outer case was stainless steel. It was likely to shine forever. It was the inner liner which was made of cobalt. That much he also remembered.

As he stood on the sidewalk in front of his RV, he started to yell. Then he caught himself. His muscles twitched uncontrollably as the adrenaline pumped.

He had found it! He had not only found Cobalt Blue, but had touched it! It was there! He was rich! He was unbelievably rich!

The next picture brought him down to earth. It was of Charley Yee in exactly the same pose. The pictures confirmed the existence of the assembly. The pictures of Charley Yee reminded Frederick that only the old Indian knew where the unit was hidden. He had taken three steps forward and two back. He wasn't exactly where he started, but close enough.

He still couldn't hand the unit over to Kwan.

In the short term, however, he knew he didn't have to hand it over to Kwan. Not right away, anyway. Kwan was somewhere overseas. At the very least it would take him two days to make it to Arizona. By that time Frederick would have Cobalt Blue in his hands. He glanced at his watch. He had to get moving to make the agreed-upon phone call.

As he bounced into the RV, a wondrous grin from ear to ear, May Frederick looked up at him.

"Okay, genius. Now where we going now? Another damn phone call?"

She thought she was being sarcastic.

"Yes, May, m'love, that's exactly where we're going. Then, we're going to pay a social call on Charley Yee."

Frank Frederick checked his watch as he aimed the lumbering RV at the on-ramp leading to I-17 south. A four-by-four pick-up pulled alongside and he locked eyes for a second with the driver. It was a light-skinned Indian with a tired-looking hat pulled low over wraparound sunglasses.

When they made connection, Frank Frederick let his good mood show by smiling at the Indian. Kwan Yamuchi returned the smile and pushed gently on his accelerator to pull away from the crawling motor home. He had to get to the appropriate off-ramp well ahead of Frederick.

Frank Frederick stepped out and slammed the motor home's door behind him. Even closed, it only partially muffled his wife's screaming. She couldn't believe he was going to make another goddamn phone call. Did he realize how much money he was spending? Let's get out of this stinking hole! Why aren't you listening? What do you think you're doing?

He was halfway across the deserted filling station's cracked parking lot before distance and the RV's walls finally absorbed her voice. That left the desert wind once again in command.

Quarter. Quarter. Quarter. Recent practice made thumbing the coins through the slot an automatic motion.

The soft oriental voice answered, Frederick went through the preliminaries and hung up. The hot afternoon sun made the phone booth into a solarium even though it was missing half its glass. He opened the door to lean against the jam. The breeze felt good.

The phone rang, but this time it didn't cause him to jump. He had been practicing the call in his mind since leaving Flagstaff.

"Kwan?" He'd asked the question before he realized how stupid it sounded. Who else would be calling a phone booth in the middle of the high desert?

"Yeah, I'll take your offer. But I've changed my mind about the cash. I'll take only half of it in twenties and fifties. Yeah, that's right. Two million. The rest I want put in a bank account in the Cayman Islands. I want confirmation that money is deposited and the cash in my hand before I turn over Cobalt Blue."

As he spoke, Frederick became more confident. More sure of what he was doing. Kwan didn't know Frederick hadn't the slightest idea how to set an account up in the Caymans. It was something he'd seen on television. He leaned against the door jamb and let his eyes roam across the hills and cacti rimming the low valley where the road to Pitacho cut under the interstate. Occasionally he'd hold up the picture and smile at his image. Even drunk and past seventy, he thought himself a handsome man. Few would agree

"**Yes, Mr. Frederick, I can set** up that account. Don't worry, I'll make the arrangements and you can confirm them by phone." Kwan's tone was just short of patronizing.

The call was being routed from the pay phone, halfway

around the world and back again. As he lay in the rocks above the filling station, the image in Kwan's binoculars was slightly out of sync with what he was hearing. Even electrons take time to cover nearly twenty-five-thousand miles. His eyes saw Frederick's lips move slightly in advance of the words reaching him. Like a badly-done movie voice-over.

Kwan smiled. He also wondered how Frederick would feel if he knew he'd just paid all that money to call less than a hundred yards.

"Yes, Mr. Frederick, I can take care of your payment conditions. But, may I suggest you call me again in, say, forty-eight hours, at the same hour?"

The image in the binoculars nodded as it agreed. Then it hung up the phone and stepped out of the phone booth looking at a picture or something in his hand. Then he returned to the phone booth as if forgetting something and he came out holding a tin can. It had held the quarters. The thought amused Kwan.

The door to the RV opened. A shrill voice escaped and reached Kwan's ears as he packed up his equipment and returned to his truck. He was in no hurry. Following the RV would hardly be a challenge.

Forty minutes later, the RV pulled off into a bare patch of brush between what Kwan recognized as a Native American hogan and the remains of a dying town. He was careful not to look at the RV as he drove past. Frederick wasn't a stupid man and FBI training never goes completely away. He might still notice someone looking at him as they drove past.

The dusty truck rolled into town and Kwan again smiled. It looked like something out of one of his favorite western movies. *Liberty Valence* came to mind. The street reminded him of the set in that movie. In his mind, John Wayne was standing in Roberta's doorway. Jimmy Stewart sat at a table inside dealing cards.

He guided the truck towards the curb next to another truck that could have been a clone of his own. He climbed out and inhaled the fresh air. He remembered another reason he enjoyed the American Southwest. His sinuses cleared up. He looked up at the clear blue sky, something he seldom saw in Japan because of the ever-present blanket of pollutants.

He again breathed deeply and pulled his hat down in front. He fell in behind two others wearing similar hats as they disappeared into the darkness of Roberta's. One looked back, his Navajo features split into a grin. Wrinkles formed at the corners of his dark eyes as he said, "Hey, bro!"

Kwan nodded silently and returned the smile. He had expected it to feel unnatural. But it didn't.

Twenty-eight

"**Are you sure there's a town down** this goddamn road?" Estavez was driving and looked across the minivan at the passenger's seat. Ladilow's eyelids were sliding towards sleep. The pockmarked Hispanic at the wheel reached across to slap his partner on the shoulder.

"Hey, asshole, wake up! Are we lost or what?"

Ladilow jumped up, pretending he could read the map with his still-dazed eyes.

"Yeah. Yeah, we're going right. It should be around the bend ahead. Or maybe the one after that." His voice was slow. They'd been driving for several hours and it was taking its toll. Cross-country driving was different than fighting cross-town traffic back in his usual haunts. No one dozed off in Manhattan traffic. No one.

"Shit man! What the hell kind of dog was that?" Estavez yanked the wheel, causing Yardley to jerk erect in the back seat.

Glancing out the window Yardley said, "That's a coyote."

The desert dog loped up an embankment. It paused to glance back at the dust-covered vehicle. It appeared to be grinning.

"No shit?" Estavez's picket fence denture work was spread across the rear view mirror at Yardley. "A coyote? You mean like with the road runner? Beep, beep and all that shit?"

The vehicle skidded slightly as a front wheel found a rut. The right side of the road dropped off several hundred feet into a rocky arroyo.

"Jesus, Estavez! Haven't you ever driven on dirt before? Stop fighting the goddamn wheel!" Yardley now was sitting up and stared over Estavez's shoulder. Hornslee leaned against a back window asleep. His head beat an audible tattoo with each bump, but his eyes remained closed.

Estavez looked up in the rear-view mirror, catching Yardley's eyes. "No, man, I ain't never driven on no dirt. Manhattan doesn't have a lot of dirt roads, ya know. They don't have none in the Bronx, neither. Jersey might have some, but I ain't going over there looking for dirt roads."

The minivan's high-tech, hyper-fuel-efficient, four-cylinder engine made asthmatic sounds as it tried desperately to suck in enough thin air to support combustion. Estavez's foot was on the floor most of the time just to keep the vehicle moving.

"Jesus, is this thing ever sick!" he whined. "I don't know if it's going to...oops, here we go!...Civilization!...I think."

The road lurched around a curve, flattening and straightening out at the same time. They passed the hogan of Charley Yee and then a tired looking RV. Ladilow rubbed his eyes and spoke.

"Okay, this is a joke, right?" The van slowed to a crawl as they approached Main Street, Pitacho. "This looks like something out of *High Noon*. Or maybe *The Twilight Zone*."

The only movement on the street was a small dust devil.

"Pull in here." Yardley said. He leaned between the two front passengers and stared at the crumbling town. His finger motioned towards several motorcycles and pickup trucks parked at the curb. The sign over the open door said "Roberta's."

"Here you go, Hornslee," Estavez yelled back, as the youngest member of the quartet awakened. "Something even you can understand."

He referred to the neon montage of mismatched beer signs in the windows. Half the neon didn't work, as too many beer bottles and airborne drunks had assaulted them. The messages still came through loud and clear.

"Jesus goddamn Christ," Hornslee was now awake. He evaluated the situation as he stepped sleepily out of the van. "What the hell is this place?"

A Native American, long black hair flowing from under a dust-covered black cowboy hat, silver belt buckle glowing in the sunlight, ambled past them into Roberta's. Hornslee's unbelieving eyes followed him.

"Shit man! That's a goddamn Indian!" His voice boomed out as he turned wide eyes on Yardley. "Holy, shit! Where the hell..."

Yardley grabbed the front of his shirt and yanked him close. The shirt was getting a permanent wrinkle in the front from repeated applications of the same motion. Yardley had never considered himself the sensitive type but he did value anonymity.

Hornslee's mouth worked as reverse camouflage. Every time he opened it, they would stand out in any crowd west of Grand Central Station. Major personnel mistake. Yardley knew it, but he had to live with it.

"How many goddamn times do I have to tell you? Shut...the fuck...up," Yardley snarled quietly. "Keep quiet. Don't say a single goddamn word unless I speak to you. Got it!"

Hard eyes stared into a young face.

Fist tightened on a rumpled shirt front.

"Got it?"

Young eyes wavered and head nodded slowly.

Ladilow appeared from behind the van, having done a walk-around to make sure nothing inside was visible. Or suspicious. He nodded at Yardley as he caught his eye. A professional. Yardley liked that and relaxed, letting Hornslee back down onto the pavement.

A motion of his hand, and the four gathered together for a moment. He flashed a photo in front of them, returning it quickly to his shirt pocket. His head swiveled slightly...eyes sweeping the street...still clear.

"That's what Frederick looked like twenty-two years ago. He'll be just past seventy now and we don't know if he still has the beard or not."

Another sweep of the street.

"He fucked up early and screwed his career, but according to his jacket, he was a good agent. Not brilliant, but not stupid. We have to assume he still knows what he's doing."

Hornslee butted in, "Come on, he's a geezer, how can he..."

"Hornslee, goddammit!" Yardley fixed him with a hard stare and the kid shut up.

"We'll go in as pairs, you all know our cover story. Geologists doing a casual survey of the area. Nothing specific. Avoid saying any more than necessary. Ladilow, you go the bar. The rest of us will take a table."

Yardley's eyes traveled from face to face as he spoke, searching each for confirmation. He received it, until his eyes landed on Hornslee. The ex-soldier's head was swiveling from side to side. He was looking up and down the street like a tourist.

Iraq must have been Hornslee's only trip outside of Manhattan, Yardley decided. He looked like a tourist because he was a tourist. Just goddamn great! A kid tourist with a killer's skills and a New York attitude. Major, major personnel mistake.

"Let's go, Hornslee you're with me."

Yardley walked through the door and went momentarily blind in the darkness. He focused on the bright light behind the bar and moved slowly while his eyes acclimated. When they adjusted, he saw he was moving through some sort of time warp. As much as he had traveled, he had never seen so many cowboy hats in one place. Or so many biker tattoos.

Roberta's, he decided, drew an unusual clientele. He already felt himself and his crew sticking out. There was no way they were going to blend in. They were too clean, too new, with too many sharp edges. Everyone else in the room had been worn smooth by the desert and mountains. The West had left its mark. Yardley didn't have to look in the bar's mirror to know the mark left on him was that of one of the coasts. Observers wouldn't know which coast, unless Hornslee opened his mouth. Then everyone would know it was the East coast.

The cover story would have to work for them. But he knew the possibility of gaining the confidence of anyone on the room was absolutely zero. Less than zero. They'd have to get their information about Frederick by looking around on their own and that wasn't going to be easy. This crowd would protect their own. Even if they didn't like them. Outsiders were outsiders and that would never change.

Yardley pulled back an aging oak chair at a table and dropped heavily into it. Dozens of eyes followed him and he felt every one of them.

As Yardley and the others filed in, a pair of dark almond-shaped eyes followed them. The eyes were nearly invisible in the slot between the hat's low brim and the top of the wrap-arounds. They watched Yardley order lunch and a round of beers.

Hornslee's voice drifted above the noon crowd. He let those around him know enchiladas were the ugliest-looking blintzes he'd ever seen. Everyone in the place immediately tagged the strangers as being from the East Coast.

Kwan couldn't help but smile. His old acquaintance, Richard Yardley, had some amateurs on his crew. He continued to smile at Yardley's attempts at keeping the younger member of his quartet quiet and under control.

The other two, both Hispanics, were obviously professionals. Their eyes gave them away. They were trying to casually look around, as if they were bored. But, they weren't. They looked at more than faces. They were watching hands. Surveying pants legs and vests looking for weapons. They didn't have to look far.

Kwan smiled. He could imagine their thoughts at seeing so many pistols in sight. It had surprised him too. As long as they were in sight, handguns were legal to carry in Arizona. More than a few in the crowd had availed themselves of that right.

When Roberta arrived to take their order, some of the thugs' professionalism slipped. They couldn't take their eyes off her. As she walked away, their words reached him. The comments were split between her body and her .45.

Kwan evaluated as he watched.

Young kid. Green. Impulsive. No discipline. A problem to his leader.

Skinny, pockmarked Hispanic. Cold eyes always moving. Snake-like. Probably enjoys inflicting pain. Very dangerous. The curiosity in his eyes as he looked around betrayed him as a slow thinker. Easily overwhelmed.

Round-faced, mustached Hispanic. Older. More experienced. Relaxed in his new situation. But aware. No military bearing showing. Probably from the streets. Covers his observations better than the rest. Not as obvious. A professional. Overall more dangerous than his skinny partner. This one could think.

Yardley. Obviously ex-military. Bearing made him an ex-Marine. Maybe Navy SEAL. He evaluated and understood the crowd before sitting down. Picked his seating position accordingly. Back to big column. Open area adjacent to move into quickly. View of the door. The group's intelligence was his. In Kwan's dealings with him years earlier, he remembered Yardley's superior had deferred to him several times. His intellect was valued. He would have to be watched.

Was there a connection between Yardley and Cobalt Blue? Coincidence? He'd last seen Yardley in the company of then-congressman Foster Ward. He'd last heard from Ward less than a week ago. The subject of conversation had been Cobalt Blue. This was no coincidence.

Invisible, as part of the crowd, Kwan watched. Yardley had scanned Kwan's position several times. No hesitation. His eyes kept moving. Not a flicker. Kwan fit in. He was part of Pitacho. The camouflage worked. Leaned back, his feet up on a chair, Kwan relaxed and watched. He had the perfect observation post.

The beer came to his lips slowly. He was conscious of his movements. And drinking from a bottle felt strange. The liquid was crude but strangely pleasing. He didn't feel as out of place as he thought he would. Some roles were easier to play than others.

Kwan Yamuchi nursed the beer for nearly an hour, watching as Yardley and the other three tried to strike up casual conversations with others in the noonday crowd. They had been largely unsuccessful. The two Hispanics had separated. Mustache went to the bar and the skinny one worked the crowd. Every time he sat down at a table uninvited, he was asked to leave after only a few questions. Neither had perfected the art of casual conversation. They went for their information with direct questions. They hadn't learned how to dance with words, letting the answers come out as an incidental part of another conversation.

"Hey, man, mind if I sit down?" Estavez was standing next to the chair occupied by Kwan's booted feet.

Kwan nodded and said nothing. His feet fell to the floor.

Kwan estimated the ultra-skinny Chicano at thirty-two years, certainly no more than thirty-six. As he looked into the sunken dark eyes, he once again saw cruelty. And lack of intelligence. The man was, Kwan recognized, a killing machine. A weapon. Probably Yardley's best.

"How 'bout, it, man? You local?"

Kwan had to smile at the crude opening to the line of questions he knew was coming. Estavez was trying to smile, as if the smile was on orders from Yardley. There was nothing natural about it.

Smile and people will like you, is what Yardley had probably said. Yardley had obviously not looked closely at the skinny Chicano's smile. There was nothing to like. The smile itself looked as if an ax had gone horizontally through a picket fence.

Kwan answered slowly. He was careful to adapt the cadence of the Native Americans he had been listening to around him. "Just traveling through."

"Been here long?"

"Couple hours."

"Oh, so you don't know a guy named Frederick."

"Nope." Kwan was proud of his easy use of slang. After so many years studying languages to get the grammar and pronunciation down, slang didn't come easy.

He was amused at the Hispanic's complete lack of subtlety.

"You a cop or somethin?" Kwan asked, as he slid deeper into his new persona.

"Nah, I'm a geoler-gist," Estavez answered, mispronouncing the word. Not very convincing.

Seizing the opportunity, Kwan decided to amuse himself, "Oh, on a seismic survey?"

New word. The Hispanic's eyes lit up for a second as he struggled with it.

"Nah, we don't much care what size they are. We're just looking around for rocks, yah know? Any old size. Well, gotta go."

Before Kwan could even touch the brim of his hat in farewell, as he'd seen them do in movies, Estavez was gone, heading for the next table.

Kwan hoped he was more adept at his Native American role than the cold-eyed Hispanic was at playing geologist.

Geolergist! He smiled to himself.

When Frank Frederick stepped through Roberta's door he was feeling financially flush. And sick to death of Spam. He'd picked up his social security and pension checks in Flagstaff when he went after the pictures. General Delivery was likely to be his permanent address.

Visions of truck loads of twenty and fifty-dollar bills also danced through his mind. He'd have money soon. A week, two at the most, and he'd never have to eat Spam again. Or drink the cheap beer.

May was back in the RV. She thought he was next door visiting Charley Yee. The two had become old drinking buddies and as odd a couple as the West had ever seen. She didn't care, as long as they left her alone to enjoy her Spam sandwich in peace.

Frederick was all too happy to let her gum away at her sandwich while he enjoyed a plate of enchiladas and a beer. Or two. Or maybe it would be a burrito. And three beers. As he waddled up to the bar, he hadn't made up his mind.

He was focused on the chalkboard menu behind the bar and didn't notice the men who sat at the table to his right. They glanced at him as he passed, but not one eye at the table tracked him to the bar. Not only was their picture twenty-two years old with a beard, but it was over sixty pounds lighter. The years and the weight had re-sculpted taut, bony-faced Special Agent Frank Frederick. Well-rounded and drooping were the current adjectives. The old Frank Frederick was several layers down inside the new one.

He went unrecognized by all but one in the room.

Kwan Yamuchi spotted Frederick the second he came through the door. He studied the face closely as he walked past. Kwan's sunglasses hid his eyes. Frederick never knew his future benefactor was analyzing him closely.

Kwan recognized the look. Frederick was well on the way to being beaten by life. Colorless, putty-textured skin. Rounded, slumped shoulders. A slow, arduous shuffle and dead eyes seeing only ahead. Frank Frederick was a human being in decline. A nearly-deserted shell of a man whose mind knew what was happening, but was powerless to stop it.

Over the phone Kwan had recognized a mind struggling to stay strong. Their conversations had contained crude traces of the intelligence which had been applied to Frederick's former job on a daily basis. But, the body was much further along in decline than the mind. Retirement, Kwan decided as he eyed Frederick struggling onto a stool at the bar, was not a healthy pursuit.

As Frederick ordered his gourmet, low-cholesterol meal of enchiladas, refried beans and beer, Yardley and his team stood to go. Their words drifted over to where Kwan sat.

"First let's do a little recon," Yardley was saying. "Frederick is here somewhere."

At the mention of the ex-agent's name, Kwan slowly swiveled his eyes around to watch Frederick at the bar. Frederick didn't twitch a muscle. He either chose to ignore it or his hearing was suffering as much as the rest of his body.

"Let's head down towards Payson and find a place to stay. Then we'll split up and come back." They were talking as they moved towards the door.

Yardley's fingers cruised idly over the top of the aged chair, on which Kwan Yamuchi had his feet propped, as he passed.

"If that old coot's in town, we'll find him." Yardley crowed.

Just out of earshot, Frank Frederick was already two swallows into a fresh brew.

Twenty-nine

Stephanie Goodlin wasn't born unattractive. She had made herself that way. Round face with pleasant features. Gray colorless eyes set in gray skin. Brittle brown hair pulled back into a bun. She looked forty-five but was little more than half that. She acted twice that. She blamed her ex. Blamed him for her chain-smoking, for the necessity of the job working in the Gila County office. For her life.

Her world was acres of large tax maps. Miles of loosely bound notebooks in Gulliver proportions. To her the county was block and lot numbers. Addresses didn't count. Topography didn't matter. Only block and lot numbers. But, there weren't all that many of them.

Most of the county was reservation or federal land. Only 15.6% of the entire state could be put in private deeds. She repeated the statistic often, showing off her knowledge. She was the keeper of who owned what. Eventually, every real estate sale in the entire county went through her. Divorces, bankruptcy, desert burn-out, she knew why every piece changed hands.

Land was the story of the people. Or was it the other way around?

The bell dangling from the top of the glass-paned front door tinkled. Forewarned, she quickly ran her hands down the front of her only flowered blouse. She'd worn it on purpose. She thought it gave her face color. And accented her lemon-sized breasts. Ted Fowler had called yesterday. Said he'd be in to give her a plat map number to look up. Fowler wasn't married.

She ran her hand over her hair, looking for strays. She missed several. One kinky strand stood up Alfalfa-fashion.

As Fowler rounded the hall corner, he was walking slowly and limping. A hand grabbed the worn wainscoting for balance. He muttered something under his breath about a guy named Robert. He glanced up and saw Deputy Assessor Stephanie Goodlin smiling her brightest. His scowl didn't change.

"Stephanie?" Fowler did his best to put on a front, but couldn't. Roberta had left her mark and it could be a month before he walked normally. White-knuckled fingers grabbed the counter.

"Oh, Mr. Fowler," Stephanie had a pained motherly tone. Pale skin bunched up between her eyes. A concerned frown. "Are you okay?"

"Yeah, yeah. I'm fine. Got thrown by a horse the other day," Fowler tried to say it slowly, with a deeper than normal voice and the touch of a drawl. "Snake or somethin' spooked him."

She couldn't know about his borderline horse phobia. He feared them. They hated him. That's why he'd never been on one.

He looked the woman in the eye. Too bad she wasn't better looking. He'd undressed her many times in his mind. Standard procedure. She didn't look good naked. And he did have his standards, after all. He wouldn't pork just anything. Still...she probably wouldn't cost anything. Maybe next week.

"Did you find the plat book I needed? It's the same one I had out a couple weeks ago."

"Yessir, I remembered." A giant book dropped onto the counter top. She flopped it open to the proper page.

Fowler stood on his tiptoes to get a good angle. It hurt, so he wrestled the book to a table. Ms. Goodlin watched from behind the counter. Her tongue darted out to wet, cracked lips. Nervous hands wrapped around one another behind the counter.

Fowler's fingers moved smoothly down the blue-lined paper, found the town outline, then Main Street, then counted backwards up the blue, square property lines. Fingers stopped, then reached for a pencil. A circle was drawn around a small square which indicated a specific piece of land. Numbers were written in a small notebook.

"Tax status reports?" Fowler only half-glanced up from the plat book at her. She scampered around the counter, mimeographed forms in hand. She laid them next to the book.

"Thanks." He didn't look up.

Scanning the forms, he flipped through several pages, each containing dozens of tax-delinquent properties. Those underlined had been deeded to, or taken over by, the county to settle tax liens. The county owned a lot of land it didn't really want.

"Yes! Yes!" Fingers stopped at a row of numbers. They were underlined. The county had once again become a landowner, whether they wanted to or not.

He really didn't need that particular piece of land. But he wanted it. Call it pay-back. He rapidly filled out the request forms necessary to get it moved into auction status. Once the county had done that, he'd come back and put in a bid on it. His would undoubtedly be the only bid. It always was.

Struggling to his feet, he handed the completed form to the eager looking Assessor. His eyes met hers. Hers lit up. His didn't. Then he faked a smile. You could never tell for sure how good the librarian types would be. Often they had a surprising amount of fire stored up in their tight little asses.

She wanted to make conversation, something she was never good at.

"Buying another piece out there, huh, Mr. Fowler?"

No response. He was putting his pencil and notebook away.

"Sure seems to be a lot of interest out there, these days." She tried again.

He looked up at her, a question in his eyes.

"What do you mean, interest?"

"Oh, a mine-owner was in here looking at the same map. They used to do that a lot. Not so much anymore, though. First time this year."

Fowler relaxed. He didn't care about mines. Useless, dangerous and polluted. Too many problems. Abandoned open land with residential possibilities....derelict city land with commercial possibilities....that was his specialty. As long as it was cheap, as in nearly free. A good day's wages was often all that was needed for one of his real estate purchases. He bought land for pocket change. Movie money he called it.

Few knew about the tax-seized properties. Or the tax sales in which they were disposed. Some properties had been on the books for fifty years and the county had given up trying to auction them off unless someone asked.

Fowler asked more than anyone else in the county. So he owned more than anyone else in the county. Not all of it was good land. But it was all his land. And he was closing the gaps between some of the pieces; creeping them closer together to make a whole.

As he turned to go, he took one more look at the county bureaucrat. She was again naked in his mind. Not a pretty picture. Still.... He smiled sincerely and winked. You could never tell.

He exaggerated his limp on the way out.

Thirty

Richard Yardley stood next to the van, in front of the motel, Hornslee beside him. Ladilow and Estavez leaned against the white two-door, economy-sized Pontiac they'd rented.

"Ladilow, you two go in first. Pitacho's too small for all of us to keep nosing around. We look like a damn mob. Besides, we're assuming Frederick is there because that's where the computers said the phone call came from. We don't know he's there for a fact. Hornslee and I'll nose around here in Payson. You cover Pitacho."

Finished speaking, Yardley opened the van's door. His eyes automatically swept the area. The scent of pine trees bordering the empty parking lot was nearly overpowering. A truck loaded with huge logs rumbled past. Traffic was light and mixed. Older sedans. Tourist RV's and rentals. A lot of well-worn jeeps and pickups with no tailgates. It wasn't hard to pick out the locals.

The two vehicles rolled out, heading in different directions. The white car turned left. Ladilow had paid attention to the roads on the way in. He knew the way back to Pitacho by heart, but Estavez didn't trust him. An open map lay on his lap.

Sitting in the shade, Kwan Yamuchi wasn't bothered by the early afternoon heat. Humidity was next to nothing. A bottle of water sat on the cracked sidewalk next to his rickety chair. The wooden chair was a dried, gray, fibrous collection of splits and checks. The desert was relentless in its ability to suck moisture out of everything. The chair had given all it had.

Hat pulled low, eyes swiveling back and forth behind dark glasses, he leaned back. Just another desert rat with nothing to do but watch the town grow older.

His hands automatically worked a length of fraying rope he'd found on the sidewalk. They were remembering knots. And splices. A hackamore took form in his hands. He'd once seen the knot in a western horse magazine. Eyes glanced up and down the street. Then a bowline on a bight. A sheepshank. His hands continued to remember. A masthead. He smiled. Perhaps those pre-teen years working on junks in the harbor hadn't been totally wasted. They definitely hadn't been forgotten.

He had a clear view of the entire street. In the distance, the dirt road connected the town with the edge of the mesa. A hogan sat next to it. Charley Yee's trinket shop. Then Frederick's bedraggled RV.

Looking the other way, Main Street faded to a narrow, sandy scar in the sagebrush. For the first fifty yards, a few broken-down buildings and a big adobe were scattered on either side like forgotten road trash. Then nothing until the road fell out of sight. The desert would soon reclaim it completely.

A cloud of dust rising from beyond the other edge of the mesa announced the arrival of a vehicle. The dust cloud was too big to be a motorcycle. Besides, it was too early for it to be a motorcycle. Motorcycles in Pitacho were usually nocturnal.

A white sedan appeared out of the sand cloud. Brand new. Economy class. No dents. A rental. The Pontiac slowed, idled past Roberta's, then turned into an alley several buildings down. Kwan recognized the occupants before the car turned. Yardley's two professionals. The game was about to begin anew.

The game was also about to get interesting. In the distance, Kwan saw the door on Frederick's RV open and the graying keeper of Cobalt Blue step out. Frederick began to walk the short distance towards town. Roberta's would again be the center of activity. Kwan put his rope down.

"I'm gonna check out the rest of this shit-hole town. You poke around the bar." Ladilow was speaking as the two Hispanics stepped out of the dusty alley where they'd parked their car. Estavez nodded and moved towards the saloon's open door.

Ladilow turned the other way. He never saw Frederick approaching in the distance. He also never saw the Native American on the other side of the street pivot out of his chair to amble slowly across the street. Kwan entered Roberta's behind Estavez while Frederick was still a block away.

Estavez was already sitting at the bar by the time Roberta's cool darkness flowed over Kwan. Moving slowly, as if trying to decide which table was best, Kwan seated himself near the bar and behind a large timber column. Frederick wouldn't see him as he came through the door.

Silence had returned to the old building after the noontime crowd vanished back into the surrounding hills. With the exception of those enamored of something named Cobalt Blue, the only other occupant was a tiny, withered old man sitting by himself at one end of the bar. Sketchy gray beard against a face the texture of hickory bark. Ragged cowboy hat. Sweat colored straw. Folds Frayed. Crown broken. Hat band a folded bandanna. Kwan had heard the busty barkeep refer to him as Snuffy. There had been affection in her tone.

"What'll it be, stranger?" Roberta's voice caught Estavez by surprise. The words were logical, but to Kwan they sounded like a line from one of his western videos. Her name should have been something like Miss Kitty. Not Roberta.

Estavez's stool was midway between Frederick and Snuffy.

"Beer. Draught!" Estavez answered.

Estavez continued surveying the mostly empty room, trying to penetrate the shadows with hard eyes. They focused briefly on Kwan. Then skipped over to the graying older man who was just then sitting down at the other end of the bar. They then homed-in on Roberta.

She pulled the exaggerated, long handle, expertly running the golden liquid down the side of the glass to keep the head to a minimum. Estavez had just wrapped his hands around the frosty glass and was about to ask a question when Roberta turned her attention to her other customer.

"How 'bout it...Frederick?...that's it isn't it? What'll it be Frederick?"

"It's Frank..." Frederick beamed at being on first name basis with a woman like Roberta. He continued with his order.

Estavez never heard the request for huevos rancheros and two beers. All he heard was the name. Frank Frederick. He turned his head slightly as he took a drink and tried not to stare.

Frederick held the long-neck bottle with both hands as if afraid it would make a run for it. His formless, beige, short-sleeved shirt hung limply over rounded shoulders and was open two buttons. Fistfuls of short, curly, pure-white hair spilled through the opening.

Estavez had studied the FBI file photo of Frank Frederick several dozen times. It was thumbtacked to his mental bulletin board. As much as he could, without alarming Frederick, he studied the face at the other end of the bar in the long mirror and compared them. Age hadn't been kind to his quarry.

Eyes, however, never completely change with age.

Frederick's hadn't either. They were the same as those which had stared at the camera twenty-two years earlier. They were the eyes of the man they had been sent to find.

"Roberta, I'll be back in a second." Frederick sounded pleased to use her name with familiarity. He wouldn't dare do that when his loving bride was with him.

The ex-agent stood and walked behind Estavez. He headed down the long hallway that eventually exited on the back porch. Another two turns would be necessary to find the outside door to the men's room. Although the corroded excuse for a rest room had absorbed thousands of gallons of recycled beer, many had tired of the walk. They simply unloaded over the porch railing. Often, the lines of golden streams redefined the term "pissing contest."

Kwan heard the exchange between Roberta and Frederick and watched for Estavez's reaction. It was subtle, but it was there. Darting eyes kept returning to the image of Frank Frederick in the mirror. Estavez had found what he was looking for.

The Hispanic swung quickly off his stool as Frederick disappeared around the corner. He was so intent on his quarry, he never saw Kwan rise out of his seat. He also didn't hear Kwan in the hallway behind him. Silent feet aren't strictly a Native American trait. Warriors in all their guises develop the skill.

"Hold it right there, old man." The words were a harsh whisper. The threat obvious. "Hands up where I can see 'em."

Frank Frederick's muscles locked instantly. He recognized the cold, blunt shape against the back of his neck. At the same time, a sharp point had penetrated his jacket. It was pricking the skin on his back directly behind where his heart should have been, but was at that moment jammed in the back of his throat. In seconds, asthma began to constrict his throat muscles.

"You ex-FBI, old man?"

A shaky nod. Trembling hands worked their way to the top of his head. Frederick coughed.

"Then you're the Frank Frederick we're lookin' for."

"You know the drill. Start walking."

Frederick took several steps, with one hand going out to the wall to steady himself as he stepped around the first corner. He coughed twice.

"Keep movin' old man. Keep..."

Frederick didn't hear the next words. Coughs exploded up his throat and his body convulsed violently. His diaphragm was trying to heave his lungs out onto the dry wood decking. The diaphragm would have won, but the asthma-constricted throat muscles kept everything down, effectively choking the old man.

He fell to his knees. The pistol against his back was no longer important. He couldn't breathe. The harder he tried, the more impossible it became. His throat would barely let air in. The tug of war tripped pressure valves all over his face. Veins stood out, purple, hard and angry. He was on the verge of strangling himself from the inside.

Fuck the guy with the gun. He had more pressing matters. A shaking hand raced to a pants pocket for his inhaler. Gasping mouth open. Two-quick pumps. A deep breath. Two more pumps. His lungs gratefully sucked air as the mist began working its magic. He'd survive. If the guy with the gun didn't shoot him.

Still on his knees, he turned his head. Where was the gunman? It hadn't been his imagination. He had been there. Grasping the saloon's rough wood siding, he struggled to his feet. He was alone. Taking several deep breaths, the wheezing in his lungs began to subside. He turned towards the men's room to take care of urgent personal business. If it hadn't been for the asthma diverting his attention from the gun, the personal business would have already taken care of itself inside his pants. But it didn't, so he still had to pee.

Kwan didn't have to say anything. The automatic pressed against the back of the skinny Hispanic's neck had been enough. A free hand cupped over Estavez's mouth dragged him silently backwards around the corner and out of sight of the convulsed ex-agent. Frederick never had a clue what was taking place behind him. Even as Kwan herded Estavez off the stairs at the end of the porch, he could hear Frederick's gurgling cough. Kwan was momentarily worried. He'd hate to have come that far only to have the key to Cobalt Blue die in a coughing seizure.

He hadn't planned on becoming Frederick's unseen guardian angel, but in his line of work, Cobalt Blue was worth ten or fifteen times what he was paying for it. For that kind of profit, he would have protected the devil himself.

"Keep walking. Don't turn your head. Hands high." Kwan's

voice was low, his words measured and distinct. He was careful to speak softly, although they had walked far enough down the row of decaying buildings they were safely out of sight and earshot of Roberta's.

"Where's your partner?" Kwan asked.

Estavez started to turn his head to answer but a jab from the automatic stopped him.

"What partner?"

A jab from the pistol.

"Don't fuck with me!" Kwan hissed.

Another jab. Estavez got the message.

"I'm not sure. He's..."

"Never mind," Kwan cut him off. Keeping the pistol in place, he yanked the spike out of Estavez's up-stretched left hand. The automatic was snatched out of the other hand. Kwan tossed the pistol into the thick brush which grew against the back of the abandoned buildings. The spike stayed rooted in his left hand.

"Walk!" he demanded.

They picked their way through the deserted lots behind the buildings. The bright light of an open alley knifed between the buildings and Kwan spotted Estavez's white Pontiac. A figure was ambling aimlessly across the mouth of the alley. It was Ladilow. He was backlit by the sun reflecting off the buildings. As he walked, he was studying the buildings across the street. He was oblivious to his partner behind him at the other end of the alley, a pistol held to his neck.

Estavez sensed Kwan's momentary distraction. Instantly, his arms whipped around and down. The spike up his right sleeve slid into his hand. Whomever was behind him wouldn't fire with Ladilow in plain sight. He wouldn't be expecting a second spike.

He was right, Kwan wouldn't risk the shot. But Estavez had forgotten one of his own spikes had gone over to the other side. He had barely begun to pivot, when his brain spasmed from lack of blood. And pain overwhelmed all thought processes.

The spike Kwan had grabbed was barely visible where part of its handle protruded from the skinny Hispanic's left armpit. The rest was inside his chest. His heart muscles had offered little resistance as the finger-sized, triangular blade slammed in one side and out the other. Blood bubbled silently past the handle. The effect was immediate.

Inertia carried a dying Estavez around. His eyes, huge and

unbelieving, focused on the vaguely oriental face under the cowboy hat. As he fell, his systems began to shut down. Glassy eyes. A hint of blood at the corner of his mouth. A brief twitching of muscles as he settled to the sand. Not so much as a whimper had escaped Estavez's lips.

Standing at the mouth of the alley, all Ladilow heard was the sigh of the desert wind and the flapping of loose sheet metal roofing. He'd catch up with Estavez at Roberta's.

Ladilow was stepping into Roberta's by the time Kwan's lock pick slid into the rental car's trunk.

Frederick bolted through the back door into Roberta's. He was shaking and stared straight ahead. He saw nothing but the front door. He didn't hear Roberta calling after him about his order. He pushed blindly between empty tables towards the door. His mind was whirling and his heart pounded.

Someone was after him! Someone knew him. But, who?

No one knew he was in Pitacho. The only people he had communicated with were Kwan and...Brad Anderson!

Anderson!

The man with the gun at his back had said "they" were looking for him. "They" was probably Anderson! Kwan was still in Japan. He had spoken to him only a day earlier. It couldn't possibly have been him. As he half-fell out the front door and turned towards his RV, he bumped into a round-faced Hispanic on his way in. For a second they exchanged glances. Ladilow didn't make the connection.

"Out of my way, old man," he snarled

Frederick didn't even focus on the face. His mind was elsewhere. If someone knew he was in Pitacho, they knew he had Cobalt Blue. Or thought he had it. Think! Think! His mind was refusing to cooperate. Think!

Kwan was his only out! He had to get Cobalt Blue and call Kwan. He'd make a new deal with him. Yes, that was it! If Kwan wanted Cobalt Blue, he'd have to get him out of the country. Kwan would be his survival plan.

But he didn't have Cobalt Blue! Charley Yee! He was the key. Yee had to take him back to the cave. But this time Yee would be the only one drunk.

Thirty-one

"Hey, it's beginning to look like a home! Sorta."

Maggie Longfeather stood in the door and evaluated the progress her brother and Sam Tipton had made with the old mine building. An enormous pile of debris was the result of their efforts. Rotten lumber, scrap iron, piles of dirt, was heaped at the back where the building's broad plank floor opened into the mine. Longfeather's pick-up was backed against the heap waiting to haul it away. It would take many trips. The Willys was parked in the middle of the huge building. With the floor cleared of junk, the building's size became even more apparent and dwarfed the Willys, which now looked like an abandoned Tonka toy.

As her voice echoed off the walls, Sam Tipton stood up from bundling new electrical wiring. He wiped his hands on his jeans.

"Hey, kid, what's happening?" He knocked the dust off his sleeves. "Here, let me help you with that stuff." He scooped the grocery bags out of her arms and deposited them on a heavy, freshly-refinished workbench. Its newly-urethaned surface had the dull glow of well-aged oak.

As he turned, his arms started up, prepared to hug her. He changed his mind. At the time he asked himself why. He gave himself no answer.

"And how do you like the kitchen?" Change the subject. Tipton grinned as he leaned back against the bench.

"What do you mean kitchen?" Maggie asked, her eyes traveling in a circle. "Where?"

"Right here!" Tipton grabbed her by the hand and led her around the bench-turned-kitchen-counter.

"This is the stove," he pointed with pride at the heavy iron forge. It had been wire-brushed until the rust was polished to a dark, reddish-brown sheen. It was not unlike a nouveau designer finish. A newly-made stainless steel grate lay across the opening. A propane bottle sat on the floor next to the waist-high unit. The smoke hood hanging over it had the same polished patina.

Maggie grimaced. "What are you planning for dinner? Fried horseshoes?"

Sam ignored her.

"And this is the refrigerator." He opened a huge, polished-rust steel cabinet. Its heavy, medieval door was bound in iron straps festooned with walnut-sized rivets. Inside, a series of frost-covered coils wrapped around a large stainless steel box. A chilly vapor rolled out to greet them.

A fluorescent-yellow sticker on the shiny box's door warned "Store Viable Organs Only."

"The outside was a powder magazine we found in the mine," Sam explained. "I don't suppose I have to explain the liner. That was in the junk we brought up from Pitacho."

Maggie was still trying to digest the refrigeration unit when Sam forcibly dragged her up the broad steps towards what passed for a second story. The platform formed a heavy timber ceiling over the "kitchen."

The steps, which were twice the width and three times the thickness of normal stairs, had been scrubbed clean and sanded. The natural wood, oil-soaked from years of industrial operations, was polished to a satiny, deep luster.

At the top, Maggie found herself standing on a broad platform attached to one of the massive walls. It was held up by enormous wooden columns. The size of two double garages, the open platform didn't have a railing and offered an unobstructed view from three sides. From that vantage point, Ivan's seated figure was clearly visible at the far end of the building.

"And this is the bedroom!" Sam pulled her across the wide floor boards and tossed her in the middle of a freshly-made double bed. The cover was a brown and red Navajo rug. The headboard was made from polished mine timbers mortised and pinned together to form a sculpture. A Joseph Longfeather original.

The night stand was a weathered cedar stump nearly three feet across. A mining lantern, ready to be lit, stood on it.

As she hit the bed, Sam fought the urge to leap in beside her. It was just as well he didn't. She had barely touched the cover when she ricocheted off like a cat to land on her feet.

"Sam! Where in the hell did you get a mattress? God, I shudder to think what's living in any mattress you could find." She backed away from it as if she had disturbed dark denizens living within.

"Eee-yuk! That has to be scorpion city!" She shuddered again.

"Relax, kid! And thank your mom. She donated it. So it's not only clean, she probably had it sterilized in a radiation chamber.

Christ, I think this is the first regular bed I've had in ten years!"

Tipton landed in the bed on his back, arms behind his head. Feet crossed.

"Want to try it out?"

Sam's eyebrows arched upwards in a Groucho Marx imitation. His voice had a laughing invitation attached to it and he acted as if he wasn't serious.

"Oh, and check this out!" Before Maggie could respond to the quasi-proposition, he rolled out of the bed. In three excited strides, he covered the distance to a heavy wooden door in the stone wall.

"For the first time in years I get to shower indoors! What a kick!" He yanked the door open to reveal a small room walled in heavy stone. An antique, porcelain and oak toilet sat against one wall and a shower head protruded from the other. The floor, although aged, polished wood, was obviously a recent addition.

Half of the outside wall appeared to be in ruins and missing. As Maggie drew closer, however, she saw Longfeather and Tipton had matched the crumbling outline with sealed wooden framing. The missing stone area had been replaced with glass, retaining the illusion of a crumbling ruin, but keeping the weather out.

The bathroom offered a hundred-mile view of the Mogollon Rim. Real estate weasels would charge in the high six figures for that kind of view. Location, location, location.

"This was some sort of chimney or flue. But isn't it great!" Sam made no effort to hide his excitement.

"Water comes from the tank on the roof. It's still cold as hell, but I can poop or shower and have the best view in Arizona." He was so proud of what he saw as a major step forward in his life, he could hardly stand still. Maggie smiled. He was acting like a kid. It was cute.

"Sam, you're nuts!" she protested. "People can see right in!"

"What people?" Sam laughed. "And, who gives a shit?"

"Besides, I've been showering in public for seven or eight years so this amounts to absolute privacy, for me."

A new voice joined in from across the bedroom.

"Yeah, believe me," Roberta said, "Everybody in town knows what Tipton's got and damn few want it."

She laughed uproariously in a deep, throaty tone. She turned slowly, taking in the rustic amenities. She nodded her approval.

"Tipton, Fowler may have done you favor," she said.

"You've really set up housekeeping up here. But, do me a favor...don't let the word get out how being sober has changed your life. You may put me out of business." She grinned.

Sam suddenly threw his arms around both girls' necks and fell into the wide bed, taking both of them with him. Wrapping an arm around both, he spoke. His tone was serious.

"Speaking of Fowler...let's make it a point to keep this place a little secret from him. That's one reason we've left everything outside exactly as we found it. We want this place to look totally abandoned and worthless." He alternately looked each of the girls in the face.

"You'll notice you didn't see the Stinson or any trucks parked out there. That's because those sheds are all open to the mine. I could taxi a bomber in there, close the door and no one would know we're home." He grinned and lost his serious tone. "It's kind of like having our own bat cave."

"And speaking of bats, Roberta, we still have a flying rodent problem in here. But don't worry. They won't come after you. Usually."

As if spring-loaded, Roberta Rodreguez scrambled frantically out of bed to stand in the middle of the floor, searching the ceiling. Sam laughed and lay back in the bed. He didn't release his hold on Maggie, and she didn't fight it.

Ted Fowler stood in the middle of the large abandoned adobe on the edge of Pitacho. The light from an open door cast his shadow across the empty floor as he spoke quietly to himself.

"Sonuvabitch!" His voice was an awed whisper aimed at no one. "He got all his shit out of here!

He paused at the door on the way out and looked back inside.

"I wonder where that piece-of-shit drunk is holed up now? Huh! Interesting!"

"I'm going to have to check on that."

Thirty-two

"**What the hell do you mean,** you lost Estavez?"

Richard Yardley paced back and forth at the foot of the bed. Right hand pinched the bridge of his nose. Red face. Bulging veins. He was not a happy man.

"Where'd you last see him?" His head stayed down as he paced. His fingers never left the bridge of his nose.

"We split up in the alley where we parked the car. He went to the bar and I went the other way to check out the town."

"When I went to the bar, he wasn't there. I waited about half hour and asked that tall broad if she'd seen him. She said he'd been in earlier, but she didn't know where he went."

"Yeah, okay, and then what?" Yardley was impatient. Head down. Still pacing.

"Well...the town isn't all that big, so I walked around for a while, couldn't find him and came back here."

Yardley stopped pacing long enough to look Ladilow in the face. Hornslee sat on the dresser in the corner of the motel room. He was grinning. He loved seeing someone else on the hot seat.

Snatching the satellite-phone off the bed, Yardley held it up in front of Ladilow's sweating face.

"Goddammit! You know I have this! So, why didn't you call me as soon as he turned up missing?" Yardley's face was inches from Ladilow's.

"Uhh...I forgot the number."

"Great! Just fucking great! We lose a team member and you can't tell anyone because you forgot the goddamn phone number?" Yardley's voice climbed in pitch. Hornslee grinned wider.

"And what about Frederick, Ladilow? Did you find anything out about him?" Yardley was standing on his tiptoes to make his eyes even with Ladilow's. His words carried a single drop of spit onto Ladilow's cheek. Ladilow fought the urge to wipe it off.

"Uh...uh...I never got around to asking about him. When I couldn't find Estavez, I forgot." Ladilow stopped talking as Yardley whirled around mid-sentence and ripped his jacket off a chair. Ignoring the others, he stomped to the door and yanked it open, half-turning as he did.

"Well, genius, coming with me? You too, Hornslee. You'll drive the white car."

He muttered under his breath as he jerked the van's passenger door open. His words flowed together into a single, monosyllabic condemnation of subordinates everywhere. "Motherfuckingoddamnidiots!"

The dust cloud behind them caught up even as the two cars rolled to a stop at the curb. Only Yardley had enough sense to keep his door closed until the light breeze carried the dust down Pitacho's main street. That early in the afternoon, the sun hadn't yet soaked the high desert and mesas with enough heat to build a serious wind.

Yardley glanced both ways down the street. Empty. He signaled his rapidly-dwindling team into the shade of a nearby sagging porch.

"Ladilow, get down to that shitty little convenience store at the end of the street. Tell the old guy...tell him you're looking for your partner because he forgot his wallet. Then, swing around behind the buildings on that side of the street.

"Hornslee, go in and talk to the bitch in the bar and don't, I repeat, do not order a beer. I'll cover the area behind the buildings on this side of the street. Meet in the bar in no more than fifteen minutes. Check the time."

Each looked at their watch. Hornslee compared his to Ladilow's and made an adjustment.

"Okay, go."

Each took off, headed in different directions.

A Native American leaning against the wall on the other side of the street interrupted his knot-tying. He took notice which direction each went. It might prove useful information. He idly noted their white Pontiac parked in the sun and wondered how many days it would be before they noticed their rental car had developed a distinct aroma.

Yardley rounded the back of the building and stopped short, caught completely by surprise. A withered old man sat amidst the sagebrush, leaned back in a rusting kitchen chair. The sun baked down on him. He was stark naked. A ragged straw cowboy hat covered his face. His body was the color of cheap tobacco. Every inch of aged human leather was evenly tanned.

This was not the first time it had seen the sun.

A pair of cowboy boots, their finish and age mimicking their owner, stood next to the chair. Faded jeans and a plaid shirt were neatly folded on top. An ancient single-action Colt six-shooter, its finish worn silver, its corners worn smooth, lay on top. Yardley noted blunt lead shapes visible in the cylinder. It was loaded.

The man appeared to be sleeping until a voice, as tanned and leathery as its owner, came from under the hat.

"Kin I hep yah, sonny?" The hat didn't move.

Yardley felt foolish talking to a naked old man under a cowboy hat, but he couldn't ignore him.

"Just looking for a friend." The ex-FBI operative tried to step past the Mogollon nudist without looking. Even so, he couldn't miss the two thumb-sized scars in the upper right chest. Obviously bullet wounds. A jagged "Z" scar ripped across his withered stomach. Even the scars were tan.

Yardley was several steps past the nature lover when the voice again crept from under the hat.

"Tall, skinny Chicano? Bad skin? Real ugly?"

Yardley stopped. "Yeah, that's him. How'd you know?"

"You're the only strangers these parts. Hard ta miss."

A skinny arm, sharply-folded skin wrapped around it, came up and pushed the hat back. The face was as worn as the boots. The hand reached out.

"Snuffy Smith's the name."

Yardley took the hand and tried not to look past it. When he did he felt as if he was looking at the oldest troll in the world. Stained, chipped teeth. Crow's feet so deep they looked painful. Sun baked lips. Bright green eyes which looked out of place in their aged surroundings.

"Yardley. Richard Yardley," he replied.

"Well, Richard Yardley, you're sure lookin' fer a friend in a strange place. How'd yah come to lose 'em?" Snuffy Smith croaked.

"Have you seen him?" Yardley asked.

"Yep," Smith answered.

"Where and when?" Yardley asked.

"Roberta's. This mornin.'"

"Where'd he go?" Yardley prodded.

"John."

"John, who?" Yardley asked impatiently.

"Not John-Who. Just john. Yah, know..." Smith grabbed his not-so-shriveled penis and laughed. "Shakin' the dew...yah, know...."

Yardley was becoming intensely uncomfortable. "Where'd he go?"

"Probably went in the urinal like most folks do," the old troll ventured. "Some don't go there though. Prefer peeing over the railing."

"No, I mean after that,' Yardley was beginning to wander if the conversation was worth the brain damage.

"Don't know. Never saw 'em come out. You checked the john?"

"That was this morning," Yardley pointed out.

"Wouldn't be the first to die in Roberta's john. Powerful strong 'n there when it's hot."

"I'll check the john." Yardley started to walk.

"You do that, Richard Yardley." The hat was back over the face. A bony hand lay casually on top the Colt.

Yardley didn't look back. The image would stay in his mind too long, as it was.

"He was in here, that's all we know." Yardley spoke quietly to the other two while half leaning across one of Roberta's corner tables. The afternoon was wearing on and several of the evening's regulars had already drifted in. They wanted to get a head start on their hangover.

Yardley's eyes scanned the room as he talked. He watched an Indian come through the door and sit by himself on the other side of the room. That early in the afternoon, the small crowd was about half American Indian, half American cowboy. By night's end, they would be balanced out by bikers and Latinos, the usual Roberta's mix.

He smiled to himself when a familiar figure came through the door. Snuffy the Mogollon Nudist appeared bigger when dressed. But, he still looked like a troll playing cowboy.

"And we still don't have a handle on Frederick." Yardley continued. "We can't keep wasting time looking for Estavez. For all we know, he's fucking his brains out in some bimbo's bedroom right now. He'll show up. If he doesn't, he doesn't get paid. Simple as that.

"Ladilow, we still have a lot of Payson to cover." Yardley stood, thereby announcing the meeting was about to move outdoors. "Hornslee, you're going to stay here."

They stepped out into the piercing afternoon sun practically feeling their way as their pupils shrank to pinholes. They stood on the sidewalk in front of the two cars.

"We know he's not in there and neither is Frederick. So, Hornslee, you park your skinny butt in the car and sit here until one of them shows." Yardley gestured at the white rental and Hornslee walked towards it, catching the keys Ladilow tossed at him with a flick of the wrist. "Don't talk to anyone," Yardley warned. "Don't follow anyone. Don't do anything until we tell you. Here's the spare phone in case something happens. I want you to sit in the car and be quiet. Think you can handle that?"

Hornslee nodded and climbed in. An assignment he could handle. He hurriedly cranked his window down and wrinkled his nose. "Some asshole left a sandwich or something in here."

Thirty-three

Frank Frederick pulled the RV's shades aside just a crack and peeked out. The old Indian was still out there. Sunset was hours away, but Charley Yee already had his usual front row seat. He didn't want his Gods to think less of him because he was late. Frederick thought fast and hard. His eyes never left the slowly rocking Indian.

"Frank! Open the damn shades! This place is like a tomb!"

Frederick ignored her which infuriated her further. He didn't care. His mind was focused on Charley Yee. Frederick had to convince him it was time for another pilgrimage to see his gods.

An empty soda can bounced off the windshield a few inches from his head. Her aim was improving.

"Frank you bastard...." The shrill words faded into the distance. Frank was someplace else. His mind was rehearsing his sales pitch to Charley Yee. He had to be convincing.

He frowned. Things had suddenly gotten very complicated. And dangerous. The gun in his back meant someone big was looking for him. And that someone was still out there somewhere. The voice hadn't been Anderson's. But Anderson had to be behind it. Only he and Kwan knew about Cobalt Blue.

Frederick's frown deepened. For Anderson's men to have found him so quickly, they had to be using Bureau assets. Anderson must have a benefactor powerful enough to ask the right people to look the other way at the right time. Frederick glanced out at Charley Yee again. It was time.

"Charley, my friend, my friend." The aging Native American didn't turn his head at Frederick's overly bright, well-practiced salutation.

"Come, I have brought us something." Yee again appeared to ignore Frederick, but he'd heard the liquid sloshing in the bottle. A sun-dried hand extended in its general direction. His eyes still stared at the far horizon.

Bottle to his lips, Charley smiled. He didn't see Frederick's smile. Frederick was thinking that another of his plans was working. This time when Charley took him to visit his gods, Frederick would remember the trip. He'd remember the way to Cobalt Blue. He patted the pad and pencil in his shirt pocket. This time he'd write the directions down. And he'd stay sober.

Charley extended the bottle at arm's length. It was an offering to his friend and old drinking buddy. Frederick took the bottle and stared at it. Maybe just one. After all, he couldn't insult his friend by not drinking. That might insult his friend's gods.

It was Scotch this time. Very cheap Scotch. It burned going down. Aged maybe two weeks. Three tops. But it would do the trick. It would put Charley in the required agreeable mood. The bottle went back to Charley. Then back to Frank. He made a short protest. Okay, maybe just one more.

"Frank, you sick sonuvabitch!" May Frederick was standing in the middle of the narrow RV hallway. Her husband was sprawled face down through the open door, his pants at half mast. Ancient, white thighs glowed in the fading light. Charley Yee lay under him, pinned face down by Frederick's weight.

"Jesus, Frank! Butt fucking an old Indian? God...!" She stomped back and forth, at a loss for words.

Frank Frederick stumbled to his feet, his pants sliding to his knees. Charley Yee mumbled a drunken chant as he lay face down on the dingy carpet. His hands were handcuffed behind him.

Frederick reeled back, barely catching himself with a free hand on the doorjamb. The other hand struggled to hold a snubnose .38 revolver and his pants at the same time. He turned big, watery eyes towards his wife.

"Butt fucking?" His voice crescendoed with incredibility. "Who's butt fucking who, you old bitch! I couldn't stumpf old Charley if I wanted to. You killed my dick years ago. I haven't had a goddamn hard-on since the last time I saw you naked. Yeah, that's what killed it."

He roared with laughter and bellowed at the sunset, "Hey, Charley's gods! You hear that? One look at her naked, wrinkled old body killed my dick! It won't work no more!"

He struggled with his pants, trying to feed the belt through the buckle.

"Shee-yit. I'm not trying to stick it up old Charley's dirtchute." He got the belt through the buckle.

"I had my trusty old revolver here in my belt and it fell into my underwear." He began to laugh again and tilted his head back and yelled.

"Thank you, Charley's Gods, for not shooting my worthless, limp dick off, when you had the chance." More laughing. "I know it ain't much, but it's all I got!"

Saliva dripped from his mouth. He laughed hysterically as he tried to climb over Charley Yee to the driver's seat. Yee was still chanting as Frederick stood up and got his foot caught between the seat and the engine cover.

"Goddamn, motherfucking...." Frederick dropped the .38 in the driver's seat and bent over to wrestle his foot free.

"Good-bye my friend," Charley Yee croaked as he rolled upright and stood outside the door.

Frederick glanced up, his bleary eyes unable to focus. He nodded a drunken nod. He returned his attention to his stuck foot, unable to comprehend that his captive was making a slow, wobbly escape.

Charley Yee was already a dark outline in the gathering dusk, when Frederick realized his plan was coming apart.

With hands cuffed behind him, and brain cells cauterized by bad Scotch, it was all the old Indian could do to stay upright, as he made his unsteady way towards Roberta's.

Frederick tried to follow. "Goddamn foot...!" He continued yanking on it as Charley shuffled out of sight into the dark.

"Roberta!" Snuffy Smith's usually quiet voice was cranked up as loud as he could make it to get the barkeep's attention. "Roberta! Charley!"

As he spoke, the cowboy troll pivoted deftly down off his usual stool. His movements were quick and smooth. And out of character.

Three quick steps and he had a supporting hand under Charley Yee's arm.

"Hold on there, old fella." Snuffy was at least a decade older than Charley. "We gotcha!"

"Christ, Charley!" Roberta had Yee's face cradled in her hands as she looked at him. The purple bruises inflicted by the Hispanic kid had healed to a queasy shade of yellow. She saw no new marks. Only his breath appeared to be the worse for wear.

"Whew!" Roberta's face squinched up as she stepped back, holding him by the shoulders. "God! What've you been drinking?"

Charley just grinned and giggled. Snuffy helped limit his swaying.

Then Roberta noticed his hands.

"What the hell?" She spun him around and tugged at the handcuffs.

"Charley, who did this to you?"

Toothy grin. More bad breath. Bright dancing eyes that couldn't focus.

"My friend. My old friend. My friend who loves my Gods." Charley Yee giggled and rolled his head on a limp neck.

"What old friend, Charley? What old friend?" Roberta leaned down to stare directly into his eyes. She softened her voice. "What old friend, Charley?"

"My friend who was going to come with me to see my gods."

"A friend wouldn't do this to your hands, Charley."

"Mine would. He has a gun too." Charley Yee laughed. "It's tiny, not big like yours." More laughing. "He needs it to protect our gods."

Roberta shot a quick glance at the door and thought about the .45 on her hip. Snuffy's free hand moved up to rest on the worn grips of the old Colt stuck in his belt.

"Charley, let's go."

The three of them moved quickly around the bar towards her apartment.

"Can Charley have another drink?" The Indian's eyes danced across the bottles as he staggered past the bar.

"No, Charley can't have another drink."

As Roberta herded Charley through her apartment door, Snuffy returned to his usual perch. His worn cowboy hat was resting on the bar. His hand was under the hat. The Colt was no longer in his belt. His eyes were on the door.

Thirty-four

Sam Tipton heard the vehicle first.

"What the hell? Who'd be coming up here this close to dark?"

Maggie Longfeather glanced up as Tipton walked to the big side door. Then she returned her attention to the grill. There were still two hamburgers to be flipped.

"It's Roberta!" Sam's voice rang out from the doorway.

He leaned against the cut-stone doorjam as Roberta's old truck rattled its way the remaining distance to the mine building. She had someone next to her who was leaning to one side.

The truck had lurched to a halt before Tipton recognized her passenger. It was Charley Yee. Tipton stepped up to the side of the truck. As he did, Roberta spoke through the open window.

"Well, Tipton. Last week you told me to consider you Charley's guardian, so here he is. Guard away."

"What're you talking about?" Tipton asked. Sam followed her as she got out and walked around to the passenger side.

She had to support Charley Yee as she opened the door. He'd been laying sideways to give his hands room behind him.

"Okay, what the hell's going on?" Maggie's agitated voice from the door beat Sam to the punch. She'd seen the handcuffs.

Sam didn't say a thing as he knelt down and looked at Yee's wrists. They weren't bruised or bleeding. The cuffs were fairly loose and hadn't been on long. Someone was either careless or wasn't that serious about the cuffs. He looked up at his friend.

"Who did this, Charley?"

"My friend." He grinned broadly. His eyes wandered back and forth.

Roberta just rolled her eyes.

"Friend, my ass!" Tipton growled. "Come inside."

Maggie was holding a cup of coffee to Yee's lips when Sam returned to the kitchen. A gigantic pair of bolt cutters was slung over one shoulder. He stepped around behind Charley Yee.

"Don't move, Charley." One end of the cutter handles was put on the floor for leverage. Tipton suddenly put his entire weight behind it, grunted and Charley's hands dropped free.

The still-drunk Indian brought his hand up in front of his eyes. The cut cuffs dangled from that wrist. The other was free. He eyed the cuffs.

"You broke my friend's bracelet!" he said in a drunken whine. "He will be angry!"

"Yeah? Then let's really piss him off!" Tipton growled. He grabbed the cuffs and repeated the process. A short grunt and Charley was again a free man.

"All right, now what's this all about?" He was focused on Roberta.

She told him all she knew, which was next to nothing. Charley had stumbled into the bar already handcuffed and talking about a "Friend" with handcuffs and a gun. That was it!

"Let's go!" Tipton was already half way to the door. "We'll take the Willys, Charley can go with you. See you at the bar!"

As he dropped into the Willys next to Maggie he turned, "Someone better have a damn good explanation for this!"

The engine barked into life before she had time to answer.

Roberta's truck disappeared down an alley to the back of the bar. Tipton took the closest parking spot he could find out front. It was a busy night.

"Are you calmed down?" Maggie asked Sam.

"Yeah, yeah, I'm okay," he snapped. "No, on second thought, I'm not. I'm pissed! Who would do this to Charley?" He threw the Willys's door open to vault up on the sidewalk and past an Indian sitting by the door. A corner of his mind admired the splice the Indian was weaving in a rope. Very nautical, his subconscious thought. His conscious mind didn't even see Kwan. It was concentrating on what had happened to his friend.

Maggie followed with Charley Yee and led him through the saloon door behind Tipton.

"Okay, Charley, show us who put the cuffs on you?" Sam softly demanded.

Charley Yee giggled again. Old eyes traveled slowly around the room. As he turned, he started to fall, but Roberta caught him.

"There is my old friend!" Charley's eyes brightened when they landed on Frank Frederick slouched back in a chair against the wall. Both feet were on the table.

"My old friend," Charley started to stagger towards Frederick, then stopped.

"Say, what happened to your shoe?" He pointed at a bare foot.

"It got stuck." Frederick slurred in response.

Sam gently pulled Frederick up by his arm. He held Charley with his free hand.

"Okay, you two, outside. We're going to talk."

Frederick rolled his eyes up at him, "Why certainly sonny. Say, have you ever thought about getting a haircut?"

He roared with laughter. Tipton aimed him at the door.

Once outside, Frederick stumbled off the curb but caught himself by grabbing the fender of a white Pontiac. Hornslee abruptly sat up in the driver's seat and swore under his breath. "Old drunk!" He started to open the door then hesitated when Tipton grabbed Frederick.

Tipton carefully set the old man down on the curb alongside Charley Yee. Yee was chanting something which Tipton thought sounded like a Beach Boys tune with only one note.

"What's your name?" Tipton was looking at the graying white man next to Charley Yee.

"My name is Franklin D. Frederick, late of the FBI," Frederick laughed at his weak attempt at an English accent.

"Where's your gun, old man?" Tipton's attitude softened as he talked.

"It is safely hidden where my wife can't find it. Say? Have you met my wife?" Frederick leaned closer to Tipton as if sharing a secret. "Sonny, she's a real bitch! A real strawberry bitch! She killed my dick!"

He roared and looked over at Charley Yee for approval. Yee, laughed and nodded agreement.

"What the hell," Tipton started, "were you doing handcuffing Charley Yee?"

"Handcuffing? My old buddy Charley?" Frederick eyes were luminescent white circles as he arched his eyebrows.

"Why, I don't know what you're talking about." He sounded like a little old lady defending her innocence after being caught in the act of shoplifting. "I did no such thing!"

He straightened his back and threw his head back in an attempt at looking proud. He nearly fell over backwards.

Sam Tipton was having a difficult time keeping a straight face. Maggie leaned against the wall behind them. Her hand was pressed to her mouth. A short laugh escaped anyway.

No one noticed the young man behind the wheel of the white Pontiac. The instant Frederick introduced himself, he lay his head against the door. He appeared to be resting. He was listening.

Frederick looked up at Tipton and insisted, "I didn't do it." Short hesitation.

"What happened to the handcuffs?" he asked timidly. "They were good ones, ya know."

"They died, Mr. Frederick. They died!" Tipton said.

Pulling Frank Frederick to his feet, he looked down at Charley Yee and back at the old government man.

"Okay, you two. Separate for the evening, sleep it off, and see if you can play nice next time." He treated them like unruly, but sweet, ten year olds.

"Good night, old Indian friend of mine. We'll go to meet your gods tomorrow." He patted Charley Yee on the head who looked up still chanting and smiled.

Tipton could have sworn Charley was chanting Ba-ba-baaa, Ba-ba-baarbara Ann.

Frederick turned, a semblance of impending sobriety showing in his eyes. "I'm going home now." He hesitated for a second.

"Which way is home? Oh, yes." He stumbled down the sidewalk towards the RV.

The Pontiac driver's eyes followed him closely.

Maggie stepped off the curb. She grabbed Tipton by the front of his shirt, putting her dark eyes close to his. "Okay, good Samaritan. It's time for enchiladas, to hell with our hamburgers." She smiled brightly, "I'm buying."

"You're right 'cause I'm broke," Tipton snorted.

As they walked into the dull roar that was Roberta's, neither noticed the white Pontiac slowly back away from the curb. The driver had a sat-phone to his ear and was cursing at the busy signal.

Thirty-five

"**You miserable bastard, where** the goddamn hell have you been?" May Frederick wasted no time in sinking her fangs into her drunk husband.

Frederick closed the RV door, stood as straight as he could, and stared at her. The walk and the night air had knocked the edge off the Scotch. He was no longer drunk enough to put up with her yammer.

"May, will you please shut the fuck up! I don't feel so good. I...." the old man started.

Neither heard the RV's door open. The Beretta nine-millimeter against Frederick's head was all that announced Hornslee's sudden appearance. May Frederick saw him first.

"OhmyGod, ohmyGod, ohmyGod." An endless stream of words vomited past her quivering lips. She couldn't control them. Her hands instantly knotted themselves into the front of her frizzy sweater.

"Yer husband was right lady," Hornslee snapped, "Shut the fuck up!"

She stared at him, her body carved of ice. Her mouth the only part still movable. "OhmyGod, ohmyGod..." The words flowed unending.

The phone was in Hornslee's free hand. His thumb would frantically jab the re-dial button. He'd listen. He'd curse the busy signal. He'd hang up.

"All right, Frederick! Tell her to shut the fuck up! Right now!" He was frustrated. The pistol was pressed against the old man's head so hard he was forced against the littered counter top. A dish and two empty Spam cans clattered to the floor.

Looking at May Frederick, Hornslee shouted, "Shut up old lady!" He was hardly paying attention to Frederick. His thumb jabbed at the phone.

"OhmyGod, ohmyGod..."

"Goddammit, I mean it! Shut up!" Hornslee was out of patience.

"OhmyGod, ohmyGod, oh..."

"Okay, I've had it with you bitch. You're history." Hornslee turned and leveled the automatic at the trembling old woman.

"Noooo!" If Frederick hadn't yelled as he leaped, he might have surprised Hornslee. But he gave too much warning. Hornslee swung his gun hand at the aged agent. Frederick's lunge was clumsy. Hornslee's swing was not. It was swift and hard. And on target.

The big automatic caught Frederick on the right cheekbone and his nose at the same time. There was a hollow sounding thump. Blood shot out of his still black-and-blue nose. He slumped backwards into the passenger's chair, his eyes glassy.

He barely saw Hornslee return his attention to his wife.

"OhmyGod, ohmyGod..." The words moved faster. The pitch increased to a scream.

"OhmyGod, ohmyGod..." Her eyes weren't seeing.

Hornslee had a slight smirk on his face, "Jesus, bitch! You're a hard one to shut up. But we don't need you so..."

His finger tightened on the trigger.

"OhmyGod, ohmyGod, ohmyGod...!"

Thirty-six

Frank Frederick opened his left eye. The right had something sticky holding the lid shut. His head pounded. The right half of his face was numb and his mouth tasted of blood. He spit over the arm of the chair, and then realized where he was and the images returned.

A pain shot through his neck when he jerked upright to look the length of the dark RV. The only light came from the half-opened refrigerator. Then he saw his wife.

May Frederick lay in a crumpled heap half on and half off the bed. Her legs were bent in a series of unnatural angles. It was as if she had relaxed and let gravity do its work.

"No! No!" Frederick's voice was a high, sad whisper. More a moaning breath than a voice. He forced himself off the chair. A shaking old hand white-knuckled the edge of the counter for support as he made his way towards the bed.

"May, May! Goddammit, no!" He reached the bed. As his weight deformed the lumpy mattress, May Frederick's limp body flowed the rest of the way to the floor.

Frank Frederick felt the life drain from him. His muscles lost all strength as he slid down next to his silent wife. He pulled her to him, her head falling heavily onto his chest. The night swallowed the nearly inaudible whisper, "No! Not now, you wrinkled old bitch. Please, not now..." A tear finished the sentence.

"Who's a wrinkled old bitch?" The smoky rasp was barely above a whisper, but sounded as loud as a shout to Frank Frederick. His eyes popped open. He felt his wife's head move.

Then he was looking into her eyes.

"I mean it, you old goat. Who's a wrinkled old bitch? I'm not old!" she croaked.

Frank's first attempt at speech ended in a choked whisper. When the words came out, they were unbelieving and thankful at the same time.

"Oh, Jesus!" He held her head to his chest for a long time, squeezing tightly.

He held her face out where he could look at her. He couldn't believe it. Then he remembered.

"Are you okay?" His eyes flashed around her disheveled dress. The refrigerator light revealed no dark splotches.

She nodded, a weak smile on her lips.

"Where...? How...?" His eyes flashed around the RV. He was suddenly afraid.

"Stay here, May!" He struggled on his knees to the small stove. Reaching under it, his hand came out clutching the snub nose revolver. Then he fell back beside his wife, crouching in the darkness like a dog protecting his brood.

"What happened?" He asked the now very wide awake May Frederick.

"I don't know," she answered. "I saw this horrible man with the gun. He hit you and then pointed the gun at me. I guess I must of fainted."

"Fainted! God, God, I thought you were dead." He put a shaking arm around her. "I'm sorry about calling you old, but..."

"Yes, but you're right, I am a bitch. And you're a bastard." She looked up into his watery eyes, "And, like it or not, Mr. Frederick, we are old. And, like it or not, we're all we've got."

Her wrinkled hand reached up to tenderly touch an age-spotted cheek. A tear dampened her finger.

"We're getting out of here, now!" Frederick struggled to his feet. He fell back into a sitting position on the bed. His head was killing him. It was a toss-up which was worse, the hangover or the pistol-whipping.

"I need to make a phone call, get a hold of Charley Yee, and then we're out of here," Frederick stated.

"Shit, where am I going to get that many quarters this time of night?" He was thinking out loud.

"Roberta's! She might have them." He stumbled towards the front of the motorhome. As he shuffled, he kicked something laying on the floor. It was glowing.

He tried to bend over but his head nearly exploded. He chose to squat instead. It was the sat-phone. He picked it up and sat down on the rear-facing passenger chair by the door.

Something hard jabbed him in the back, as he sat down. He reached behind his back. It was the Beretta. He fell back into the chair, the automatic in one hand, the phone in the other.

It didn't make sense. What had happened?

Staring at the phone, he decided it didn't make any difference what had happened. He had to force the plan and make it happen immediately. He and Charley had to get Cobalt Blue tomorrow. His deal with Kwan would include airline tickets out of Phoenix tomorrow night. If Charley wanted, he could come with them.

Twenty-four hours and it would all be over. He desperately wanted it over.

He glanced back at his wife. Suddenly he was ready to forget the entire thing. Just start the motor home and leave. But, if he did that, they would have a future exactly like their present.

May Frederick was still sitting on the edge of the bed watching him. The narrow wedge of light from the refrigerator hit her directly in the face. She didn't look nearly as wrinkled as he remembered. Nor as old. He smiled at her. It had been too long since the last one.

He began punching numbers into the phone. Let the transoceanic call show up on someone else's phone bill. At this stage of the game, who gave a shit?

The phone vibrated in his vest pocket and Kwan pulled it out. Flipping it open, the lighted number pad cast a green glow on his face. He was smiling. He glanced over at Hornslee who was wrestling the wheel of the rental car. They hit a bump and the ex-G.I. grimaced as one of Estavez's spikes in Kwan's left hand accidentally pricked his rib cage under his right arm. He hadn't known Kwan was even on the planet until he felt the spike against his ribs just as he was about to put two 9mm slugs in that screaming old lady.

"Yes?" He had been expecting the call, but not so quickly.

"Yes, Mr. Frederick. And how are things going for you there?" Kwan continued smiling in the dark. He knew exactly how things were going, which is why he expected the call.

"Why yes, I think we can arrange to have everything in place. Tomorrow evening will be difficult, however, because of the amount of cash. How about the next evening...Yes, sir, that would be forty-eight hours"

Frederick continued to push. Kwan could sense the desperation in his voice. He understood. The wolves were closing in. Something told Kwan to wait. At least one wild card had showed up. Where did the old Indian fit in? Why was Frederick trying so hard to attach himself to him.

"I'm sorry, but I guarantee the money will be there in two days. If you want, we can have it waiting for you at the airport along with the airline tickets," Kwan was just short of being patronizing.

As he listened, he gestured with his left hand. He wanted a left turn made. Rocks and scrub oak danced sideways through the headlights.

"Yes, I understand you are in great danger. I will send one of my men to you to help with that problem. I have one nearby and he can be there to assist you sometime tomorrow. He will also be empowered to receive Cobalt Blue and deliver a portion of the money."

Kwan remembered the two bulky knapsacks back at his camp on the mesa. It had been his traveling money, a half-million dollars in small bills. It would do Frederick for a start, if need be. He wrinkled his nose. The smell was disagreeable. He could hear a subtle buzzing in the car. His driver appeared not to notice the dozen or so flies flitting around his head. His eyes were riveted on the headlights. He wasn't smiling.

"In the meantime, Mr. Frederick," Kwan continued, "the best thing you can do for your own safety is to get to a very public place. Whomever is after you will not try anything with other people watching."

Another gesture, another turn.

"Mr. Frederick, please feel free to call me at any time...That's okay, I'm glad to help." He smiled again. Frederick bordered on being a buffoon, but something in his helplessness touched Kwan. He was old. He was desperate. Those were qualities Kwan's culture had taught him to respect.

He also appeared to have Cobalt Blue, or at least knew where it was. That alone was enough for serious respect.

Kwan flipped the telephone closed. He dropped it into his vest pocket and leaned forward, reaching for his pistol laying on the dash. Despite the spike against his ribs, Hornslee picked that moment to make his move.

Hornslee threw the steering wheel to the right, forcibly burying the Pontiac's right fender in a rocky bank bordering the dark road. Hornslee was wearing his seat belt. Kwan wasn't.

Kwan's was still reaching for the automatic when he was slammed against the dash. The automatic clattered to the floor.

Kwan saw stars as his head impacted the windshield hard enough to crack it.

In that split instant, Hornslee threw himself at Kwan.

Hornslee grasped Kwan's left hand, using all of his strength to keep the razor-sharp spike from doing its job. Still dazed, Kwan was late in countering the move. The spike fell from his hand and under the front seat. In a single motion, Hornslee released his seat belt and popped the door open to roll out.

Kwan scrambled across the seat and out the door right behind Hornslee. He snagged a fleeting pants leg while still prone in the seat.

Hornslee fell, but sprang back to his feet. Hundreds of hours of hand-to-hand combat training had paid off. But he wasn't quick enough. He was barely on his feet before Kwan's right foot caught the side of his head. As Hornslee came up off the ground, he grasped at his right boot.

The headlights flashed off a long knife in his hand.

"Okay, you fucking Indian, let's see what you got. I don't know who you are or what you want, but you're mine now," Hornslee snarled.

The two combatants circled each other in the dark. Crouched and ready. The headlights cast long, hard shadows which danced against rocks and brush.

"Young man, I want nothing." Kwan said quietly, "and if I thought you would walk away and I'd never see you around Mr. Frederick again, you could live."

Kwan spoke as he circled. He felt the stiletto up his sleeve but rejected it. This would, he knew, be an unequal match as it was. Having a knife himself would only make it that much more uneven. This was not a fight he wanted.

"I don't suppose you would consider leaving this place tonight and never coming back?" Kwan posed the question already knowing the answer. Hornslee was leering. A twisted grin bared his crooked teeth. The lights flashed off the blade as it snaked back and forth.

"Goddamn, man! I heard Indians was dumb," Hornslee taunted, "but you're flat stupid! This, in case you haven't noticed, is a knife." He made a quick lunge at Kwan who side-stepped easily away.

"It's a knife and I plan on killing you with it. But before you die? You know what I think I'll do? I think I'll take your fucking scalp like I seen 'em do in the movies," Another lunge which wasn't even close.

"Yeah, then I think I'll cut your balls off." Saliva oozed from the corner of Hornslee's mouth.

"What is worth dying for, young man?" Kwan was still circling, arms bent and moving in a smooth, crisp rhythm in front of him. Hands rigid. Fingers curled. Ready to strike.

"Ain't nothing worth dying for, man," Hornslee replied, "but, since I ain't the one dying, who cares?"

Another lunge. Another sidestep.

"But why Frederick? Is he worth dying for?" Kwan asked. "You are going to die, young man. Please reconsider your actions." Kwan spoke quietly and matter of factly, as if counseling a co-ed as to whether it was wiser to take English Lit or Philosophy 101.

"Fuck you, Indian!" The lunge was the answer Kwan had expected. His left hand parried the knife thrust, redirecting it harmlessly into space.

His right hand, cocked and ready by his hip, flashed upward at Hornslee's face, heel of the palm forward. Fingers curled back out of the way.

Hornslee never saw the hand coming. He probably heard the crunching of bones as the heel of Kwan's palm caught the bottom of his nose at an upward angle. The blow was aligned precisely with the bone which formed the bridge of his nose. The force transformed that bone into a battering ram which instantly punched through the rest of the bone structure. Before Hornslee's head had a chance to snap back from the blow, the bones of his nose were buried deeply inside his brain.

By the time an obnoxious young man from New York City landed on his back in a remote part of the Arizona desert, he was dead. Residual neuron flashes caused several muscles to twitch. Then it was over. Kwan Yamuchi had solved Richard Yardley's personnel problem for him.

Kwan dropped the body by the rear bumper while he retrieved the trunk keys from the ignition. He was glad it was dark. He knew what he would find when he opened the trunk lid. The buzzing was faint, but distinct in the stillness of the night. The red glow of the taillights helped him find the lock.

As the deck lid popped open, he ducked. A black cloud

bloomed out of the trunk. The taillights reflected off the cloud, turning each fly a dull red. Hundreds. Thousands. Drawn to and created by death. Four days of heat had turned Estavez into a breeding ground.

Kwan breathed shallowly, so the stench wouldn't invade his lungs permanently. He bent to pick up Hornslee. First, he rolled him on his back. Hornslee wore a shocked expression. Eyes wide and round. Blood oozed out of the corners of his eye sockets.

Kwan squatted and cradled the body. He took another deep breath and dropped it in the trunk. Hornslee's staring eyes would greet his discoverers. Even in death some consideration must be given to proper presentation.

Residual taillight glow inside the trunk revealed only a little of what was happening to Estavez. All Kwan could see was a black blanket of flies and a wriggling, seething mass of what looked like fat rice.

He gratefully slammed the deck lid.

Turning the car around, he was acutely aware of the increased sickly sweet smell inside the car. The impact of dropping Hornslee's body on Estavez had ruptured the putrefying carcass and the stench was becoming unbearable.

Ten long minutes later, Kwan Yamuchi pulled the car to the side and got out. It was less than a mile walk back to his truck from there. He was careful to wind all the windows closed to capture the full effect of what was happening inside the Pontiac. Again, it was all part of proper presentation.

He left the keys in the ignition. No reason to be inconsiderate.

.

Thirty-seven

"**Jesus, I'm getting tired** of this dump!" Yardley spoke out of the side of his mouth, as they stepped into the dark and din of Roberta's. Ladilow grunted his agreement. The usual clientele was up to its usual rowdiness. Individual curses and shouts blended together to form a solid wall of noise floating on the sour-sweet smell of spilled beer.

They walked to the bar and Yardley surveyed the crowd.

"I almost expected to find Hornslee passed out in here," he said as they pulled chairs up to a table. He continued to look around. Each table was analyzed in turn. The old couple, the man holding a damp towel to his face, held no interest for him. The old woman looked scared and had been crying. No matter. Everyone had their problems.

"If Estavez hadn't decided to disappear, I wouldn't think anything about Hornslee not being here. He's such a flake. I should never have left him alone. But, now I'm worried. Something's going on," Yardley surveyed the crowd as he spoke.

He caught Roberta's eye behind the bar and held up two fingers. He made a pulling motion with his hand. She nodded and took two glasses from the rack, filling each in turn from the old-fashioned beer spigot.

"Estavez has been gone for four days. Hornslee hasn't checked in since noon." His eyes continued around the room. "Where do you suppose that little shit could be?"

Roberta made her way between the tables. She fended off a butt-pinch while balancing two draught beers on a tray. As she set them down, Yardley asked, "You haven't seen one of my guys in here this evening have you? Late-twenties, short hair, medium height, sort of clean-cut? He was driving a white Pontiac."

Roberta frowned and shook her head, "I haven't seen anyone like that. As for the Pontiac, I haven't been out front since noon."

Looking at the next table, she shouted, "Hey, Sam Tipton! You or Maggie seen this guy's friend? Driving a white Pontiac."

Tipton could barely hear but caught the part about the white Pontiac clearly. He yelled back, "Yeah, earlier this evening. Maybe three hours ago, there was a white Pontiac sedan parked out front. Didn't look at the driver though. Sorry."

Roberta looked down at Yardley, shrugged her shoulders, and headed back to the bar.

If she been looking at Yardley when she shouted Sam Tipton's name, she would have seen an instantaneous reaction. She had barely turned to leave when Yardley leaned across to Ladilow. He spoke in a low, incredulous voice.

"Sam Tipton? Christ! I don't believe it!" He looked past Ladilow at Cowboy Tipton. He was excitedly explaining the finer points of something or other to Maggie. His hands were moving excitedly and his eyes were dancing.

"It's hard to tell because of the beard, but his age and size are right." Yardley had to force himself not to stare.

Ladilow stretched and yawned, using it as a cover to shift his chair around to observe Maggie and Sam.

"I never saw him up close, so I can't tell for sure either," The round-faced Hispanic answered, "Besides, that was ten years ago. But how many Sam Tiptons can there be in the world?"

Yardley stood and walked over to Sam and Maggie's table.

"You saw the Pontiac, huh? Mind if I sit for a second?"

Sam nodded and Richard Yardley dropped into a chair.

Yes, Tipton had seen the car just before sundown and no, he didn't talk to the driver. Yes, it did appear to be a rental, so it was probably your friend, but we didn't see which direction it went when he left. Yardley, however, needed other information.

"So," lied Yardley, "My name's Jack Sergeant, I'm a geologist doing a casual survey of the area. What's your line of work?"

Tipton introduced Maggie and danced around the work question with his usual answer, "I sorta specialize in machine work."

He looked over at Maggie, grinned and took a drink of ice tea. Since sobering up he was acutely aware of not being able to explain what he did for a living. For reasons he couldn't explain, he found it a little embarrassing.

"I hear a little accent," said Yardley still fishing for information. "You from back East someplace?"

"Nope! I'm a Zonie by birth. Spent quite a few years in D.C. though." He surprised himself. It was the first time he'd been able to mention that period of his life without some emotion. More than just his alcoholism was on the mend.

"You don't strike me as a government guy," quipped Yardley.

"We all change. I used to wear white shirts, ties, and everything." He grinned self-consciously and Yardley stood to go.

"You know, you look familiar," Yardley said. "You wouldn't have been in the Navy in the early Seventies, would you?" Yardley was asking a pivotal question but Sam didn't know that.

"Nah! Marines. Aviation. Same time frame though." He had given a pivotal answer. He didn't know that either.

"Thanks for your time folks, Semper Fi and all that." Yardley turned back to his table as Sam touched his brow in a two-finger salute.

"Damn, it's him!" Yardley was careful his back was to the other table. He didn't want Tipton to see the expression on his face. "That's actually Sam Tipton! I don't goddamn believe it!"

He was fishing in his jacket pocket for his phone, as he spoke. Furiously punching numbers. Fingers drumming on the table. Impatient. Foot tapping. A voice answered. He cupped a hand around the phone to shut out the background noise.

"You are not going to believe who I just talked to...Sam Tipton! ...Yeah, that Sam Tipton...no, I'm absolutely positive. Ex-Marine, machinist, worked in D.C, the whole thing.

"No I don't know how, or even if, he's tied into this thing, but I thought you ought to know." Yardley motioned at Ladilow and pointed at the table. Ladilow frowned. He threw a five and two one-dollar bills down. He stood as Yardley, just finishing up his phone call, also stood. They walked directly to the door. Yardley looked around only once to memorize Tipton's face and the Native American girl with him.

Two tables over and directly in line with Yardley, Kwan Yamuchi had been practicing his lip-reading. What he visually overheard was interesting. Very interesting. Something about this man, Sam Tipton, upset Yardley greatly. Why? Did it have anything to do with Cobalt Blue? Also interesting was that Yardley hadn't yet figured out what Frank Frederick looked like even though Frederick was in plain sight. Kwan looked in Frederick's direction. His wife had finally stopped crying.

Yardley had just stepped out the door when Kwan picked his length of rope up off a vacant chair and stood. He wanted to see which way Yardley went.

Thirty-eight

Yardley and Ladilow had walked past Tipton on their way out of Roberta's. Out of curiosity, Tipton's eyes followed them. Earlier, when Ladilow's jacket shifted, Sam glimpsed the shoulder holster under his left arm. That didn't surprise him. Half the state had a gun within an arm's reach. Something about the two, however, was definitely different.

They had an aura about them. The way they moved. The way their eyes showed more than a casual interest in those around them. Something told Tipton the pistol was offensive armament, not defensive.

The two were reminders that the real world still existed down that rutted dirt road back to civilization. Men like them didn't often visit Roberta's. They made Tipton uneasy. He'd seen their type many times before. In another life. In another place.

Maggie caught him tracking the two with his eyes.

"Do you know those guys?" she asked.

"No, but I sure as hell know their type." he answered.

"What do you mean?" Maggie asked, "He said they were geologists. That's what they told Roberta too."

"Yeah, that may be what they say, but trust me. They aren't. They couldn't tell a rock from a horse biscuit. I'd also be willing to bet which side of the law they're on." Tipton took another sip of tea.

"You worried about them?" Now Maggie was curious.

"Nah, just interested. You know, strangers in town and all that small-town Western stuff," Tipton replied.

"Listen, I'm finished." Sam stretched, his hands high over his head. "I'd say let's go for a walk, but there's no place to go."

"That's okay," Maggie's eyes flashed a shade brighter, "Let's go anyway."

Sam was caught by surprise. "Hey! I was just kidding. Walking means, well, it means walking, which is too much like exercise."

"Let's go Mr. Couch Enchilada, you promised me you'd start exercising. It's part of the new, healthier you, remember?" Maggie quipped.

"Shit! I was just getting used to the old me." He ran his fingers through his long hair and shaggy beard. "Next thing you'll be asking me to shave!"

"Never," Maggie said in mock amazement, "It would ruin your chance at winning the Grizzly Adams look-alike contest."

"You drive me nuts, Sam Tipton!" She was being half serious and very frustrated. "Somewhere under that hair is a good-looking man," she hesitated and appeared to be thinking, "I hope!"

"Okay, you win. I'll walk you to your car," Tipton reached across and grabbed her wrist to read her watch. As their hands touched, Maggie's eyes flashed down at the table for a split second. Then back up to stare directly into Sam's eyes.

Sam felt her blue eyes as they stared at him. They then flicked back down to the table. She pretended to be looking at her watch along with him.

"Wow, you're right! It's late! And I've got an early day at school tomorrow." A slight stammer slowed the first several words. "The contractor is coming to set up the new publishing system." For a second she forgot Sam and drifted off in another direction.

"I'm going to have twenty gigs of memory, six hundred megs of speed and more RAM than I know what to do with!" She was excited. "We'll be able to do graphics we never thought possible. The kids'll love putting out their own newspaper."

Sam pulled his hand back. He was glad for the beard. It kept her from seeing he was flushed. He was confused by what he was feeling. He could still feel the warmth of her hand against his and was glad she started the tech talk. That he could handle.

He joined in, "Will you be able to use it to do your leather catalog and all that stuff?"

"Yes, but it'll hardly be a catalog," she laughed. "I'm not that big yet. Just a fold-over mailer listing the four or five different styles of moccasins I make. Someday I'd like to do a catalog, but not now. Between teaching all day and sewing leather all night, it's all I can do to stay awake.

"And speaking of staying awake," she yawned, "it's a long drive back to Payson. Besides, my cat has probably clawed a hole through my front door." She shouldered her purse, as she stood.

Sam eyed the purse. "One of yours?"

"Yep," Maggie smiled proudly. "Just finished it last night. Check it out!"

She tugged gently at the end of the purse. An opening

appeared with the ripping sound of reluctant Velcro.

"There's the hidey hole for a pistol that you suggested. Very feminine. Very secret. You like it?" She was obviously proud of her work.

"Perfect!" Sam replied, as he handled the soft leather bag. "Now all Longfeather and I have to do is get you to start carrying something in there for your own protection."

"Why Mr. Tipton, I do believe y'all worry 'bout lil old me." The phony southern accent sounded ludicrous coming from the beautiful Native American face that was Maggie Longfeather.

"...Well...it's just that..." Sam let the sentence trail off as Maggie turned towards the door. It was a sentence he was glad he didn't have to answer. A few weeks earlier, the booze in his system would have made him willing to spit out any words he had in his head. He glanced around. He was suddenly reminded how good a beer would taste right then. And given enough of them, he could hide behind the glow they produced.

He slapped a hand down on the table, as much to break his mood as to leverage himself out of the chair. He didn't like those kinds of thoughts. They worried him. Maggie was already disappearing through the door and he hurried to catch up.

Maggie's van was down the block and across the street. White with the Navajo symbol for life painted on the door in dark gray, it glowed yellow in Roberta's neon.

Tipton caught up with Maggie Longfeather in the middle of the street.

"You in some kind of hurry?" he asked.

"Nope, you're just naturally slow. Always have been." She was laughing softly.

Her hand came up, thumb and finger spread. The fingers captured her hair to pull it back from her forehead. Black as the night around them, it fell to her shoulders. She tossed her head slightly to make it lay straight. It was a ritual repeated periodically, part of being a woman. Unconsciously, she rubbed her lips together as she did it. Sam found the moves very cat-like. And very attractive.

They reached the van together and she turned to lean against it after opening the door.

"Be around tomorrow?" she asked.

"Why, yes," Sam sing-songed his words, "I don't think I'm

off for Paris until later in the week. Hell, yes, I'll be here. Where else would I be?" The sarcasm was heavy.

"Oh, I don't know," Maggie was trying to recover. "I thought...I don't know what I thought." She laughed nervously and took a step forward.

She was half-a-head shorter than Sam and as she moved closer he could smell her hair. Strawberry. It was always strawberry. Only inches away, the warmth of her body radiated between them, as if they were already touching. He felt ridiculously light, as if he would float off the ground at the slightest touch. His legs felt funny. His breath came in short, quiet bursts, as if he was holding it.

She wasn't looking up at him, but stood staring at his chest, her nose nearly touching it. He was afraid she would look up.

His lips barely brushed her hair. And the top of her forehead. His arms were telegraphing phantom movements to his brain. Although still hanging at his sides, they felt as if they were already wrapped around her. But his brain refused to send the signal to move. It was confused, caught in the rush of warmth. The rush of new feelings.

Intellectually he knew what the next move should be.

Emotionally, he wasn't ready for the next move.

She tilted her head and looked up at him. Sam stopped breathing for a second. The neon threw deep shadows on her face and set fire to her already-luminescent eyes. They moved slowly around his face and settled on his lips.

Her eyes stared at his mouth and didn't move. She bit her bottom lip.

She moved forward just enough that her breasts brushed Sam's chest.

The electricity started low in the back of his legs, flashing upwards to his diaphragm causing it to catch. The feeling was so strong, he nearly jumped.

He tried to think of Marilyn's face but all he could see was Maggie's.

Then the image of two Native American children roughhousing with a white boy leaped into his head. He saw the little girl's face. Then his mind cleared. His eyes saw the same face, now a woman, staring at him. It was inviting him. He heard his own breath racing in and out. His left arm moved of its own accord. It floated slowly up. It hesitated then his hand caught the door and held it.

A voice came out of his mouth and it sounded far away. And as if it belonged to someone else.

"Yeah, well...you have an early day tomorrow. Better get moving."

He stepped back, his body in a cold sweat.

Maggie blinked as if coming out of trance. She smiled. Almost relieved.

"Yeah. See you tomorrow." The words were soft and slow. She climbed into the seat and closed the door as if she was a robot. She moved with muscles that were numb.

"If you decide to go to Paris, you will let me know won't you?" She was smiling automatically. A hundred different feelings were interwoven. She was overwhelmed.

"Oh, I will...." Sam was amazed at the inane answer. His brain had decided to coast. It couldn't cope.

Maggie backed into the street, waved and was gone. Sam stood in the middle of the street watching her taillights float past Charley Yee's hogan. Then they were gone. Still he watched. He stood in the middle of the street for several long minutes. Finally, he spoke out loud as he walked slowly towards the Willys.

"Dumb, Sam! Really, dumb!"

Across the street, Yardley and Ladilow were just getting ready to leave. They found the episode very interesting.

Thirty-nine

Kwan was walking in the shadows, following Frederick towards Yee's hogan, when he saw Yardley's mini-van drive past on the way out of town. He'd followed them before and knew which road they were likely to take. He knew they couldn't miss the Pontiac. He smiled when he thought of them opening the trunk. He wondered what message their discovery would deliver.

Frederick disappeared around the hogan. As Kwan came closer, he could hear the old man's voice from the other side. He was talking to the Indian, Charley Yee.

They were too far away to hear carefully but it had something to do with Yee's gods. They were going to meet them the next day. Frederick was nervous and kept looking around. He wasn't taking the advice Kwan had given him about staying in public places. That too came up in the conversation. Frederick wanted Yee to come with him out where it was brighter and where there were more people around.

Kwan leaned against the hogan and tried to make the pieces fit. Charley Yee was an obvious piece. Frederick had been spending too much time with him. As frightened as he obviously was, he was willing to take the risk of standing in the dark trying to reason with a half-crazy Indian. It didn't make sense. Frederick was negotiating for four million dollars and here he was socializing with what appeared to be the town character.

Yee was a key piece in a puzzle. Kwan knew that. However, he didn't have a any idea what the puzzle was supposed to look like so he had no idea how the pieces fit. Roberta's neon cast a dim, yellow glow on the sign in front of Charley's hogan. Kwan read it several times. He glanced around the building at the two old men. They were still involved in their animated conversation. Satisfied, he ducked through the blanket into the hogan.

It took only seconds to completely analyze the gift shop. Low quality. Some bordering on comical. No possible way to make a living from such merchandise. Kwan had seen Roberta's affection for the ancient Native American. If it weren't for the barkeep's kindness, he suspected Yee would be much skinnier than he already was.

Pushing aside the second blanket, he glanced inside the "shrine." He recognized the signs: a self-appointed holy man who had given his life over to a deity no one obviously cared about. The signs were the same worldwide. Popular religions were cash cows and the clergy showed it. Unpopular religions bore benefits only within the minds of the true believers. Kwan correctly assumed this was a church with a congregation of one.

Being careful not to disturb anything, he surveyed everything. He was attracted to the antler arch and what was obviously the item of most ceremonial importance.

He found it curious that a box, an empty box, would be at the center of Yee's religion. Then Kwan bent down and read the engraved brass tag. He recognized the designation as being the same he'd seen when hacking into a Washington computer. It was the official designation for Cobalt Blue.

Suddenly it made sense! Now he knew why Frederick had attached himself to Charley Yee. It was the weird High Priest of the Mogollon who had Cobalt Blue. He obviously didn't know what he had and probably didn't care.

Frederick knew exactly what Yee possessed and how much it was worth. Not that it would make any difference to Charley. Yee didn't look like the type of holy man who would sell his religion for a paltry four million dollars. Frederick hadn't yet learned that the real world has no leverage on a true holy man.

Kwan stepped out into the cool evening. He was suddenly struck by its cleanliness. The herbs of the desert, sage, mesquite, juniper, entered his memories through his nostrils and he thought of the first "master" he had known as a child. He was a swordmaker. A national treasure. A national treasure who owned nothing and wanted nothing. His humble dwelling often had very much the same aroma which wafted over him at that moment. The desert perfume transported him back to his youth.

Kwan walked though the scattered brush and squatted at the edge of the mesa. Far to the south the subtle glow of Phoenix barely smudged the horizon. The big city was trying to convince the world that it was the true representation of civilization in the desert. Inhaling deeply, he knew better.

Kwan turned so he could see the two old men quietly arguing in the distance. Civilization was hunting both of them and would hurt them, if found. Kwan felt the presence of the weapons about his body. The obsessed children of every god need a protector to stand between them and reality. Kwan had performed the function before. He knew he would do it again. For a profit, if at all possible.

Kwan squatted in the dry brush and watched as Frederick, apparently achieving some form of success, herded Charley Yee into his RV. Kwan dashed across the dark desert when the RV's engine coughed into life. They were leaving! Kwan had just begun to lope towards his truck when the big vehicle U-turned onto Main Street and lumbered slowly towards Roberta's. Kwan stopped, stood in the shadows and watched.

The motor home pulled parallel against the curb directly opposite Roberta's and stopped. The engine died. The lights went out. Three figures, one of them Frederick's wife, exited and walked into Roberta's. Frederick was nervous. He looked in all directions at once. He had taken Kwan's advice and was staying in a very public place.

Kwan walked slowly down the dark sidewalk towards Roberta's.

Charley Yee sat on the curb outside Roberta's. Kwan walked up behind him and quietly sat down on the curb next to him. Neither said a word. Neither acknowledged the other's presence.

Kwan pulled the rope out of his back pocket and began to tie a series of knots.

A few minutes passed and Charley Yee picked up the loose end of the rope. Twisting it backwards, the individual strands broke free until the old Indian had unraveled over a foot of the coarse rope. Silently, his gnarled hands began to work. They wove the strands into a pattern the rope had never seen. Kwan stopped what he was doing and watched intently. Strands dove into small openings within the rapidly-building bundle, to reemerge on the other side. Then other strands disappeared to resurface. The old hands never stopped, but had a deliberate rhythm and pulled hard on each strand as it came back into view.

The mass became increasingly dense as the strands became part of the bundle. In a few minutes, the strands were used up. They were reduced to twisted tufts barely sticking out of a hard, knitted ball several inches in diameter. Using a worn pocketknife, Yee snipped the tufts off flush, leaving the ball perfectly symmetrical and smooth. He swung it in a whistling arc over his head and smacked it down hard in the dusty street. He handed it back to Kwan and uttered only a single statement.

"Good for killing rabbits. Better if done in leather."

He never once turned his eyes towards Kwan, but kept looking out at the distant horizon.

Kwan turned the ball over and over in his hands. Studying. Remembering the moves. He then took the other end of the rope and handed it to Charley Yee.

"Do it again?"

Charley took the rope and smiled. His hands began working and Kwan Yamuchi never took his eyes off of them.

The water flowed cold against Kwan Yamuchi's skin as he sat in the small, sand-bottom stream. He casually rubbed himself with a cloth as he let his mind wander. The night was blue-black, decorated with pure white specks of startlingly-clear light. Kwan imagined himself sitting at the center of the universe. His mind tried to see himself from the perspective of one particular star out on the far edge of the galaxy.

He'd never seen such a huge sky. Or felt as naked. Or as small and insignificant.

He stood and used the edge of his hand as a squeegee to whip water from his skin as though shaving a layer of skin away. The movements were quick and sharp. He heard the droplets leaving his skin and impacting the surface of the stream. He heard the water flowing silently between rocks in the tiny stream. The sound of a lizard scurrying through the sand was clear. His senses were keenly aware—tuned-in to everything around him.

As he lay on his blanket beside the stream, the cool air accentuated his nakedness. He closed his eyes and let himself float upwards towards his star as the soul of the West flowed in and joined with his own.

Forty

After making the drive so many times from Payson, Ladilow had finally figured out a shortcut that didn't require going all the way down to the main highway and then back. There was only five miles of really bad road, but the minivan hated every second of it. The dark made it even less fun.

They hadn't gone a mile when their headlights bounced off a white sedan pulled off the side of the road.

"Shit! It's the Pontiac!" Ladilow said. He pulled over behind it without being asked. He left the lights on and the engine running as he stepped out.

"Looks okay," Yardley commented as he walked up to it. Shining a flashlight inside from the passenger side, he said, "The keys are in it."

Ladilow opened the door and reached for the keys. As he did, several dozen flies flew past him, "Damn, it smells in there!" With the keys in his hand, he slammed the door. He wrinkled his nose. "Whew!"

Yardley recognized the smell. Ladilow obviously didn't. Ladilow had never been in a combat zone, much less one that was weeks or months old. If he had, he wouldn't have been so eager to check out the rest of the car.

"What the hell's in the trunk?" Ladilow said as he twisted the key in the lock.

Throwing the trunk open, the car lights behind him reflected off the inside of the lid. Ladilow clearly saw what the darkness had mercifully hidden from Kwan. A cloud of flies engulfed him. When they cleared, Ladilow saw Hornslee staring up at him from a bed of maggots. What remained of Estavez had begun to putrefy and purge fluid ran all over the floor of the trunk. Everything was coated with maggots.

Instantly, Ladilow wheeled around and vomited his guts out in the ditch.

Yardley didn't have to look to know what was in the trunk.

"Are they both in there?" He asked. Ladilow was still bending over. He nodded as he spit repeatedly to clear his mouth.

"How were they killed?" Yardley asked.

Ladilow ignored him for a full minute. His face had lost all color. He walked around behind the mini-van taking the long way to avoid looking into the trunk again.

"I don't have the slightest damn idea how they were killed. If you want to find out, look for yourself. One thing is damn certain, though, Yardley," Ladilow paused to spit several more times, "They didn't crawl in there and get rotten all by themselves."

"I'll tell you somethin' else, boss," Ladilow said, "Hertz is really going to be pissed about the car!"

Yardley ignored him for a second as he thought.

"We have to get them out of there," he said thoughtfully.

Ladilow laughed a short, explosive laugh, "In your goddamn dreams! There is no fucking way I'm even coming close to them. Dead is one thing. Falling-apart rotten is something else! You're on your own if you want them out of there!" His face was contorted. He had a continual urge to spit. The smell was so intense, he could taste it. The thought made him gag.

"If it was me, I'd just push the goddamn car off in the closest gully," Ladilow said. "You didn't rent it in your name, so who gives a shit?"

Yardley thought for another few seconds and looked over the edge of the road. It was so black it could be a thousand feet down.

He reached for his telephone. He started punching numbers, as he said to Ladilow, "Okay, drive it over here and push it over the edge."

Ladilow laughed, "Fuck, no, I'm not going to drive it over there! It stinks so goddamn bad in there and..."

Yardley cut him off, "Five hundred bucks...!"

Ladilow grinned and started for the Pontiac's door. He was swinging the keys on his index finger.

By the time the call went through, Ladilow already had the car's front wheels over the edge of the deserted dirt road. He'd also thrown up again.

As the car disappeared in the darkness and the sound of bending metal echoed in the canyon, a voice answered the phone. Yardley didn't give them time to speak. "Okay, listen to me," his voice was emphatic. "The ante just went up out here. Someone just stuffed two of my team in the trunk of our rent-a-car...

"Hell yes, they're dead! What a stupid fucking question! I'd let you talk to the maggots but they're busy eating!

"We need more people out here, right now! We have some

serious competition and I'm willing to bet it's Sam Tipton."

He listened for a few minutes before continuing.

"...Yeah, I think it's a little too coincidental, too. Since we haven't found Frederick yet, there's the real possibility Tipton already has Cobalt Blue."

The voice on the other end ventured an opinion. Yardley didn't agree.

"...I don't care what you think. Get me some more people."

There was a long pause, as he listened.

"Yeah, yeah, yeah, I'll call you in the morning."

He didn't bother to say good-bye and flipped the phone closed. His anger showed. Ladilow was leaning over the ditch spitting and Yardley snapped, "When you're finished acting like a goddamn pussy, can we please get the hell out of here?"

Forty-one

Brad Anderson was not enjoying the conversation. He paced back and forth in front of his office window, pausing only to watch a fender-bender knit Washington, D.C. traffic into an impenetrable snarl. He grimaced. Every word coming out of the speaker-phone on his desk delivered more bad news. He spoke to Richard Yardley on the other end.

"I thought your so-called hand-picked team was unbeatable. How'd Tipton manage to get two of them?"

Yardley's voice sounded tinny, an imitation of the real thing. Even so, the aggravation and worry were evident. "First of all, we don't know it was Tipton, although he seems the likely candidate," Yardley said. "Second, we don't have a clue how or where they were killed. They just showed up in our trunk as maggot-bait. Estavez looked as if he was at least four days gone."

"Was he in the trunk all that time?" Anderson asked.

"Looks that way," Yardley's disembodied voice said.

Anderson stopped pacing just long enough to look across the room at another who was listening quietly. Anderson's disgusted look was returned in kind.

"So, you're telling me you drove around for four days with your man rotting in your trunk," Anderson's sarcasm was unmistakable.

A noticeable pause preceded Yardley's answer, "Yeah. There wasn't any reason to look in the trunk, so we didn't. Our second guy, Hornslee, hadn't been there more than three, maybe four hours. He had checked in that afternoon."

"Okay, let's say I send you some more men. What's your plan?" Anderson asked.

"Right at the moment, I'm not certain we have one," Yardley replied. "Frederick hasn't surfaced and I'm wondering if Tipton hasn't somehow cut Frederick out of the deal. For all we know, Frederick could be dead and Tipton's calling the shots." Yardley was thinking out loud.

"I've got to tell you," Yardley continued, "I find it damn coincidental we're out here and suddenly Sam Tipton shows up. You don't suppose he could know who Ladilow and I are, do you? Shit that was ten years ago! When I heard his name, I couldn't believe it. I wanted to make sure it was him, so I watched him last night messing with some Indian girl. There's no doubt. It's him."

Anderson didn't reply immediately but kept pacing. Occasionally he'd look up at his visitor.

The speaker cut into Anderson's thoughts, "Anderson! You still there?"

"Yeah, I'm still here. No, I don't think Tipton could have made the connection. There were no witnesses. If there had been, the police would have been all over them," Anderson left the thought hanging in the air.

"There could be a connection with Cobalt Blue, though," Anderson said. "He was an engineer and known to be an expert with things mechanical. Maybe Frederick brought it to him to fix. One thing is positive, however, we can't ignore the possibility he's got it."

A waving hand on the other side of the room caught Anderson's attention.

"Yardley? I'm going to put you on hold for a second. Just hang on."

Anderson punched a button and looked across the room.

"This is not good!" Secretary Ward's voice was tense, "Tipton can hurt us, whether he has Cobalt Blue or not. If he has it and makes the connection, he's doubly dangerous. I've told you this before and I'll tell you again," Ward continued, "do not underestimate Sam Tipton."

Ward was leaning forward in his chair, rigid in his posture as he made his point to Anderson, "We have to focus on two fronts now, Cobalt Blue and Tipton. They may be one in the same, but we can't depend on that. We have to make damned sure we get them both."

Brad Anderson nodded. He remembered Tipton from several projects during the early Eighties. They hadn't worked together closely, but he had known him well enough and had been in a position to watch Tipton in action. He'd been impressed. Tipton was an unusual combination. He may have been an engineer, but he was a creative thinker as well. He would have made a good spook, but, as Anderson remembered, Tipton had wanted nothing to do with the intelligence community. He'd made no secret of that dislike.

Anderson also remembered how Tipton had won the regional karate matches without breaking a sweat. On top of that, he was a mini-legend for his escape from the jungle in Viet Nam after being shot down. He saved several brass hats and himself in the process. No, he wasn't about to underestimate the man.

"I want you out there tomorrow morning at the very latest." Ward said.

The tone of the conversation left no room for Anderson to make comments.

Ward continued, "We don't know if Tipton has Cobalt Blue or not, but we can't take a chance. I want to make sure you understand this. I want Cobalt Blue, but I want Tipton more. Get out there and clean this thing up."

Finished, Foster Ward leaned back in his chair and continued frowning.

Anderson punched the speaker-phone back into life.

"You still there?" He asked. A grunt answered him.

"I'm on my way out there. What's the closest airport?"

"Payson," Yardley replied. "That's where we're staying."

"I'll call you en route with an ETA. I'll also bring a couple of hired hands with me. Do we need any other assets?" Anderson asked.

"A couple of helos wouldn't hurt," Yardley replied.

Anderson answered, "I'll get them in the works. We'll talk later."

He hung up the phone and looked across the room. The chair was empty. Secretary Ward had delivered his message and Bradley Anderson clearly understood it.

Forty-two

This time she'd make her move. Ted Fowler had called asking for the same tax book as before and Stephanie Goodlin made up her mind. He was single. She was single. And she'd seen him looking at her. She was certain that look wasn't something she had imagined. She was certain he was interested.
This afternoon she'd do something about it.

Staring at the tax book open before him, Ted Fowler thought how idiotic it was. Until last month, he had never even been to Pitacho. He hadn't known it existed other than flipping past it when perusing other tax maps. Now, he owned a piece of it. Sam Tipton's adobe. And he would own more before the month was out. That would teach that big bitch to screw with him! He fantasized for a few seconds. He was walking into Roberta's, the deed in his hand, the sheriff backing him up. Let's see her smart-talk her way out of that. This was going to be fun.

His fingers found Main Street and identified the correct block and plot number. Now, if only the same sequence of numbers was on the tax sale listing indicating the county had taken it over.

Stephanie Goodlin reached over his shoulder. She dropped the sale listing and the appropriate bid forms on the table. She leaned against his back in the process. He felt her breasts against him. He smiled. She left them there for a second. Rubbing. Lingering. Making certain he knew what he was feeling.

As Ms. Goodlin looked over his shoulder, she turned her head. Warm breath in his ear. Perfume. Cheap perfume. And too much of it. She was being too obvious.

He smiled again.

Ignoring her for a moment, he scanned the county's confiscated property list. There it was! He jotted the figures down on the bid form. It didn't look like much money for a piece of land and a building. But, it would be enough. It didn't have to be much, since he would be the only bidder. As he always was.

When he stood, finished with his paperwork, Ms. Goodlin was leaning against the counter. She smiled what she thought was a seductive smile. Fowler smiled back, suppressing a laugh.

She'd seen too many bad movies.

His eyes wandered up and down her dress. Well, at least she'd tried. It was still her usual cheap cotton dress, but at least it was solid blue. Not the usual Forties floral pattern. It showed her shape, such as it was. Very average face. Square, bony shoulders, bowed forward. Slightly sunken chest. Considering her young age, much of her had drifted south. Lots of hips and butt.

Still...she was there. And she obviously had something on her mind. So, why not?

"Say, Ms. Goodlin," Fowler smiled his best crooked smile. He thought it made him look sexy. "Would you like to go out to dinner tonight?"

Ted Fowler was sweating. His heart pounded in his ears from the exertion. He looked down and the lights from the other room reflected off Goodin's moist, naked body.

Her eyes were closed. Her lips curled back in a silent snarl. She was loving it.

He pumped harder, moving his hips from side to side. Up and down. Pausing now and then to tease.

He pictured how the two of them looked to the cat watching from atop the book case. He was glad Goodlin's eyes were closed. Otherwise, she would have seen the smothered laugh on his lips.

She began that low moan again. He now knew it would build to a choked scream deep in her throat as the orgasm peaked. It would be her third.

He was still working on his first.

Then he felt it building within himself. He had to concentrate or it would retreat like it had before. He closed his eyes and conjured up an image. The fantasy was of a woman in one of the videos he had rented the night before. He'd watched one section over and over. The woman was very good with her mouth. Unfortunately, Stephanie Goodlin wasn't that good. In fact he had given up on her and climbed on top. Maybe the missionaries were right.

Finally, he felt it rising up in him. There!

It came and went quickly.

Mediocre, at best.

He rolled off onto the bed and wished he smoked. It would give him something to do. And a way to avoid speaking to her.

She stood and walked across to the bathroom. The light caught her from the side, throwing shadows across her body. It accentuated the extra rolls of flesh and bumper crop of dimples.

Then he noticed it.

Her breasts weren't the same size! He couldn't stop staring. It wasn't a big difference, but they were definitely different! He felt a small giggle starting in the back of his throat.

Stephanie Goodlin glanced over and saw him smiling. Then she turned towards the bathroom.

He broke out laughing.

"Ted? Ted, what's wrong?"

He couldn't stop himself. The laughter poured out. He finally grabbed a pillow and buried his face in it. When he did, his toupee shifted. Finally, the laughs stopped and he looked at her.

She was still standing in the light. He took one look and started laughing again.

"Ted, what are you laughing at?"

Fowler finally regained enough control to say, "Oh, nothing really. It's minor." He giggled. "But, did you ever notice your boobs are different sizes?"

He started laughing again.

Goodlin's face went pasty white. She snatched a robe off the door and fought her way into it. One sleeve was twisted and tears ran down her face while she wrestled with it.

"Get the hell out of here, Ted Fowler!" She was screaming and sobbing at the same time. "Out! Get out and go to hell!"

Fowler was still laughing. He would alternately bury his head in the pillow, stop laughing, then break down again when he raised his head and saw her.

"Fowler, you're a cruel, nasty person." Her background had never taught her the right kind of words to say how she really felt. "And you look absolutely ridiculous in that toupee."

She snatched it off and threw it. It landed on the bookcase where the cat immediately began playing with it.

"Oh, knock it off, bitch!" Fowler regained his composure and went after his toupee. The cat fought him for it momentarily. The cat was playing. Fowler wasn't. "You're no prize piece yourself. The only reason I'm here is charity. This was definitely a pity-fuck."

"And it was pretty pathetic!" He was just building up verbal momentum as he adjusted the toupee. Without a mirror, he couldn't know it sat askew on his head, like a small, sleeping animal.

"Goodlin, you stink at sex! And I'm glad you put your clothes back on because I was about to get sick!"

Stephanie Goodlin's voice rose to a scream that made her cat scurry under the bed. "Ted Fowler, you get the hell out of my house right now or...or I'm going to get my gun and shoot your penis off. And then...and then...and...!" Her imagination had run out before her anger. And frustration. She didn't know what to do with herself and couldn't remember what she'd done with her pistol anyway. "Get out!" Sobs racking her body, she stomped into the bathroom and slammed the door.

Fowler struggled into his clothes and walked towards the front door.

"You'll be sorry, bitch!" he yelled. "No one else in town would be willing to stick his dick into you! You ought to be thanking me!"

He slammed the door so hard a picture fell off the wall.

Fowler was still backing his BMW out of the driveway when Deputy Assessor Stephanie Goodlin came out of the bathroom. She picked her briefcase up and threw it on the rumpled bed. Putting her reading glasses on, she thumbed through a note pad. Finding the number she was looking for, she dialed the phone and waited.

"Hello, I'm sorry to call so late. Is Mr. Mandell in please?"

Forty-three

Yardley didn't recognize the first man out of the Citation biz-jet. Shorter than average. Early thirties. Close-cropped, stylish blond hair. Fashionable blue blazer tailored to fit big shoulders. Tan slacks. Open-throated, striped, button-down shirt. Tanned. Good looking. A jet-setter to most observers. He stepped out, scanned the area, then put his head back in the airplane cabin to say something. He took up his post by the door with arms crossed and right hand near the blazer's lapel. Yardley didn't have to guess why.

Brad Anderson stepped through the door. He looked haggard. It had been a long, rushed trip. They'd been in the air most of the night. He walked directly to Yardley without looking in either direction. Bending close, though they were alone on the ramp, he said, "Bring a car around. I don't want to spend any more time out here than necessary."

Motioning the blond over, he made the introductions, "Richard Yardley, this is Gunther, he's your back-up. Also, we'll have two helos, a Bell 206 and a Hughes 500, standing by. The Bell will be here, the other in Prescott, so they don't attract too much attention. Each will have a complete team on board."

Anderson had always been good at planning, Yardley remembered. The jet started its engines as the men finished loading the minivan.

Gunther looked over at Yardley, sizing him up. He grimaced. Yardley didn't impress him.

Yardley smiled while he analyzed the younger man. Gunther! This guy looked like a Gunther. Yardley wondered how the teutonic pretty-boy would handle the desert, drunk bikers and naked old men. Gunther didn't impress him.

Gunther sat in the middle of the second seat. Anderson rode shotgun. Anderson hadn't been in the field for twenty years and Yardley knew it. Anderson's boss must be really worried to put his lap-dog in harm's way. Yardley resented Anderson's presence. When the shit came down, the last thing he'd need was a three-piece suit from the ivory tower mucking up the works.

"What is that smell?" Gunther's voice had a distinct accent Yardley couldn't exactly place. It was German, but it wasn't. Yardley glanced up in the mirror to see curiosity in the young man's pale blue eyes.

"Smell?" Yardley returned, "Oh, that's just the pines. In an hour, you'll forget it's there."

While looking in the mirror, Yardley saw the black, Royalite golf-club shipping cases standing up behind Gunther. He glanced over at Anderson.

"Planning on doing some serious golfing?" Yardley quipped. He knew there wasn't so much as a golf ball in the heavy shipping cases.

Anderson looked over, a tired, slightly bored expression on his face, "Yeah, right! Golfing! Gunther here is a tactical weapons specialist and he brought his own special tools along." He accentuated the world "special."

"Any more on Tipton?" Anderson asked.

Yardley slowed for traffic before speaking. "No. We saw him and his lady friend night before last, but haven't been up to Pitacho today. We couldn't make the round trip and be here in time to meet you."

"We have to be careful," Brad Anderson said slowly. "Back in Washington, Tipton met me on at least two occasions and we were probably at other functions together. We have to make the assumption he'll recognize me on sight."

They were coming into town and Yardley slowed. The early morning rush hour didn't amount to much, but that far out in the country, turn signals were seldom used by most drivers.

"Stop here!" Anderson startled Yardley with the abruptness of the order. He was pointing to a small cafe nestled back in a stand of pines. Yardley wondered how Anderson had managed to even see it.

"We haven't eaten since yesterday afternoon."

Pretty-boy in the back grunted his agreement.

Yardley pulled the van into the narrow parking lot driveway. He'd have to remember to get something to take back to Ladilow.

Their booth was in the far corner opposite the door behind a line of knotty pine planters. The small cafe was decorated in woodsy art-deco. It reeked of vacation-America, circa 1952. It reminded Yardley of the rustic restaurants his folks had taken him to in the Peekskills. Knotty pine dominated. The ceiling. Tables. Booth seats. The walls were natural-finished peeled logs.

The instant they stepped inside Yardley realized they were indeed off the beaten path. The patrons were all locals. That meant the food was bound to be good and it smelled good. The See-America-First crowd had apparently moved down the street to Denny's.

Suddenly, he was hungry again.

"**Two eggs, sunny side up**, a little runny, side of whole wheat toast, hash browns, OJ and coffee, black." Anderson rattled off his order as though he'd been rehearsing it.

Yardley was studying the menu when he glanced past the waitress at the front door. The young woman standing at the bakery case next to the cash register looked familiar. He couldn't hear her order but saw the waitress loading a paper bag with bagels and assorted small pastries.

The dark-haired woman turned to point into the case and Yardley got a clear view of her face. His eyes snapped into immediate focus. It was Tipton's girl friend, the pretty Native American he had been standing with in front of Roberta's bar!

Silently Yardley reached across the table and took Anderson by the wrist, squeezing hard. He looked him straight in the eye and moved his head subtly from side to side. The waitress, plump and red-faced with a checkered apron, saw the move and stopped writing. Her stubby pencil poised expectantly above the pad.

"Miss, I'm sorry," Yardley said quickly, "but I just remembered we have to meet someone across town."

As he spoke, he let his eyes flick past her towards Maggie Longfeather. She had finished paying her bill and was packing up to leave.

As quickly as he could, without disturbing the confused waitress, Yardley stood. Maggie was at the front door.

He threw a five-dollar bill on the table and started after her. Anderson had gotten the silent message and was right behind him with Gunther. By the time they reached the front door, Maggie Longfeather was already in her van. It was rolling out of the parking place when Yardley jumped into their vehicle.

"Anderson, I'll explain in a second. Move!" Yardley careened out of the parking space and easily made the corner in time to jump into the sparse traffic while she was still in sight.

"That, gentlemen," Yardley said, "is Sam Tipton's lady friend! One of the guys at the bar told me her name is Maggie Longfeather."

He adjusted his speed to keep a pickup and an aging Cadillac between him and the minivan. It wasn't hard to keep her in sight.

"Anderson, you said we don't know how, or if, Tipton figures into this thing, but we still need an edge on him. I'd say she's it. Why don't we just tag along and see what happens."

Anderson and Gunther had nothing to add and settled back to watch.

Maggie Longfeather reached into the passenger seat. Her hand was into one of the bags, trying to guess which was a cinnamon-raisin bagel by feel. Finally she gave up and set the bag in her lap. She peeked in, as best she could, without causing an accident. The bag felt warm where it touched her.

Glancing down, she identified her choice and pulled it out. She was still munching on the first half when she turned in at the sign announcing the Rim Country Middle School. It was time to go to work. And deliver the baked goods.

She didn't see the minivan behind her slow as it passed the school entrance then continue on its way.

Anderson wrote on a pad even as they continued down the tree-lined street. He pulled a phone out of his pocket and dialed information asking for the Rim Country Middle school. Receiving the number, he first wrote it down then punched it in as Yardley turned the van around.

A matronly sounding voice answered and Anderson said, "Good morning, this is, ah, David Sinclair at Sears. Yes, I'm just calling to verify employment for a credit application...yes, the name is Maggie Longfeather."

He looked at Yardley, his eyes questioning the name. Yardley nodded.

"Is she currently employed there?...Oh she is? Well, thank you very much for your trouble."

Anderson handed the phone back to Gunther.

"Call the same number and ask them when school is out so you can come pick up your son."

Gunther punched the redial button and did as he was told.

Finished, he announced, "Two-thirty unless they are engaged

in sports, then it is three-thirty."

"Okay, we'll be back here at two-thirty," Anderson decided. "Yardley, you take Gunther and head up to Pitacho to see what Tipton's up to. I don't want to go up there until we know for sure I won't be seen by him.

"I'll come back here with Ladilow and have a little discussion with our Miss Longfeather. We'll tail her home and see if we can't put together a little negotiation that Sam Tipton won't be able to refuse. If he has Cobalt Blue...we'll deal. If he doesn't, the result will be the same. Either way, we'll finish the project we started ten years ago."

Maggie Longfeather was tired. It had been a long day. As she killed the lights in the computer lab, she smiled. She watched the street lights playing with the square outlines of her new high-tech toys and she felt like a kid at Christmas. Publishing the newsletter was going to be so much fun! And she'd already mocked-up a dummy catalog sheet. It had been a productive day.

Her mind was still on the new computers as she guided the van out the drive and towards home. Only a few blocks up and into the woods. Very convenient. One of the many reasons she liked her little cabin. That and the isolation it offered her leather studio out back.

She was too tired to notice headlights behind her slowing at the entrance to the drive.

Moccasin patterns hung across the back of the workbench. Each represented a different traditional style. Beneath them, a long line of completed and semi- completed moccasins were arranged, each waiting for a specific operation. It was a rudimentary assembly line which was powered by Maggie Longfeather's delicate hands.

As she sat down to work, fatigue was forgotten and another part of her brain kicked into high gear. The warm smell of fresh leather filled the room. The languid rhythm of traditional flute music joined the tempting aroma at the push of a button. She was in her world and drifting deeper every second.

She began to slowly run a curved needle and waxed thread through the pre-punched holes of an unfinished moccasin. In. Out. Pull hard. Back in. Back out. Pull hard. The rhythm was hypnotic. She completely lost herself in the process. She was in the zone. It was a near out-of-body experience brought on by intense concentration and fatigue. She was so deep in her work that she never heard the door behind her slowly swing open.

"**Miss Longfeather!**" Maggie jumped so hard she stabbed her finger. She swung around to find two men, one pale and middle-aged with average features. The other, a younger, round-faced Hispanic. They were standing casually by the door as if they had been invited in. But they hadn't been.

"Who are you?" Maggie blurted.

"Miss Longfeather," Anderson began, "it isn't so much who we are as what we want." He spoke carefully, his courtesy floating on veiled threat.

Maggie backed against the bench, her hands behind her. Although the words were innocuous. The tone was threatening. She thought about the Walther automatic laying on the shelf beside her right shoulder.

"I said, who are you and what do you..."

Anderson held up his hand as if to shush her. It was done in a scolding manner.

"Please, Miss Longfeather! Let me ask a few questions and then we will determine how our evening together progresses." Anderson's tone was now condescending.

"Mr. Ladilow, would you be so kind as to escort Ms. Longfeather to our vehicle?"

Ladilow took one step forward and Maggie Longfeather's right hand became a blur. It flashed forward, catching Ladilow in his surprised face. His head snapped back for an instant. He grunted in pain.

His left hand instinctively grabbed his cheek where it hurt. It found a moccasin dangling from heavy, waxed thread which was anchored to his cheek by a curved needle. The needle pierced completely and out of his cheek.

Maggie continued around, her hand sweeping the small automatic off the shelf. Half crouching, she turned to level it at the intruders. She never made it. As she crumpled to the floor, the automatic fell from her hand onto the carpet.

Anderson kicked the Walther away from Maggie Longfeather's limp hand and dropped the short, lead-filled leather baton back in his pocket.

She lay on her back, her shirttail half out. The top blouse button popped.

Standing in front of a mirror, Ladilow growled. He gritted his teeth and pulled. The needle hung up for just a second before sliding back out. Throwing the moccasin and attached thread against the wall, he turned towards the inert form of Maggie Longfeather.

"Fucking bitch!" He stepped quickly, his booted foot recoiling to kick hard.

"Ladilow," Anderson's voice was just short of yelling. It caught Ladilow mid-swing.

"Hold your temper. You'll get your chance to play your little games. But not now."

"Be patient," Anderson said. "First Tipton. Then her."

The note simply said, "We have Ms. Longfeather and she will be as dead as your wife and daughter, unless you give us Cobalt Blue. We'll call."

The note was clipped to the outside flap of Maggie Longfeather's purse as it dangled from the old mill's door hasp. A satellite phone protruded from the side pouch.

Dragged out a deep sleep by someone banging on the door and not yet half awake Tipton tried to focus on the note. He blinked in the early morning sun. When he re-opened his eyes, he expected to be in bed. The nightmare would be over. But it wasn't. The note was still there.

He shivered. The blanket wrapped around his bare shoulders wasn't enough for the early-morning chill. He stared at the note. The words made no sense. Taken as a whole, they were just too incredible. Even in sections, the words said too much about too many things, but still made absolutely no sense.

"...Ms. Longfeather will be dead..."

That meant one thing.

"...as your wife and daughter..."

That meant something quite different.

His mind felt something he hadn't felt for ten years. The last time had been while coming back from a funeral. Their funeral. Something was slipping away, he could feel it. His life was slipping away.

It couldn't be happening again!

"...give us Cobalt Blue..."

What the hell did that mean? Cobalt Blue?

The sat-phone rang and he jumped so hard he nearly dropped the blanket. As he answered it, he heard the beat of a helicopter in the background.

"Who the hell is this?" Sam shouted before anyone had a chance to speak.

"Oh, please Mr. Tipton. You really don't expect an answer to that, do you?"

The voice was smooth and far away, digitized and carried through space. Electronically sterilized.

"What the hell do you want and where's Maggie?" Sam didn't realize he was shouting.

"Mr. Tipton, you are getting entirely too agitated. This situation is really quite easily solved. You give us Cobalt Blue and we'll give you Miss Longfeather. There! That's simple, isn't it? If you delay or try to find us, we will deliver her to you one piece at a time. And you, Mr. Tipton, will die, as well. This time we won't miss."

Sam leaned back against the door, dropping the hand holding the phone down to his thigh. "...This time we won't miss?" What the hell?

He took a deep breath. Then two. Remain calm. Think. Try and figure out what they want. He felt his nerves lashing at his common sense. Calm. He had to remain calm. Cobalt Blue? He had no idea what they were talking about. But play along. Buy time. Be strong.

"And what makes you think I'm going to give you Cobalt Blue?" His voice was calm. His mind was not.

"Well, Mr. Tipton, we don't think you want to see Ms. Longfeather hurt. Or have her otherwise damaged. You know, she really is quite beautiful. One of our people is especially attracted to her. You wouldn't want him to consummate their friendship, now, would you?" Short laugh. Caustic.

Deep breath, Sam. Breathe deeply and think before speaking. Don't let panic dictate words. Or actions. He heard his own voice inside his head. It was giving him advice as though he was someone else.

"Look asshole! How badly do you want your precious Cobalt Blue?" It was "B" movie dialogue and he knew it. "Bad enough to come for it yourself?"

"Oh, please, Sam. You don't mind if I call you Sam, do you? You are hardly in a position to bargain with us. We're not very nice people. We'll give you a few hours to think about this and call you back. Have a nice day, Sam. I'm certain Miss

Longfeather will."

The phone went dead. He stared at it in his hand for several long minutes before forcing himself to go inside.

He stared out the open window. The rising sun chased the mesa's shadow across the desert miles below but Sam Tipton didn't see it. His thoughts weren't connected to his eyes. They weren't connected to anything. They whirled aimlessly around, trying to sort out intertwined images.

Marilyn. Maggie. Melissa. He idly wondered if there was significance in the alliteration.

A single name kept cutting in, obliterating all other images. Cobalt Blue! Something named Cobalt Blue had put Maggie in the hands of someone who would hurt her.

His head fell back, his neck limp. He stared straight up. He saw Ivan Petrovitch sitting above him.

"Ivan. Hey, Ivan! You listening? What the hell is going on?" His voice was tired. It was tinged with a hint of hopelessness. He looked down at the bottle in his hand. Sun coming through the window turned the Scotch into a brilliant, liquid bronze. It appeared semi-solid and languid. And so smooth.

The top was still in place.

He held the bottle out at arm's length. He turned it, letting the light play with it, watching the refraction of the sun's rays as their edges changed colors while passing through. His thoughts continued to tumble over one another. The confusion refused to lift. He felt it sucking him in, taunting him with its chaos, challenging him to reach in and sort it out, to apply logic to the situation and make it work.

Old feelings invaded his thoughts. He resisted, but he was tired. Tired of fighting. Tired of having things go wrong. Tired of trying to cope. Just plain tired.

He knew the way out. Temporarily, at least.

His fingers tightened around the bottle cap and he gazed out at the Mogollon.

"Well, Ms. Longfeather, I do hope you are feeling better after your little nap."

Maggie didn't feel like talking. She turned her head on the pillow and immediately wished she hadn't. It hurt. A lot! Her brain was on fire. She reached up to touch her head. One hand wouldn't move and she looked up to find it handcuffed to a cheap veneered headboard. Her eyes and head moved as if in slow motion. God they hurt!.

Her free hand explored the lump hidden in her hair. How could anything be that big and not burst through the skin? Touching it immediately shifted the hot spot to that point. She felt no blood. Just a gigantic lump. It was well above the hairline. Thank God, because she was going to have one hell of a bruise. She then realized that was a damn silly thought for someone in her situation.

She shifted her eyes towards the speaker standing next to the bed. It was the same man who had been at her studio. Average height. Stocky. Skin the color of someone who spent too much time indoors. Early fifties. Short, respectable-businessman haircut, graying at the temples. Pale, featureless eyes spaced tightly to a nose too thin for the face. His tan cardigan sweater was one size too big and buttoned at the bottom where it met khaki slacks.

No fashion sense, she thought. Another dumb thought.

Her host stood patiently waiting for her answer. Screw him. Let him wait.

Suddenly, she wondered where she was and looked around. It was a small bedroom in what she recognized as a vacation cabin. The usual walls of pecky cedar had been varnished so many times that the natural yellow was dulled to the color of old motor oil. Cheap lace covered small, multi-paned windows. The varnished, pine-board door was open and she could see the central living room. There were probably at least two or three more identical bedrooms arranged around the living room.

Although she'd never actually been in that particular cabin, she knew it well. Hundreds of nouveau-rustic rentals like it nestled in the trees up and down the Mogollon. She could be anywhere within seventy-five miles of Payson.

Her host was definitely low budget. Or low profile. Or both.

Seeing that she was awake and not hurt seriously, Anderson turned and walked to the door. Turning as he paused to close the door behind him, he said, "You will make yourself comfortable won't you?"

Maggie silently mouthed her mother's least favorite four-letter word at him.

The sound of Anderson's minivan had barely faded down

the drive when Maggie again heard the key in the lock. She quickly sat up on the bed as the door swung open. Ladilow let it swing free and he leaned against the jamb. He was trying to look pleasant, but he was failing. Two Band-Aids plugged needle holes in his cheek. Pants zipper at half mast. Cheap plaid shirt hung loosely on his rounded body. He had been wearing the shirt entirely too long. Without taking a breath, Maggie knew he smelled like he looked. Not good.

She also knew the expression on his face. Every woman did. Also, not good.

"Hey, woman," he grinned. "It's just you and me. What 'cho think?"

Maggie said nothing. He didn't look or act drunk. His eyes weren't doing a drug dance. He appeared normal. Which also was not good.

Dealing with a drunk was one thing. Dealing with a stone-sober man intent on what many men are intent on was something entirely different.

"You know, my boss is not such a nice guy." Ladilow moved inside to lean on the wall. "In fact, I think he probably plans on killing you once we have this Cobalt Blue thing."

He hesitated to see the effect his words had on the object of his affection.

Maggie Longfeather made certain he saw none. She did her best to make her face appear neutral. But she didn't like the words she had just heard. She tugged on the handcuff chain holding her right hand to the headboard.

"Don't bother, lady," Ladilow stepped to the edge of the bed. "You're stuck."

He grabbed her hand and pulled against the handcuff. It hurt her wrist. She showed no emotion.

He stood close in front of her. She was right, he smelled.

"You know, I may be able to help you, though," Ladilow towered over her. A hand reached out to play with her hair. The smell grew worse.

"I don't even know what this Cobalt thing is your boyfriend and Frederick have got. All I care about is the money. But, I can help you. All you got to do is help me." His hand ran his pants zipper the rest of the way down.

The smell became overwhelming.

"Cho know what I mean?" Ladilow leered.

Maggie faked a smile. Ladilow returned it, a light in his eyes.

"Yes, I think I know what you mean," Maggie licked her lips. And held her breath.

Ladilow relaxed and positioned himself in front of her. She made a move with her head, as if closing the distance between them. Ladilow didn't notice her left hand moving closer. In an instant, the same strong fingers that spent hours and hours cutting and stitching leather found their mark. Maggie brought her hand up under Ladilow's crotch and grabbed him. Hard!

Ladilow's first instinct was the wrong one. His muscles told him to jump back and free. With Maggie holding on to his crotch, all he succeeded in doing was falling backward. The pain was so intense, his legs didn't want to hold him up. And she wouldn't let go. No mercy.

His guttural screams made the window lace move. On the way down, he swung clumsily. One fist hit Maggie a glancing blow on the side of her head. Then he was all done swinging and concentrated on moaning. Both hands wrapped themselves around Maggie's wrist, but there was no strength in them.

"Please, lady, please," He moaned.

"Ladilow!" A new voice from the door.

Maggie jerked her head around. She didn't release her grip.

Yardley stepped in and stood beside her, looking down at Ladilow squirming on his back. Maggie had to half-kneel to maintain her hold, with the other arm stretched out to the headboard with the cuff biting into her wrist.

Maggie could see a grin working at the corners of Yardley's mouth. He found the situation amusing but was trying not to show it.

"Miss, you can let go now, I think I can guarantee Ladilow won't bother you again," Yardley said.

She wouldn't release her grip.

"Ladilow! Tell the lady you'll leave her alone!" Yardley raised his voice like a father scolding a child.

No answer. Ladilow was concentrating on other problems.

"Ladilow!! Tell her!"

"Okay, okay! I tell her. I'll leave you alone...ow..ow...ow! I promise!" The words came between teeth gritted so tightly Maggie expected to see porcelain flaking off.

She let go. Ladilow curled into an embryonic position and hugged himself tightly.

"Miss," Yardley started, "I'm sorry to see you got caught up in the middle of this. But...." He made a gesture denoting helplessness. She knew the feeling.

Ladilow used a chair and table to get to his feet. He made it into a semi-crouch. His legs didn't want to straighten out.

"Since you're stuck with us, the least I can do is keep the hired hands under control. I promise no more problems." Yardley smiled slightly as he backed towards the door pushing the hunched-over Ladilow behind him.

As she heard the key in the lock, Maggie Longfeather grabbed her belt buckle with her free hand and pulled. She didn't like the situation and was about to change it.

"Damn, Tipton! What the hell was that?" Longfeather blurted.

Fragments of glass showered out of the air and the short crack of the nine-millimeter still echoed off the cliffs surrounding the valley. The broken neck of a bottle, just completing a high arc, landed in the grass.

Joseph Longfeather's startled eyes popped around the edge of the heavy door and peeked into the old mill. His friend was still standing at an adjacent window, his outstretched arm just lowering a worn Browning automatic to his side.

"What the hell was that?" Longfeather again asked.

"That, my good friend," Tipton was being very dramatic, "was me, fixing myself a drink. A full bottle of Scotch with a nine-millimeter chaser."

"Looks like it would leave a helluva hangover!" Longfeather didn't know whether to smile or frown. His friend had obviously just been through something.

He smiled. Proud of himself. It had been close.

"J, take a look at this," he laid the note in front of his friend. "Tell me what you make of it."

Longfeather scanned the note in seconds.

"Is this some kind of sick joke? Why in the hell would anyone kidnap Maggie? And what's Cobalt Blue?" He spoke without raising his head. His eyes still glued to the note. They skipped back to the beginning several times. Reading. Re-reading. "This makes absolutely no sense!"

Sam quickly threaded his arm into a worn leather flying jacket and started for the door. The Browning Hi-Power was stuffed into the back of his belt.

"Where are you going?" Longfeather asked.

"Damn if I know. Roberta's? Payson? I don't know, but I can't hang around here!"

Halfway through the door he had a thought and stepped back inside to grab the sat-phone off the table. "We'll need this."

Then he had another thought and pushed the re-dial button on the phone. He listened as it was answered. The voice on the other end said words that registered surprise on his face. Then understanding.

"What number is this?" he said while gesturing wildly for a pencil. Longfeather obliged.

Tipton caught the ball-point while he apologized to the gracious-sounding lady on the other end for dialing a wrong number. It wasn't wrong. And he wasn't the one who had dialed it last. He scribbled the number twice on a pad laying on the table. He tore the bottom number off, stuffed it into his shirt pocket and was gone out the door.

Longfeather glanced at the pad on his way past. He didn't recognize the number. It had an out-of-state area code, 202.

Thank God for overly-protective brothers, Maggie Longfeather said to herself as she whittled at the bed post.

The belt buckle had been an insistent Christmas gift: Joseph Longfeather had given it to her for Christmas then insisted she wear it. She always thought having a belt buckle that pulled apart to reveal a small, but substantial knife blade was being paranoid. No longer.

The stout blade protruded between her fingers as she grasp the buckle portion in her palm. Slowly the blade worked into the joint where the two top pieces of the headboard met. It was cheap woodwork. But solidly glued.

Her mind went into the zone where it lived while lacing moccasins. Push! Work the blade. Push! Again and again! Her hands worked automatically.

Then, movement! Something in the joint gave as the blade wedged it a millimeter apart. Push! Twist!

Freedom! The top piece sprang free with a quiet crunch and Maggie Longfeather slid the handcuff off the headboard.

Now what?

She dropped to her knees to look at the antique door lock. She smiled. Either her captors hadn't looked at the door closely or they thought of her as "only a woman." It took less than ninety seconds with the knife blade to remove both lock screws and pull the lock plate loose. The door creaked open with it. She slowly pulled it open and peered through the opening. Nothing!

The big, open living room was classic rental lodge, circa 1948. The varnished, two-story, log walls were interrupted only by a huge, smoke-streaked stone fireplace and a balcony which ran all the way around the room. Bedrooms opened on all four sides of the second story. It was a nice lodge, as such things went, but she wasn't in the mood for sight-seeing. She walked quickly towards the front door.

She was halfway across the thick, handmade rag rug when heavy footsteps thundered up the outside porch steps. A voice swore loudly about always forgetting something.

Suddenly the door was yanked open. Ladilow was two steps inside before Maggie registered on his distracted mind. They were less than ten feet apart. His eyes disappeared in a squint as he frowned.

"You goddamn bitch!" Ladilow lunged at Maggie, who easily side-stepped him. As he thundered past, she spun around, her elbow out.

The point of her elbow caught the Hispanic hard in the kidney exactly the way her brother had showed her. Ladilow fought to keep his balance. His face was twisted in pain. His back arched.

"Yardley!" He screamed. "Yardley, she's loose!" There was nothing wrong with his vocal chords.

Maggie's blue eyes swept the room. A car door slammed outside. She heard another voice yelling. It was also swearing as it drew closer.

No other doors. Two men with guns. She knew better than to stand and fight and raced to the balcony stairs. She was halfway up when Yardley burst in the room.

"Stop! Goddammit, stop or we'll shoot!"

Maggie didn't bother to look back as she continued to run. She assumed he had a gun in his hand.

Yardley thumbed the Beretta's safety off, bracing it in a two-hand hold. Maggie's flowing black hair was in his sights, even as she made it to the balcony.

Then Yardley let the hammer down. Where was she going to go? He already knew what she was about to find out. This was a very secure cabin, owned and rented out by very insecure people. It was a fort. Or a prison. The definition depended on whether you were on the inside or the outside. Maggie Longfeather was on the inside. It was a prison. Yardley didn't need to shoot her.

The first bedroom door on the balcony was ajar and Maggie saw the light of a window beyond. The door slammed against the wall as she rushed to the window and ripped the curtains apart. Damn! Bars!

The feet on the stairs were heavy, but in no hurry. Her captor obviously knew about the bars. No reason to rush.

She was trapped! Eyes frantically searching. Nothing. A weapon! Something she could swing. A lamp. No! A chair.

Her eyes ripped around the room in search of something to help and swept across the ceiling. There! A framed square outline broke the even expanse of the cedar paneled ceiling. An access panel to what? An attic? A crawl space?

She jumped up on the bed. Footsteps echoed on the balcony.

She couldn't quite reach the edge of the opening. It was too far away from the bed. Footsteps closer.

She bounced on the bed one time, leaping out with both hands extended. Her fingers knocked the panel cover aside and locked on to the edge of the framing. This, she remembered is what drove Tipton and her brother nuts when they were kids. She swung only once before easily pulling herself up into the small opening. Neither Tipton nor her brother could do that on the best day they ever had.

The bedroom door slammed open below and Yardley walked slowly through, automatic in hand. He wasn't prepared for an empty room.

Where was she?

His eyes caught the black square in the ceiling.

"Okay, Miss Longfeather, you can come down now! You have no place to go!" He circled the opening, staring as far as he could into the blackness above.

Maggie stayed at the panel opening just long enough to see Yardley staring up at her. She then crawled carefully away from the opening, inching along on the narrow, dust-covered board walkway bridging the rafters. A few feet from the opening, the light died. The blackness of the low ceiling attic settled around her. Dark rafters above and below encircled her like ribs in Jonah's whale.

    The guy with the gun was right. There was no place to go.

Forty-four

Joseph Longfeather leaned over and picked up the moccasin. The curved needle dangling from it caught under a table leg and he bent to work it loose.

"Hey! Look at this!" His words rumbled through the tiny workshop and out the open door.

Sam Tipton grunted as he brushed pine needles from his knee. Longfeather was holding a single moccasin attached to a large sewing needle by a length of thread.

"There's blood on this needle!" He held it up in the light so Sam could examine it. While Tipton took the needle, Longfeather bent and fingertipped several dark spots on the carpet. Still on his haunches, he looked up at his friend.

"Could be blood!" He indicated the carpet spots.

Tipton didn't bother to check it himself. What ever Longfeather said would be true. It always was.

His eyes continued to scan the place. The door had been open when they arrived. The only sign of a struggle had been a chair laying on its side. Nothing dramatic other than a bloody needle and a wayward moccasin. Then, he kicked something under the edge of the workbench.

Bending over, he retrieved the little Walther PP automatic from its accidental hiding place.

"Where'd she normally keep this?" He asked.

"Bottom shelf on your left." Tipton glanced over at the shelf as he dialed the phone. No way Maggie would have let the pistol lay under the bench on purpose. Something didn't compute. The phone answered.

"Give me Sheriff Rickert." His words were uncharacteristically short. He had neither the time nor the temperament for pleasantries.

Forty-five

Maggie wanted to sneeze and cough at the same time. Everything in the attic was fuzzy with fifty years of dust. She willed herself to do neither. The voice below the ceiling was still yelling at her and she could hear the telltale sounds of furniture being moved. They were coming up after her.

Her eyes had grown accustomed to the near-dark and she looked around. She was kneeling on a loose board walkway barely two feet wide. Either side was a dark swamp of wooly looking insulation broken regularly by stout-looking rafters. Overhead, the roof structure climbed to a teepee climax.

She could make out slivers of light coming from the far end of the attic. She felt her way through clumps of crumbling cardboard boxes. Christmas ornaments crunched under foot. Dusty clothes from another time grabbed at her ankles.

As she drew closer to the end of the building she could see the source of the light. It was a fragile looking louvered vent being blocked by a large, dust covered pile of what were now antique steamer trunks. At the time they were put in that pile, they hadn't been antiques.

"Miss Longfeather! You might as well come down. You know there's no place to go. No place at all." The voice sounded distracted, its owner's mind on something else. More sounds of furniture moving.

In the dark, the pile of trunks looked foreboding and huge. She put her back against the rough-hewn studding of the building's end wall and pushed at the pile. The trunks teetered, then cascaded off the other side of the walkway. A shaft of light broke the darkness where a trunk fell noisily between the rafters and through the ceiling into a bedroom below.

The voice by the trap door said, "What the hell was that? Go check it out!"

Heavy feet ran down the balcony in her direction.

"She threw something through the ceiling!" The voice boomed up through the hole left by the trunk.

Maggie jumped, it sounded so close. She backed up and her

foot flashed out at the louvered opening. Broken wooden slats obligingly showered into the sunlight outside the building.

By the time Yardley's head poked through the trap door, his quarry was no where to be seen.

Maggie Longfeather was already down to the main crotch of the big old sycamore at the end of the building and jumping lightly to the ground when Yardley shouldered his way up on to the walkway. He could clearly see light at the end of the building.

"Goddammit!" He yelled down to Ladilow. "I think she's gotten out. Get out front. Now, dammit!"

The hushed crunching of fallen leaves was the only sound as Maggie sprinted around the side of the building towards the main road. The white van was still sitting where Yardley had left it. The driver's door was open and the engine was running. Yardley had been in a hurry.

There was only one other vehicle in sight, a newly-rented jeep. She paused and kneeled as she passed it. Her blade pierced the side wall of the right front tire and an angry hiss erupted.

She and the white van were already out of sight by the time Yardley got to the front door. Only gravel, still raining through the underbrush next to the lodge, said she'd ever been there. Maggie Longfeather had also been in a hurry.

As she hit the main road, it was decision time! Her mind was whirling. She remembered snatches of conversation she'd overheard between Anderson and Yardley and tried to fit them into her immediate future. Should she go to the police? Or should she go find Sam and Longfeather and warn them? Decision made, the tires screeched as she careened out onto the main road.

Houses and roadside businesses began to dot the roadside. Turning hard right, she followed the sign to the airport.

The small airport was nearly deserted. As she walked briskly, just short of an all-out run, to the end of the hangars, she noticed a shiny Bell 206 helicopter tied down in the corner of the ramp. Several men sat on the bumper of a Humvee next to it watching her.

The men yelled at her but all she heard were bits and pieces including the seemingly obligatory salutation, "...hey, baby..."

As far as they knew, she had ignored them. She started

around the end of the hangars and Barney Glass's bedraggled old Super Cub came into view. He wouldn't mind if she borrowed it.

The men at the helicopter didn't even look up as she taxied out to the runway. She was already out of sight before they received a phone call to be on the look-out for a good-looking Indian girl.

The morning air was so clear, Maggie had Tipton's valley above Pitacho in sight while Yardley's men at the helicopter were still on the phone catching hell from their boss.

The helicopter blades began slowly winding up long before the phone conversation was over.

forty-six

"**Anderson!...yeah, we** can't be more than a few minutes behind her." Yardley's free hand struggled with the helicopter's seat belt as he spoke. The other held the sat-phone.

"These bozos you hired with the chopper think she may have been in some sort of Piper Cub. If that's the case, we're almost twice as fast as she is. Yeah...we'll head straight for Pitacho and that biker bar. She'll probably wind up there."

The screaming turbine lifted the machine off the short stretch of road near the lodge and Yardley had to yell to be heard. "Get this goddamn thing moving!"

Yardley dusted himself off as he walked through Roberta's door. Ladilow followed him in. The chopper sat behind town, hear the edge of the mesa, its rotors still winding down.

When his pupils finally opened up to let enough light in, he could see the bar was mostly empty. What would normally be considered "the lunch crowd" had yet to arrive.

An old couple was in the corner arguing. The old man was a regular. Yardley had seen him every time he'd been in the bar. The same Indian he'd noticed before tying knots on the sidewalk was nursing a beer not far from them. The only other patron was the Mogollon Nudist, Snuffy, who was welded to his usual stool at the end of the bar. Maggie was no where to be seen. As Yardley turned to leave, the old man began yelling.

"Goddammit, May! We can't leave, not yet!" The old man was screaming at the top of his lungs. Normally his tantrum would have been lost in the roar of Roberta's crowd. This time, however, it echoed off the stone walls. It was the kind of scene which was hard to ignore and was guaranteed to make bystanders uncomfortable.

Roberta stood on a short stepladder rearranging bottles on an upper tier of the back-bar. She stopped what she was doing and listened without turning her head. She didn't like marital discord. It hit too close to home. She turned and leaned against the shelves.

"Hey, Frederick! Frank Frederick!" Her shout caught the old man's attention. "Either pipe down or take your problems outside! Some folks are trying to have a peaceful drink in here!"

The only open beers in sight were Kwan Yamuchi's and Snuffy's. Neither looked as if they gave a damn what the Fredericks said in public.

Yardley stopped mid-stride just inside the door. His hand shot out to grab Ladilow's elbow and he leaned close.

"That's Frank Frederick! Damn! He's been right under our noses all along!" He stared hard at the old man, made the mental connection, and spun around to step back through the door. He fumbled for the telephone in his inside pocket even as he turned.

"You aren't going to believe this," He said quietly when Anderson answered. He could hear road noise of the Humvee in the background. "We may not need Tipton. Frank Frederick is here in the bar!" As he talked, he moved further away from the door.

"Okay, we'll meet you at the Interstate turnoff with the chopper! We're on our way now!"

He diverted his attention to Ladilow and said, "I can't believe it! That old geezer has been here every single time we've set foot in this place and none of us made the connection! Damn!

"Let's go!" Yardley said, "It doesn't look as if he'll leave here until they run out of beer. We'll work out what to do with Anderson on the way back."

They walked quickly down the street in the direction of the helicopter. If they had looked over their shoulders, they would have seen a single Native American, rope in hand, leaning in Roberta's doorway. He was watching them and heard the helicopter's turbine winding up.

forty-seven

Frank Frederick stepped out of Roberta's and looked up to watch a helicopter disappear in the distance. It was low.

"May, listen, I can't tell you what this is all about," he was explaining to his wife, as they walked, "But, believe me it's worth a lot of money to us. First, I have to talk to Charley Yee. Then we're going to pack up and get the hell out of here!"

May Frederick smiled at the prospect of leaving Pitacho behind. She let the smile show. It felt good to smile. She hadn't done that much lately.

They continued walking in silence. They hadn't done that much lately either.

Charley Yee was bent over his workbench. A piece of sharpened mesquite in his hand was scribing a triangle in the damp clay of a teapot-shaped piece of pottery. He looked up as Frederick walked in. A faint smile crossed the old Apache's face before returning to work.

Frank Frederick began to talk.

"Charley, listen to me." His voice was weak with a tight quiver around the edges. "We have to go meet your gods. You may not understand this, but they have something which is very dangerous."

He paused, as he tried to think of the right things to say. He found doing this while sober to be very difficult.

"This thing could hurt your gods. In fact, it could hurt them and everyone else, if it's not properly cared for."

Charley's hand hesitated for an instant.

"Charley, we're friends. You know that, don't you?" Frederick found it difficult to say those words because it dawned on him that at some level, he meant them.

"I want to help you and I want to help your gods. I want to make sure they, and you, live long happy lives." Frederick said those words. He meant those words. At the same time however, a little voice in his head was counting up how many trucks it would take to carry four million dollars in small bills.

Charley Yee continued to work, ignoring Frank Frederick.

Frederick continued to talk, his voice smooth and low. He was trying hard not to be pushy. He tried to put himself in Charley's position and that was becoming increasingly easier to do.

The old Indian seemed unmoved and Frederick was tired. He couldn't bridge the gap and reach Charley Yee. He sat down on a low bench and leaned heavily against the wall. Silence filled the dark interior of the hogan. A small, lemon-colored gecko scurried up the wall next to him.

"Come! We go!" Charley's voice was soft, yet firm. His words were both a statement and a command. Even as he spoke, he pushed back from the workbench. He was standing in the door before Frank Frederick had a chance to absorb his words.

"Where are we going?" Frederick asked.

"To see my gods. But, first, do you have something to drink?"

Seconds later, the old RV coughed into life and rumbled down Main Street.

Kwan Yamuchi watched from a distance. The instant the RV came to life, he started for his truck. Too much was happening, too many paths crossing, for him to let both Frederick and Yee out of his sight at the same time.

forty-eight

"Hey, Tipton!" **Maggie's** voice echoed off the walls of the old mill. She broke into a run and ventured a few yards into the cavern at the back. No lights.

"Yo, hey guys!" The only answer was a great horned owl as it moved deeper into the mine where it wouldn't be disturbed.

She ran back outside, squinting in the sunlight. A few seconds later the Super Cub's tires were skimming the grass and she shot out over the edge of the mesa. Pitacho was less than three minutes away and it was all down hill.

Where were those guys?

"**Maggie!**" **Roberta's** voice boomed above the noon day crowd of desert rats and cowhands. She raced around the bar, meeting Maggie before she was across the floor. A bear-sized hug picked her friend's moccasins off the floor.

"Where in the hell have you been?" the tall barmaid asked. "Tipton blasted in here early this morning, said you'd been kidnapped and split for Payson to find you! He looked batshit!"

"Kidnapped?" Maggie echoed. "How could he know I was kidnapped already?"

"He got a ransom note," Roberta explained. "I don't know what was in it. He said it made absolutely no sense to him, but he was going to find you."

Roberta continued, "So, what the hell is going on?" She had both hands on Maggie's shoulders. They stood in the middle of the floor, ignoring the rumble of Roberta's regulars around them.

"I don't have the slightest idea what this is about," Maggie said. "Some guys showed up at my studio and...Here feel this!" She took one of Roberta's hands and put it to her head.

"Damn, kid! Does that hurt?" Roberta yanked her hand back.

"Yeah, it hurts! A lot! And I have a helluva headache, but it's no big deal. The next thing I know after getting this is I'm handcuffed to a bed in some log cabin out towards Heber."

Roberta started to make a smart remark about Maggie having all the romantic luck, but thought the better of it.

"The guys who did this are all carrying guns and they all

have a definite attitude problem. I've seen at least two of them in here before" She went on to describe them and Roberta pointed out that the descriptions fit about half the males in Arizona.

"Okay, look! Something super-serious is coming down and Sam and I are somehow in the middle of it. Can I borrow your thirty-thirty, just in case?"

Roberta nodded and they retired to the back room.

Maggie rhythmically thumbed cartridges into the loading gate in the side of Roberta's old Winchester carbine.

"I don't think we have a war in the works, but this just seems to make sense." She indicated the carbine.

"Well, that being the case..." Roberta turned and pulled two loaded .45 magazines from a drawer and slid them into a back pocket. "Like you said, it seems to make sense."

"So, what now?" Roberta asked as they walked back through the bar.

Maggie tried to carry the Winchester so it wouldn't be obtrusive, but no one cared. It was just another gun.

She said, "I'm going to take the Cub back to Payson and see if they're at my place or maybe at the school. If they show up here, tell them I'll be back in about an hour and a half."

They had been paying more attention to their conversation then they were to where they were going. They didn't see the two men about to enter the bar until they nearly ran into them.

"Maggie!" Sam's words were superimposed over Maggie saying his name.

She jumped into his arms. Then reached out and wrapped an arm around Longfeather's neck. The tension of the last twenty-four hours finally found an outlet and she cried.

Hugging the two tightly one last time, she stepped back, wiping her eyes on the sleeve of her denim shirt. She was embarrassed at the outburst and smiled sheepishly. "Damn! I didn't mean to do that. Sorry!"

Sam kissed her on the forehead and wiped the tears from under each eye with a gentle thumb. Then, an arm went around her shoulders. He took the Winchester from her and led her to a vacant table. They sat down, Maggie looked across the table at Sam, and started crying again.

Forty-nine

"**All I know is I heard them** talking about you and Frederick." As she spoke to Sam Tipton, Maggie held a plastic bag filled with ice to her head. Periodically, when it got too cold, she changed hands.

"I clearly heard them saying something to the effect that either you or Frederick had Cobalt Blue, and they were going to make you give it to them. That's why they grabbed me."

"I don't have the slightest damn idea what they're talking about. Cobalt Blue?" Cowboy Tipton held his hands, palms up, in the air. The universal sign for "...what the hell?..."

"But, we've run into Frederick before," Tipton said. "Remember? He's the old guy who handcuffed Charley. Said he was ex-FBI, but he was so drunk, it'd be hard to believe him." Heads around the table nodded.

"He and his wife were in here just a little while ago," Roberta said. "The old man was really raising hell with her. I chased them out and they headed back to that beat-up RV."

Sam stood, saying, "I think it's time we go have a serious talk with Mr. Frederick."

Snuffy, who had been sitting silently behind Roberta, said, "He ain't out there no more. Half hour ago they headed up-mesa in the RV. Charley was with 'em."

"Then," Sam said, "I suggest we track them down and find out what's going on. That road's hard traveling for something like that old motor home. We should catch him easily. If we have to, we'll take the Stinson."

Ladilow braked the Humvee to a stop at the end of the street. He didn't like what he had just seen while driving in. Yardley and Anderson were going to be pissed. Really pissed!

"That goddamn old man's motor home is gone!" he said. "It was there when we left. Now it's gone. Shit!"

The Austrian nodded from the passenger's seat.

"You're right, this is not good." His accent made the words seem artificial. "Perhaps, we should see if he is inside," he indicated Roberta's with a gesture. "You go, I will wait."

That settled, Ladilow headed towards Roberta's. He turned to scan the sky for the helicopter. Yardley had said he and Anderson would be back in town in a few minutes. What had taken the Humvee nearly forty minutes to travel would take the Bell less than ten.

Instinctively, he reached in and loosened the Beretta in the shoulder holster, making certain it was ready. You never know.

Maggie Longfeather was sitting with her back to the door when Sam decided it was time to go after the lumbering RV. The group stood in unison and, as Maggie turned towards the door, she ignored the man just coming in. She couldn't see his face anyway. The early afternoon sun made him a black shadow outlined in incandescence.

Ladilow didn't see her either because his eyes had yet to adjust to the dark.

Their eyes acclimated at exactly the same time.

"Sam!" Maggie nearly screamed, "That's one of them. That's one of the guys who grabbed me!"

Even as she spoke, the black form at the door reached into his jacket and fell to the side. Two huge blasts of light blossomed out of the dark, blinding those looking at it. The muzzle blast deafened the rest.

Ladilow had heard her voice and saw Tipton make a sudden move beside her. He reacted instantly, but both shots went wide.

Pandemonium erupted as several dozen desert dwellers either dove over the bar or dropped to the floor, knocking tables, chairs, glasses and beer in every direction. Everyone felt the need to yell at the same time but none of their words had room to be understood. It was stereophonic chaos.

The first shot had barely cleared the barrel when Sam threw Maggie to the floor. Longfeather ducked into a crouch. Snuffy didn't even bother changing position in his chair.

Roberta, who was already standing, made only one movement. It was a sudden move with her right arm and hand. A single explosion, much louder than the other two, rattled glasses on the back-bar. Instantly, the sound of a body being slammed against the wall by a slow moving, thumb-sized slug reverberated through the near-dark.

Roberta stood straight. Feet apart. Right arm at her hip, .45 in her hand. She waited for a response.

The response was the dark outline of a man tumbling into a disheveled heap in the doorway. The heap moaned a low, guttural moan. Part growl.

The entire episode hadn't taken two seconds.

The slug had pulverized most of the right shoulder joint. The collarbone hung free. The arm dangled loose and without control. Ladilow's rotator cup no longer existed.

Roberta holstered the big automatic and walked slowly up to where Ladilow lay in the doorway. He moaned through gritted teeth. Roberta gracefully leaned over and scooped up the Beretta. While down at Ladilow's level, she looked him in the eye.

"No one shoots up my bar, but me!" She grabbed him by the nose. "Got that, Baco?"

The sounds had barely subsided before the throaty roar of a vehicle rolled through the door as Gunther floored the Humvee on his way out of town. He'd seen Ladilow collapse in the door.

Partner, it's a damn good thing I plugged my share of bullet holes in 'Nam," Joseph Longfeather said to a less-than-responsive Hispanic who had just retired from the gun-fighting business. "Otherwise, you'd bleed to death before we got you to a doctor."

Longfeather looked down at Ladilow laying on a red checkered oil cloth on Roberta's largest table. He was proud of his handiwork. The bandages were tight and neat. The flow of blood appeared to be quelled for the moment.

"Incidentally, I don't think I'd plan on picking my nose with that hand for a while." Longfeather laughed quietly. Ladilow didn't reply.

The internally-administered Scotch painkiller was beginning to work its magic. Ladilow was past feeling pain of any kind. In fact, as Sam Tipton approached, he appeared to have forgotten that most of his right shoulder was now a formless mass of gristle and hamburger.

Sam looked down at him and said, "Okay, do you want to tell us what this is all about?"

Maggie stood behind Sam. Roberta and Longfeather stood on the other side, looking down. Snuffy was sitting on his stool at the bar, watching the proceedings from familiar surroundings. The rest of the crowd had gone back to drinking their lunch. The festivities forgotten.

"Fuck you!" Besides deadening his pain, the Scotch had given Ladilow an over-abundance of bravery.

"Lighten up!" Tipton said, "We'll help you, but we want to know what this Cobalt Blue thing is and what it has to do with us?" Tipton knew he was making a mistake. He was trying to speak logically to a man who was at least three drinks and one bullet past being logical.

"Tipton, I don' know who d'fuck you think you are. We missed last time, but this time, you're a dead man!" Ladilow had trouble forming the words but they were unmistakable.

Sam didn't understand what he was hearing. This time?

"What're you talking about...this time? When was the last time. Viet Nam?" he asked.

"Don' play stupid Tipton. You know. Back in D.C., when we wasted…." Ladilow started coughing and laughing at the same time. "Yeah, when we wasted your old lady and kid!" Ladilow was laughing, "only, you not home!

His voice crescendoed, becoming high and hysterical, "We shot the shit outta that place! Shit! I heard we even got your goddamn rat dog!"

Ladilow's laughing was the only sound in a building filled with stunned silence. A quiet gasp escaped Maggie. Her hand went to her mouth. Longfeather clinched his fists and stared across the table at his friend.

Sam "Cowboy" Tipton stood stone still, not breathing. Not hearing. Not seeing a blood-soaked Hispanic laying on a barroom table in Shithole, Arizona. What he saw was the same image he had seen a thousand times. A million times. Until very recently, he had seen it every time he closed his eyes. Two caskets. One smaller than the other. He remembered the drizzle. The coldness of the casket's metal to his lips. The emptiness of the dark house. The feeling of broken glass crushing under his feet.

He thought back to his vision quest. The image of a growing daughter he would never see. A wife he would never again hug. He had begun to put the pain in its proper place. He was finally appreciating what he had.

But now? He looked down on a piece-of-shit thug who, for some incomprehensible reason, had ruined his life once and was trying to do it again. A decade of pain and blurred thoughts whirled through his mind. He felt lightheaded. Slowly, out of the fog, a single thought formed. A question only the man laying on the table could answer.

Joseph Longfeather steeled himself to protect his friend from himself. He had seen the pain from the outside. He could only imagine what it was like from within.

Tipton leaned over the table, a hand on each side of Ladilow and moved closer to the Hispanic's sweating face. The question came through his vocal chords in a single, whispered, syllable.

"Why?"

Ladilow didn't appear to hear and continued giggling.

"Why?" Tipton repeated, his voice was louder and firmer.

No response.

"Why?" Nearly a yell. White knuckles on the table edge. Veins standing out on his neck. Eyes boring holes through a stranger's face. A stranger who had re-written his entire life. Then Sam Tipton lost it.

"Why? You miserable, goddamn, sack of shit! Why? Why? Why?" Tipton was leaning over. Nose to nose. His voice a razor-edged, maniac scream. The scream of a man re-living the worst moment of his life.

Longfeather was ready to jump. Ready to help his friend by keeping him from doing something which would make his long list of regrets that much longer.

Sam Tipton released his death grip on the table, his hands trembling and taut. They came up before Ladilow's laughing face and poised over his throat. They continued to hang there, physical manifestations of the emotional isometrics going on within Sam Tipton's soul.

Longfeather relaxed. He recognized the signs. Sam was having an argument with himself. As long as he took the time for that argument, the result would be the right one.

Then, without warning, Sam relaxed. The tension dropped from his muscles and he turned around to sit on the edge of the table. He took a deep breath. Then another. Then a third. A hand came up and felt the scrap of paper with the phone number on it.

Things were beginning to make sense. The phone number made sense. Pieces were falling into place.

Every eye in the room was on him. There was no sound, other than quiet breathing.

Turning, he again went nose to nose with the groggy Hispanic. This time his hands weren't on the edges of the table. His left hand rested gently on the bandaged shoulder

"Hey, asshole!" Sam's voice was almost whimsical. "All we want to know is what the hell is going on?"

"Hey, I tol' you man, fuck off! We goin...ow...ow...ow" Ladilow winced in pain.

Sam's hand on the shoulder was no longer gentle.

"Okay, I'll ask you again. Why did you kill my family?" There was no hint of anger or rage in his voice. Only a coldness. His hand tightened on the shoulder.

"Ow..ow...ow! Hey, I don' know it all. I was just part of the crew hired," Ladilow was close to whining.

"Who hired you, asshole?" Sam squeezed again.

"Ow...ow! I don't know. I was just told some big D.C. dude wanted you dead 'cause you was digging dirt on 'em."

Tipton stood up for a second and thought. He turned and ignored Ladilow's pained breathing behind him. Turning around again, Sam continued.

"Different subject. Same process. What is Cobalt Blue and why come after me for it?"

Another gentle squeeze.

"All right, all right, all right! I don't know what the blue thing is, but it's worth lots. We think either you or Frederick got it. We gonna take you both."

"Frederick! Why Frederick?" It was no longer necessary to squeeze. Ladilow had gotten the message.

"Hey, man, I dunno. Just that he was the fibbie in charge and somehow he got it back again. He dealing with big guy in D.C. He hire us. We...we..."

Ladilow's voice was getting slower. Gradually he closed his eyes. He let out a long breath and his head rolled to the side.

Maggie gasped, "Oh, God!"

Longfeather leaned over him. The bar was quiet as death. Longfeather listened to Ladilow's breath. Felt his heart, then looked up with a grin. "Relax, sis, you've seen drunks pass out before. You've just seen another one. He's okay."

All eyes turned to Sam Tipton who was quietly sitting on the edge of the table. His thoughts were somewhere else. His shoulders slumped as if the load was too much.

Abruptly, Tipton stood and stomped to the bar and around behind it. He spoke over his shoulder. "I need a drink in the worse possible sort of way."

"Sam!" Maggie sounded alarmed. She tripped after him,

arriving at the exact time he reached under the bar and uncapped a bottle in a single movement.

"Anyone else?" He looked brightly around the room. His friends stared back.

"Roberta, where do you keep the limes? Club soda is damn near undrinkable without 'em."

His voice was light, but there was no mirth in is eyes.

"Hey, my friend! What is this shit!" Charley Yee was holding the bottle up and looking through it. The amber liquid danced in the afternoon sun, its motions reflected the boat-like movements of the motor home.

Frank Frederick fought the dancing wheel to stay on the rutted dirt road and looked over at his traveling companion and drinking partner, "What do you mean, Charley Yee? Does it taste really bad?"

"Oh, yes, Mr. Frank Frederick, sir. It taste very bad!"

"Then," returned Frederick, "that means this must be very, very good."

Both laughed hysterically. Frederick hit the brakes momentarily to keep from running off the road.

"Hey, let's sing," Frank Frederick said it with a crooked grin. "I used to be a helluva singer."

He tested his voice, "...la, la, la...!" He laughed again.

"No, really, Charley, listen....Mule traaaaiiin! Clippity, cloppin' over...what's a'matter Charley Yee? Why're you laughing?"

The old Indian was convulsed in the right seat.

Frederick looked over at his Native American audience of one and said, in the most serious tone he could muster.

"Charley, I certainly hope your gods like music 'cause I'm goin' to sing 'em deaf!"

Kwan didn't like driving with the windows up. He'd come to appreciate the intoxicating pine scent of the mountains. He thought it mingled well with the right kind of music. As the window was being closed, Mozart fought to escape through the diminishing opening.

The window had to be closed. Even though some distance from the snail-like motor home ahead, with the window open he could still hear Frederick singing an inane song about a trained mule. Uniting with nature wasn't worth the verbal suffering.

The window hit the stop and sealed out the audio pollution. Mozart was trapped and filled the truck's cab. Kwan Yamuchi smiled. This was the way to enjoy the Mogollon.

His tired-looking, but mechanically spirited, four-by-four barely idled as it climbed the Mogollon. Even with his foot off the gas, Kwan had to hit the brakes periodically to keep from catching up with Frederick's lurching ark.

He turned the tape player up one notch and smiled again.

Yee and Frederick had to be found, on that they all agreed. That oddest of couples apparently held the key to understanding the chaos which had suddenly descended on their lives.

"Snuffy, you're now the official bartender," Roberta was talking as she threw her leather jacket on over a well-worn Led Zeppelin sweatshirt. Because of her physique, the "Led" was stretched far away from the "Zeppelin."

"And you're official jailer, too," Sam Tipton added as he headed for the door. "Keep an eye on our friend here," he indicated a heavily-bandaged and thoroughly drunk Ladilow.

The Hispanic had lost much of his color and was propped up in a chair. Silver duct tape wound around his good arm and both legs, securing him to the heavy oak structure. His useless arm was taped across his chest in a crude sling. He stared around with angry eyes.

"And don't let him go out dancing," Tipton warned.

Ladilow didn't look like he'd be in a dancing mood anytime in the coming decade.

Snuffy stood behind the bar and grinned. He liked the idea of his new jobs. A weathered hand rested on the old Colt in his belt. The concept of a bartending jailer seemed somehow logical to him.

Longfeather stepped into the open front door from the outside and shouted, "Hey, let's shake it! They have too much head start as it is! Let's go!" Longfeather was known for his impatience when it was time to hit the road.

When the entire crew finally assembled in the early afternoon sun, Tipton said, "Okay, this is the drill. Maggie, you and Roberta take the Willys and head up the road after them.

"Longfeather and I will take Roberta's truck to the valley and grab the Stinson. From the air, we'll know for sure which road they're on. If we see they've taken one of those tiny forks, we'll circle you at treetop level and then circle their position until you find them. If we don't catch them before they get up on the rim where the road flattens out, we'll just land on the road in front of them and wait. Simple as that."

"Let's do it." His voice was curt and commanding. Tipton's days as a Marine had resurfaced briefly. This was a mission and would be treated as one.

As an afterthought before getting in Roberta's truck with Longfeather, Tipton walked briskly to the Willys. Maggie glanced up from behind the steering wheel, her smile adding more brilliance to the afternoon.

"Be careful, kid!" Sam reached in and tweaked her nose. Hoisting the Winchester easily in one hand, he levered a fresh cartridge into the chamber and let the hammer down to the safety notch.

He handed it through the window to Maggie Longfeather and said, "Don't hesitate to use this. I don't think we're playing with very nice people." He leaned down and looked across at Roberta sitting in the other seat. She nodded and smiled, as if telling Sam she'd take care of Maggie.

He was concerned but not worried. Both ladies were more than capable of taking care of themselves. Still....

Tipton stood for a second with his foot on the running board of Roberta's truck, watching the Willys as it disappeared in a cloud of dust.

"Get the hell in!" Longfeather yelled from behind the wheel. "Charley's going to die of old age before we get there."

Longfeather popped the clutch, even as the door slammed.

The sound of the helicopter beating the hot afternoon air into submission arrived ahead of the machine itself. Gunther leaned against the Humvee next to the dirt road just out of sight of Pitacho. He shielded his eyes as the chopper let down through a self-induced dust storm, and he started towards the helicopter assuming the unnecessary stooped-over stance people invariably develop near a helicopter.

Yardley and Anderson, accompanied by several recruits Gunther didn't recognize, were out of the chopper before he got to the door.

"Are they still here?" Yardley had to yell to be heard.

"No, sir!" Gunther yelled in return. As they spoke, Anderson inserted himself into the conversation, their heads forming a tight huddle.

"I checked the bar a couple minutes ago," Gunther said, "and the place is practically empty. There's an old man tending bar and Ladilow is taped to a chair. He looks like he's been shot. There's no sign of either Tipton or Frederick."

"Dammit!" Was all Yardley said.

The huddle broke up long enough to scramble on board the olive drab Humvee, a near clone of those used by the United States Army. Inside, the trio no longer had to shout. The two hired guns sat on either end of the back seat. Silent. Eyes moving like gecko's. Soldiers waiting for the fight.

As Roberta's come into view, the subtle sound of weapon safeties being clicked into the "off" position briefly filled the vehicle.

Snuffy Smith saw them coming. Gunther was first through the door. His body language warned the old man. He knew a threat when he saw one. The next two stepped immediately to either side of the door and disappeared.

A wrinkled hand tightened on an ancient .44 Colt behind the bar. The barrel pointed at the new arrivals.

Two men, older than the rest, were last in. One wore a white dress shirt under an expensive-looking windbreaker. Snuffy correctly guessed that Anderson didn't spend a lot of time being casual. He did it poorly.

Anderson's face was an irritated frown. His walk was quick and impatient. He arrived at the bar first.

"What'll it be gentlemen? A beer?" Snuffy Smith, temporary barkeep and jailer, displayed his Sunday-go-to-meeting smile. He looked Anderson in the eye. The Colt behind the bar was cocked and ready. So was Snuffy. He'd been there before.

"We're looking for a Mr. Frank Frederick and Mr. Sam Tipton." Anderson's speech was clipped and loaded with attitude. Snuffy took an instant dislike to him.

"Well, lemme think..." Snuffy spoke slowly on purpose. He needed time to analyze what was coming down. "I knew a Sam Lipton once. That was down in Nogales. And a Stan Frederick over in Bumble Bee, but I don't think I know..."

What little patience Anderson had when he walked in was gone. He cut the wizened cowboy off short.

"Don't play with me old man! I'm not in the mood for games. Where have they gone?" Anderson was leaning over the bar, a hand wrapped in the front of Snuffy's frayed plaid shirt. He pulled him so close Snuffy could smell his cologne.

Smith's wrinkled face twisted, becoming a knot of aged skin, as it prepared for a sneeze. The cologne was too much.

The sneeze was a classic and Anderson didn't have time to avoid the inevitable. He leapt back. Too late! A linen handkerchief instantly appeared in his hand. He wiped frantically at his splattered face.

"Gheez, mister. I'm sorry!" Snuffy was not entirely successful in hiding his grin.

Anderson turned red. He was even less successful in hiding his rage.

"Where'd they go, old man?" His voice was tight. Anger drew his eyes into slits.

"Who?" Snuffy said. In his peripheral vision, he saw two shadows move, one against each wall.

"Tipton and Frederick."

"Lipton? Thought he was in Nogales."

Anderson's face went white.

The wrinkled hand on the Colt tightened.

Anderson glanced over at Ladilow, who grinned broadly. Even in a semi-stupor the Hispanic recognized his friends. Anderson then realized he may not need a local tour guide after all. He could get his information elsewhere. He turned towards Ladilow.

"Hey, amigos!" Ladilow's well lubricated voice was that of a ten-year-old glad to see his classmates after summer vacation. "I got shot! And it hurts!" Watery eyes went from face to face.

Anderson yelled at the Hispanic, "Ladilow! Do you know where Tipton and Frederick went?"

"Yeah, sure. They was talking about it while the big Indian patched me up," Ladilow slurred.

"I got shot, you know." He grinned. The Scotch was still doing its job.

"Tipton and Frederick!" Anderson was on the edge of reaching down Ladilow's throat and physically pulling the words out. "Where did they go?"

"Oh, those two?" The lights appeared to come on in Ladilow's half-pickled mind. "Tipton took off up the rim after

Frederick and some old Indian in that dogshit motor home."

Anderson returned his attention to Snuffy. He quietly said, "Is that right, old man? Did they go up there?"

Anderson stared at Snuffy.

Snuffy stared back. He answered even more slowly than before, knowing the response ahead of time.

"Did who go up where?"

Anderson abruptly spun and stepped two long paces away. Ashen face. Clinched fists. Feet spread wide. Back to the bar. His head turned to one of the shadows on the wall.

"Kill him!"

The first shot broke the only full bottle of Chivas Regal in the bar. Minute traces of blood ringed the hole the copper-jacketed slug left in the wall behind the crumbling bottle.

Snuffy Smith's skinny chest had barely slowed the jacketed nine-millimeter slug down.

The second shot erupted a nano-second later from behind the bar. The old Colt's voice boomed, as a blunt, lead slug ripped a hole in the face of the bar. The wood deformed the lead into a vague mushroom shape and slowed it only slightly. Instantly, a dime-sized black hole appeared in the face of one of the shadows. It was less than an inch to the right of his nose. He slammed against the wall. The still-smoking Sig clattered to the floor.

Snuffy had evened the score.

"Shit!" Anderson started to run for cover. He pulled an automatic out of a shoulder holster as he ran. It was the first time he'd actually pulled a weapon in twenty years. Very few Washington secretaries demanded such extreme measures.

Yardley ran past him to the bar, his pistol went over the bar first, his eyes right behind it. He relaxed. The wrinkled old man was sitting on the floor, his back against a rack of empty glasses. His eyes were closed. Blood pooled in the middle of his shirt. He was out of the fight.

"Donohue's dead!" Gunther's voice came from the side of the room. He was kneeling over the downed gunman.

"Who's Donohue?" Anderson asked. Gunther pointed at the corpse on the floor.

Brad Anderson turned his attention to Ladilow.

Anderson held Ladilow's round, limp face in his hand as he looked down at him still taped in the chair.

"Ladilow!" languid eyes tried without success to focus on Anderson, as he spoke. "Do you know which road they took?"

Anderson's words were loud, as if volume made him more understandable. The pistol still hung at his side.

Ladilow struggled with the question. His slow-moving mind first had difficulty understanding the words. Then it fought to form new ones into an answer.

"Think so," He looked up at Anderson. "They were talking about the...ah, you know...the road that goes out of town the other goddamn direction."

Gunther stepped forward to cut the tape around Ladilow's arms and legs. Anderson waved him off.

"We've got what we need," Anderson snapped.

Gunther stepped forward again, a folding knife in his hand.

Anderson again stopped him.

"Don't bother," he said.

Anderson leveled the pistol, and pulled the trigger.

The back of Ladilow's head vomited its contents out on the table behind him. As he slumped down, a trickle of blood ran between his open eyes.

"Let's go!" Anderson was impatient.

Yardley glanced at the corpse on the way out and frowned.

Fifty

The afternoon had settled into the high valley, and hawks, expending no effort at all, rode thermals while looking for an inattentive rodent. Their wings seldom moved. When they did, they pushed gently against what appeared to be a tangible blue substance that was the sky.

Longfeather and Tipton were too busy to enjoy the afternoon. They hurried back and forth between the sagging old Stinson and the sagging old mill prepping for a mission.

An orange, zip-up, heavy-duty duffel bag lay next to the airplane. It looked well-used. The bag was always loaded and within an arm's reach. When they headed into the desert on a scrounging trip, they didn't have to think about what they'd need. It was all in the bag. Everything to survive and prosper in any situation was there, from tools and a hand-held transceiver, to water and Fig Newtons. All the basic necessities of life.

"You want to put these in back?" Longfeather cradled a long, handmade leather case and an old bolt action rifle in his arms.

"Yeah, why not?" Tipton grabbed the leather case, pushed a heavily-tarnished peso doing duty as a button through its slot, and opened the end flap. For a brief second, the sun glistened off Ivan's old single-shot Remington before Tipton slid it back in. He knew he didn't need to check the rifle. He just wanted to look at it for a moment. Maggie had made the thick leather case for him along traditional southwest lines. A single silver concho and leather tassel dangled off the small end.

"How much ammo you have?" Longfeather asked.

"I don't know," Tipton answered. "Maybe forty, fifty rounds. We didn't load much. How much do you have for the o-three?" Tipton pointed at Longfeather's old military bolt action, a 1903 Springfield. Standard issue during World War One.

"About the same." Longfeather laid both rifles in what had been an ambulance litter bay and pulled bungee cords tightly over them. He looked around at Sam Tipton and then back at the old rifles.

"Boy! I hope those guys aren't as serious as Maggie makes them sound. We're not exactly set up to go against a squad of bad guys with M-16's," Longfeather said.

Tipton snorted. "Yeah, if it comes down to that, I guess we'll have to rely on that well-known Longfeather creativity."

The muscular Apache ignored him and dug a coin out of his jeans pocket.

"Heads," Tipton called, as the sun flashed off the spinning coin.

"It's all right, you can tell me," Tipton shouted to be heard over the engine. "It's got two tails right? You can tell me." Longfeather sat up front and ignored him while he checked the airplane's controls.

Sam Tipton was not happy about losing the coin toss. He was a lousy passenger. In fact, with the exception of Joseph Longfeather, he generally refused to accept that role. Longfeather he would trust. No one else.

In seconds, the trees on the rim fell away instantly as the Stinson shot off the edge. No sooner were they clear, Longfeather banked gently left. Tipton smiled. Nice touch. An airplane, his father always said, interprets a person's personality and inner soul, translating them into three dimensions. Making them easy to see. A pilot, Samuel Tipton, Sr. liked to say, flies an airplane exactly the way he lives his life, but it's more obvious in the air. The Stinson said Longfeather had a precise and caring soul.

Tipton looked down the rim, searching for the road which zig-zagged its way up towards the rim. Somewhere along that road was Frank Frederick and Charley Yee. They held the answer to Cobalt Blue, which in turn appeared to be an important link in a chain of events which went back to the most terrible day in his life.

As the Stinson slowly cruised the edge of the Mogollon Rim, not far behind it men raced towards a waiting helicopter. They too were looking for two old men in a rotting motor home.

Fifty-one

Frank Frederick suddenly remembered the other song he knew and he reached over to punch Charley Yee back into full wakefulness.

"...Waltzing Matilda, waaaaltzing Matilda, You'll come a waltzing...." Frederick was singing at Yee, as if the old Indian actually cared.

On top the rim, the road snaked in and out of heavy forests alternately crossing shallow, open valleys and plains before disappearing into tall pines again.

Charley Yee leaned heavily against the window. He was dancing with booze-induced sleep. It was a pattern. His eyes would go slowly closed, then spring back open. Then the pattern would begin anew.

Suddenly Charley sat bolt upright. Eyes wide open. Head swiveling all directions. He jumped up and ricocheted off cabinets and walls as he raced unsteadily towards the back of the small motor home.

Yee climbed frantically over a sleeping May Frederick to stare out the back window.

"Go away Frank, I have a headache," Mrs. Frederick mumbled, as Charley scrambled back over her.

"Frank, my friend, Frank!" Charley stumbled forward and leaned on the engine cover separating the two front seats.

"Frank Frederick," he was frantically shaking the driver's shoulder. "We have gone too far! We need to turn back! Our road is behind us!"

"...Waltzing Matiiiiiiilllda, come waltzing with...me!" Frank had to get his dramatic ending in before he'd recognize his friend yanking on his shoulder. His performance over, he lifted his foot off the accelerator. As the lumbering motorhome slowed, he turned to look at Charley Yee. Yee was so close, their breaths commingled and formed a nearly visible alcohol cloud.

"What do you mean? Our road is behind us?" Frederick hadn't had as much as Charley Yee to drink, so scattered fragments of his brain still worked. "Jesus, Charley! Can't you find it when the sun is up?"

"We should have turned back...there." Charley's skinny arm and gnarled finger pointed at May Frederick's prone, but now squirming figure. She was waking up.

"Where?"

"Back there!"

"How far back there?"

"A ways!"

"A long ways?"

"No, a medium ways"

Frank Frederick turned and slumped into the seat while he considered the situation. He looked up at Charley Yee still standing behind him.

"Okay. A medium ways is okay," Frederick announced.

By this time the RV had coasted to a halt in the middle of the narrow, dirt path that some long-ago rancher had once used often. Weeds grew between the tire tracks which at that point ran through a relatively flat, grassy valley surrounded with trees.

Frank Frederick looked off the side of the road and began to calculate how to turn the ragged behemoth around.

The road behind the motor home climbed gradually up a slight grassy incline before the forest again closed over it. A dirty four-by-four pickup sat idling in the forest shadows. Kwan Yamuchi leaned against it. Binoculars were nested to his eyes. Beethoven drifted quietly out of the open truck windows. As he watched the white, cube-like vehicle a mile ahead, it stopped. Then it began a slow, slicing dance in which the driver obviously was attempting to turn around.

What were they doing? Were they lost? Had they decided to go back to town? Kwan still had no idea what the two old men were doing wandering around the landscape in the first place.

Charley Yee was chanting an ancient song of thanksgiving in counterpoint to Frederick who was once again mutilating Mule Train. As they inched their way up the valley and the coolness of the forest closed over them, neither gave an inch in their musical battle. The fragrance of the pines had barely closed in, when the sunlight of another small valley burst upon them.

"Frank Frederick! What is that ahead?" Charley Yee stabbed the windshield with his finger and grimaced in pain.

Frederick squinted. It was a maroon pick-up truck on the

opposite side of the road. It was a scene of distress. The hood was up. A figure in jeans leaned over the fender. Its head was buried in the engine compartment.

As the motor home rolled within several dozen yards, the figure looked up. Then it stood and waited until they pulled alongside. It was a Native American. Halfway between five and six foot. Worn cowboy hat pulled low over his eyes. An easy grin split the face and accentuated the fine boned features. The teeth were unusually white for that part of the country.

Frederick leaned out of the open window.

"Got a problem?"

"Yes, the distributor rotor is broken," the Indian answered.

Frederick looked past him into the engine compartment, as if he could diagnose the problem from that distance. The distributor cap was off.

"Got a spare?" Frederick was feeling signs of sobering up. His head was beginning to ache.

"Unfortunately, no. Can you give me a ride?" The voice was unusual, Frederick noticed. A little more controlled. More refined than he had been hearing in the area. It didn't flow easily. He ignored his thoughts.

"Yeah, sure. Jump in." Frederick was still drunk enough he hadn't given any thought to what he was going to do with an extra Indian when they got where they were going.

"Let me grab my stuff." The Native American disappeared to the back of his truck. When he reappeared he was carrying a canvas duffel bag over his shoulder. A short, bulky rifle scabbard was in his hand.

"Thank you, sir, for picking me up." Kwan said closing the door behind him. "You can just let me off when you have to turn." He sat down in the side-facing seat and said no more. Kwan thought his performance had been acceptable.

Frederick immediately forgot about him and urged the cubical ark into motion. Charley Yee continued chanting and didn't even turn to look at their passenger.

"**Here, here!** Turn here!" Charley was pointing off to the left, towards the sharp edge of the rim which lay several miles away. A barely worn path in the grass of the small valley was all that indicated anyone had ever been there.

Frederick slowed and obediently cranked the wheel hard

over. Frederick was drunk enough that Yamuchi was continually braced for a crash. It would not be an honorable way to die.

The motor home had barely made the corner when the pounding sound of helicopter rotors beat through the fragile structure. An amplified voice boomed down from above and demanded, "Stop! Where you are." A full automatic weapon barked and a dozen bits of dirt jumped out of the path in front of the RV.

Frederick slammed the brake pedal to the bottom. Charley Yee bounced off the dash. Pots and pans tumbled forward in a clattering wave. May Frederick groaned as she rolled off the bed to land in the hallway.

"Don't do anything stupid!" the voice above announced.

The down wash of the rotor blades hammered the motor home so hard, it threatened to knock windows out. Frederick and Yee, both confused, put their faces to the windshield trying to locate the source of the voice.

The helicopter dropped down in front of the stationary RV, its rotors kicking up a dust cloud. The dust cleared the second the helo touched. Men were crouched in the open doors holding submachine guns. They leaped out before the skids were firmly on the ground.

Kwan Yamuchi began busying himself the instant he saw the helicopter. The rifle scabbard was hurriedly zipped open. A magazine was slammed into the rifle, the bolt snapped back and a live round leaped into the chamber. He hid the rifle under the couch cushion just inside the RV's door. The H & K automatic was checked before being returned to the small of his back. He was ready. He sat down again.

"Out, everybody out," a man shouted, as he yanked the RV's door open. He held a stubby machine pistol, its long magazine curving out of his left hand where he held it. The muzzle moved in practiced arcs back and forth. Everyone was included in the arc.

Another young man physically dragged Frank Frederick out of the driver's door. By the time Frederick hit the ground he was breathing hard. His asthma threatened to kick in. He was suddenly stone sober, the effect of fear and adrenaline.

"Line up, goddammit, line up." One of the younger men bullied everyone into position next to the RV. The other had his head inside checking it out.

"Nothing in there but an old broad out cold on the floor." He stepped out, leaving the door open, and assumed a guard position behind the line of prisoners with his back to the door. The other stood in front of them. Both played their machine pistols back and forth in a deadly rhythm.

Anderson and Yardley approached from the helicopter. Neither had their weapons out. They didn't need them. That's what their hired guns were for. Gunther walked casually behind them.

"Well," Anderson began, "It looks as if we meet again, Mr. Frederick. When was the last time? '72? '73?" Anderson was relaxed. The situation was under control. Two submachine guns and five men should be enough to handle two wrinkled old men and a short Indian.

"Who's your friend, Frederick?" Anderson indicated the Indian in the cowboy hat.

"I...I...don't know. We just picked him up." Frederick's voice was shaking. His skin pale. An occasional cough escaped.

"Sorry, wrong place and the wrong time!" Having passed sentence on the hitch-hiker, Anderson redirected his words to Frederick.

"Frederick, you surprise me, yet you don't surprise me." Bradley Anderson sneered as he stood face to face with the old man. "You surprise me because you had the guts to try and deal with me. You don't surprise me because you fucked this up just like you fucked up everything else you've touched."

Frederick's only response was a small cough followed by a longer one.

"Okay, now let's get down to business. Where is Cobalt Blue?" Anderson moved closer yet to Frederick, as he spoke. The old man tried to answer.

"I..I'm not sure. That's where we were going. To get it. Charley has it hidden." Frederick whimpered.

Yee looked over with a question in his eyes. Frederick coughed. Once, then twice.

Every time Frederick coughed, he turned his head. When he did, he saw the guard behind him, his back to the open RV door. Yee was standing in front of the guard, his face a mixture of confusion and fear. The hitchhiker stood on the other side, his head down, as if afraid to look anyone in the face. No expression showed around the sun glasses.

Frederick's next cough was a deep one. Then another. And another. In seconds, he was doubled over, coughing and wheezing, fighting for breath.

Anderson stood back in disgust. Frederick sounded like a dying man struggling for his last, desperate breath.

All eyes were on Frederick's fight for life.

No one saw May Frederick as she stepped into the RV's doorway. She had the universal pissed-wife weapon in her hand: A cast iron frying pan. The guard literally never knew what hit him. But Kwan did. From where he stood, Kwan was looking across the door at the coughing ex-agent when the pan flashed out.

The others had barely heard the "bong" of the pan flattening a crew cut, when Kwan acted. His hand flashed under the vest. Before the other guard had time to even tense his muscles, two nine-millimeter slugs caught him in the middle of the chest. Double tapped! Dead center!

Neither guard had hit the ground before Kwan side-stepped from the group, his automatic aimed primarily at Gunther. Kwan recognized where the threat lay. The other two were obviously leaders. Administrators. Gunther was a soldier.

"I think the time has come to re-assess the situation." Kwan spoke quietly and with authority. "I do not want to kill any more of you. But, it is necessary we continue our journey." Frederick had inadvertently just told him where they were going. To get Cobalt Blue. And that was why he had traveled halfway around the world. They were making progress.

May Frederick had retrieved her husband's inhaler and he was nearly recovered. He took one more drag on the inhaler and he looked at Kwan with a mixture of thankfulness and question.

"Who are you?" His voice was raspy from coughing.

"I am a friend," Kwan said without taking his eyes off Gunther or the other two. "Now, you must guard these for a second. Do not hesitate to shoot." Kwan pressed the automatic into Frederick's hand as he reached inside the RV for his rifle.

The instant Frederick had the pistol in his hand, Gunther saw his chance. For several precious seconds, he was being guarded by a wheezing old, ex-agent who, according to Anderson, had been a foul-up from the beginning. That kind of man couldn't possibly hold a professional soldier captive. Not even for a few seconds.

Gunther made his move. His hand was just flicking towards his shoulder holster, when the pistol in Frederick hand spat flame one time. The Austrian fell back, his hands clutching his thigh. Blood spurted between his fingers.

"Next time, it'll be a knee cap," Frederick's watery old eyes were alive. Revitalized. "The time after that it'll be between your goddamn eyes."

Kwan had snapped around the instant Frederick fired. He smiled slightly then went about his business.

Stepping from the motor home, Kwan kicked the unconscious guard over on his back and yanked the pistol from its shoulder holster and the submachine gun from his limp hand. He felt his pants legs for hide-out guns. He found a small revolver in an ankle holster.

He tossed the weapons into the motor home, as he said, "Okay, everyone else. Toss them on the ground here." He indicated a spot on the dried grass between them.

The Mini-14 Ruger continued to convince the captors-turned-prisoners it was in their best interest to obey. Gunther tried to quell the flow of blood while he rid himself of his armament.

"Mr. Frederick, if you would be so kind, would you throw all the weapons inside?" Kwan asked .

Frederick moved stiffly as he carried out the request.

Charley Yee just looked around with a dazed expression. None of it made sense to him.

"Okay, Mr. and Mrs. Frederick, Mr. Yee, please get back in the RV," Kwan asked politely.

He kept his eyes on his prisoners, which now included a woozy guard with a gigantic lump on his head.

Addressing the prisoners, he said, "Please walk over and stand on that rock."

He indicated a knoll some distance away. As they walked. He watched them carefully. He then turned his attention to the helicopter.

The rifle barked, two, three, a dozen times and the full-jacketed slugs tore into the helicopter. Kwan Yamuchi knew its soft spots. At least half of the rounds ripped through the turbine section in the engine and tore turbine blades from their mountings. The rest punched clean holes in the fuel tanks and fuel lines leading to the engine.

He was looking at his captives, when he heard the quiet "whump" of spilled turbine fuel catching fire.

He backed slowly into the motor home and stood in the doorway and asked over his shoulder, "Please proceed, Mr. Frederick."

As the motor home continued to move, the prisoners grew smaller with distance. Their position was clearly marked by the oily plume of flames which was converting money to smoke.

What Kwan Yamuchi could not see, was Richard Yardley speaking rapidly into a hand-held radio.

"How far out is the other helicopter? Five minutes? Okay, that's good. Just keep the Humvee coming on that road. Believe me, we're not hard to find. Just look for the smoke.

"Part of us will go with the chopper. The rest with you in the Humvee. By the way, there's an Indian with them that not only knows what he's doing, but he looks familiar to me. We'll talk about it when you get here." He clicked the radio off and stared blankly at the disappearing motor home. The damn helicopter better hurry.

The second helicopter, a Hughes 500E, was on-site ahead of schedule. Yardley and Gunther scrambled aboard, joining two others already strapped in.

The Bell was burning furiously as the Hughes lifted off.

Yardley shouted into the intercom, "They're down this road and couldn't have more than a few miles on us. Lean on it!"

Speaking to the Humvee via his handheld radio he said, "Anderson and the other guy are waiting by the burned chopper. Pick 'em up and step on it."

Gunther tightened a makeshift bandage on his thigh and pulled a submachine gun out of a case on the floor. His anger was obvious. The pain forgotten.

"I will kill dat foocking Indian myself," he half-whispered.

Fifty-two

"**What the hell is** that?" Longfeather twisted his head and yelled back at Tipton who, at that moment, was a disgruntled passenger.

A narrow column of jet-black smoke marred the landscape five miles ahead. Tipton leaned forward so he wouldn't have to shout so loud over the engine.

"Something big! Head for it." Longfeather had anticipated that and was already turning.

"Hey, look down there. Just coming out of the trees!" Longfeather had opened his side window and was pointing downward. The unmistakable squat outline of a Humvee was leaving twin rooster tails of dust behind as it blasted down the very road they were following.

"They're in a hurry to get someplace!" Longfeather shouted.

A second later he again yelled.

"There's the Willys!" He turned the old airplane slightly left, giving Sam a clear view ahead and down. Just short of the column of smoke, the boxy-looking Willys could be seen leaving its own rooster tails. Maggie wasn't wasting any time either.

Longfeather cut across a sweeping curve in the road and caught up with the girls in a half-minute. By that time he had the Stinson down to tree top level and blasted past low in front of the Willys. Female arms waved out of both windows.

Tipton and Longfeather had no way of telling them about the Humvee several miles behind them.

"That's a helicopter burning down there!!" Longfeather was so amazed he didn't have turn his head to be heard.

As he spoke, he pulled the Stinson around and circled the burning chopper. He let his eyes travel down the path running away from the burning wreckage. Even from that low an altitude he could see the path ran clear to the edge of the Mogollon Rim. Past that point, the forested landscape abruptly disappeared as it dropped thousands of feet in only a few miles. The desert mountains and plains were blue in the distance.

He spotted the white square of the motor home and turned towards it. Hopefully, Maggie would see and follow.

"There's the motor home!" He yelled back at Tipton.

Tipton saw it and one other thing. He leaned forward, putting his mouth close to Longfeather so he couldn't miss it.

"Yeah, and look just above and behind it! There's another chopper!"

Even as they looked at the helicopter, it slewed sideways and the two Stinson pilots saw dust leaping off the path in front of the motor home. Flashes could be seen in the helicopter's doors.

"Hey! They're shooting at the motor home! What the hell?" Longfeather looked at his friend in the back seat with raised eyebrows, as if asking, what now.

"That could be a Police or D.E.A. chopper, for all we know," Tipton shouted.

"I'll pull up alongside and see," Longfeather answered.

The old Stinson roared a little louder as Longfeather urged it to catch up with the slow-moving helicopter ahead. More muzzle flashes were seen even as they closed.

Then the helicopter began to grow in size as they closed the distance.

"They're going too slow! I don't think I can stay with it!" As he spoke, he yanked up the long handle by his left hip, dropping the flaps, and cranked furiously above his head drooping the ailerons, as well. Both were features that made the Stinson such a good bush plane.

The old flying machine staggered along, slowly closing the gap on the helicopter until almost even with it. Even though they were still just a little too fast, they could easily see what was happening. Men in the helicopter were firing ahead of the motor home in an apparent attempt to stop it. Just as the Stinson came up on the helicopter and only a hundred feet separated the two craft, Sam saw one of the shooters look over his shoulder. He'd seen the Stinson's shadow on the ground and knew the helicopter wasn't alone.

Longfeather and Tipton were close enough to distinguish the man's features when he pivoted around. Suddenly they were looking directly at muzzle flashes.

"Holy shit!" Longfeather slammed the throttle forward, dumping the nose and bringing up the flaps at the same time. As they dropped towards the ground, barely skimming the trees, the airplane regained airspeed and they were out of range in seconds.

"What the hell was that all about?" Longfeather yelled, as he circled around, keeping the helicopter in sight.

It was still shooting at the motor home.

"That's not a good-guy helicopter, that's for damn sure," Tipton yelled. "Let's go down and hassle them and see if we can discourage them!"

"We're going to get shot at!" Longfeather yelled.

"Just try to stay high," Tipton returned. "They can't shoot through their own rotor blades. Let's find out how serious these guys are."

The noise of the wind through the open windows combined with the roar of the Lycoming to make normal conversation nearly impossible. Neither Longfeather nor Tipton noticed the noise, however. Adrenaline had a way of drawing the focus down to the job at hand. Longfeather pulled the airplane up and around. He wanted to be above and behind the chopper where he could drop down and threaten it. Past that, he couldn't do much else. They weren't exactly flying a fighter.

"Where's a Phantom, when you really need one?" Tipton yelled.

Longfeather was part way around the circle when the helicopter suddenly broke up and away from the motor home.

"They've seen us," Longfeather yelled, "and it looks like they've changed their priorities!" As he spoke, muzzle flashes winked in the dark of the open side door.

"Yo! We've just gone defensive!" Longfeather pulled the nose up and towards the helicopter.

"That thing's faster than we are and can turn on a dime. I think it's time for some of that Longfeather creativity!" Tipton yelled. The Browning automatic came out of his belt even as he yelled.

"I have exactly fourteen rounds, Longfeather, you'd better do some of that 'pilot shit,' as they say in the movies."

Longfeather didn't answer. He was trying to figure out what the helicopter's next move would be. The chopper gunners could only fire out of their doors and they couldn't fire up through their rotors. The helicopter pilot's disadvantages were Longfeather's only advantages.

Running wasn't an option to be considered. Sam and Longfeather couldn't abandon the motor home. Besides, the Hughes could run them down. They had the snake by the head and couldn't let go.

Maggie hadn't seen it coming and jumped when the Stinson flashed by barely above windshield level. As she watched, the Stinson circled the black column and continued around headed towards the rim.

"I'm going to follow the guys, assuming there's a road up there," Maggie announced.

Roberta nodded. Under power, with the windows down, the Willys was only marginally quieter than the Stinson and Roberta didn't feel like yelling.

"Wow, that's a helicopter burning!" Maggie exclaimed, as they closed in on the source of the smoke. Both girls stared in amazement.

"There're some guys on the other side of it," Roberta pointed out, "And it looks like they're headed this way."

Anderson and one of his hired guns, sans guns, were running towards the path in an effort to cut off the Willys.

"Screw 'em," Maggie said as she downshifted and hit the gas. She slid through the corner and onto the path. The men blocked it and looked like they weren't going to move. Maggie upshifted and kept her foot in it.

Anderson and his stooge dived out of the way at the last moment.

"Damn pedestrians!" Roberta yelled. Female hands slapped together in a high-five. "Yeehaah!"

"Look at that!" Maggie yelled. She was looking upwards, directly above the path where it disappeared over a hill.

The Stinson was clearly outlined against the sky as it pulled hard and high, presenting a perfect top view to the girls. Then it rolled over and came back down. There was a dark-colored helicopter inside its turn closing on it. They could hear the gunfire. The sounds were out of sequence with the flashes because of the distance.

"God, I don't believe it! What're they doing?" Maggie said in disbelief.

"Keep countering to the outside of the turn," Sam yelled, We want to stay in front of their nose! They can only fire out the side doors!"

Each time the chopper got far enough off to the side, muzzle flashes winked at them. Even though the air whipping around in the cockpit was cool, a rivulet of sweat ran down the back of Longfeather's neck. The concentration was intense.

Yank, bank. Read every movement of the chopper and try to anticipate its next move. To survive, he had to keep the Stinson close and above the chopper using the rotors to shield them. But the Hughes was much too fast. Longfeather would put the airplane in position, only to have the chopper whip away, gunners firing all the while.

"Okay, I've had it with this shit! We're going offensive," yelled Tipton. "Cut across his turns, I'll take the shots and hope we don't get hit."

Longfeather tightened the bank, cutting the corner, and the helicopter grew larger.

Tipton held the pistol with both hands, steadying as best he could in the turbulence.

On the first pass, he snapped off four shots as they flashed past. No effect. The muzzle flashes from the helicopter had been fierce. Torn fabric and splintered wood showed where the Stinson had taken at least a half dozen hits in the right wing.

They flashed over the helicopter and turned hard trying to stay above it in the safe zone. The chopper veered off, uncovering them. More muzzle flashes. No hits.

Another pass, half a dozen shots. Tipton was frustrated. It was like trying to catch a goldfish with a fork. By the time the bullets got there, the helicopter was someplace else.

Another pass, four more shots, and the slide on the Browning was stuck open.

Sam yelled. "I'm out of ammo and can't get at the rifles. But I've got an idea."

"I sure as hell hope so!" Longfeather yelled back.

Tipton twisted around and dug around behind the back seat on the floor. His hands came up holding the airplane's wheel chocks. One set for each wheel. Each set was two yellow-painted blocks of wood a foot long, joined by a length of light chain.

"See if you can make a pass right down their middle from behind." Tipton held one of the chocks up where Longfeather could see it. "I'm going to try to drop these into the rotors."

Longfeather turned around with a silly-looking grin, "Getting a little desperate aren't we?"

"Options?" Tipton yelled.

"Okay! On this pass," Longfeather yelled back.

This time the gunners were getting their range and two holes appeared in the skylight over Tipton's head. They were exit holes. The bullets had come in the open window just over Longfeather's shoulder. Too close!

Longfeather pulled hard as they came over the turning helicopter, forging ahead momentarily.

"Now!" Tipton yelled, as he threw out one set of chocks. He watched as the yellow blocks, clearly visible, flashed harmlessly past the helicopter a good twenty feet above it.

"Okay, I've got the range and angle," Tipton yelled. "You have to be almost at rotor level and about two lengths in front. Otherwise the blocks have to fall too far."

Since the helicopter could literally pivot around, rather than turn, Longfeather had only an instant to make it work.

Steep bank, nose down, pulling hard. Helicopter growing larger. More muzzle flashes. Closer, closer. More flashes.

Suddenly hot liquid hit Tipton in the face. Smoke swirled around in the windblown cockpit. He glanced up to see oil streaming up the windshield, running through holes in the Plexiglas. The engine had taken a solid hit.

"Longfeather!" he instinctively shouted.

"I'm okay! I'm okay! Do it!" Longfeather yelled.

Joseph Longfeather fought with the controls as they flashed over the helicopter, using what was left of the airplane's energy to drop down, nearly in front of it.

"Bombs away!" Tipton yelled.

He held his breath as the wooden blocks flashed backwards. They looked on target, then skimmed barely over the top of the helicopter's rotor disk and disappeared.

"Dammit!" He yelled.

"I'm putting this thing down, right now!" Longfeather, yelled.

Trailing a thin stream of smoke, the stricken Stinson curved gracefully towards the path where it crossed a narrow meadow. It was going to be tight.

Twisting around, Tipton could see the helicopter closing on them from the rear. Longfeather set up the approach. The speed dropped. The helicopter closed. It had a perfect target.

Sam could see two figures in the door. Both held submachine guns. He held his breath.

The muzzle flashes began.

As the helicopter drew closer, Sam could see something he hadn't seen earlier. Something yellow flapped around at the rear of the tailboom, near the tailrotor.

The wheel chocks were dangling from the tailrotor shaft by their connecting chain. He had barely focused on the blocks when one disappeared in a flash of yellow splinters. It had been struck by a tailrotor blade.

Instantly, the helicopter began yawing. Dancing back and forth as the fragile, high-speed tailrotor went further and further out of balance. The chopper pilot had his hands full and banked away, looking for a quick place to land. If the rotor disintegrated, which it would any second, all on board were doomed.

The last thing Tipton saw of the helicopter, before the Stinson dropped below the trees, it was spiraling slowly as the pilot worked to put it down. It looked as if he had it under control. More or less.

Then cool, moist, surface air flashed through the Stinson. Grass under their wings. Total silence except for the whistle of the wind rushing past the open door. The oil pressure gone, Longfeather had killed the engine to save it. In the back seat, Sam could see nothing straight ahead. It was up to Longfeather. The tires hit once. Then twice. The brakes nearly stopped the tires as they tore desperately at the grass trying to stop the airplane. In seconds, the airplane lurched to a stop. Then the silence was broken by the sound of two men exhaling breaths taken sometime earlier and light "tinging" noises as a hot engine cooled off. Oil was dripping off everything in the airplane.

"Nice, J.! Really, nice!" Tipton breathed quietly.

Longfeather was the first out and he looked back at his disgruntled and oil-soaked passenger.

"Thanks, but, I feel bad about winning that last coin toss," Longfeather said, as he surveyed their situation, "so, you get to fly it out!"

As Sam tumbled out onto the ground, he saw they had landed in a space about a third of what they normally used. A line of trees was less then twenty feet from their nose. He wasn't certain there was enough room to fly it out.

Fifty-three

Yardley nearly fell out of the open helicopter door as he reached for the step with his foot. The floor of the chopper was carpeted with empty brass casings like marbles on a linoleum floor. The smell of gunpowder overwhelmed even the kerosene smell of the turbine winding down. His submachine gun lay on the floor, its barrel smoking as lubricating oil was vaporized from the heat.

He looked back at Gunther. The teutonic super-soldier sat, seemingly frozen, in the back seat. Eyes stared straight ahead. His skin as pale as the upholstery. He had discovered he hated flying at the exact moment the pilot announced he was going to ditch the helicopter.

"Where are you right now?" Yardley spoke into a hand-held radio. He had no idea where either the Humvee or the motor home was. A short section of the path they both were traveling was clearly visible a hundred yards away at the other end of the small clearing.

Anderson's voice on the other end confirmed both the helicopter and the airplane had gone down well in front of the Humvee. Anderson said, as far as he could tell, the motor home and Willys were somewhere between the downed helicopter and the advancing Humvee.

"Then just keep coming and pick us up," Yardley barked.

Suddenly, he was bone tired.

The sound of a vehicle drifted through the cool afternoon air. Good, the Humvee was almost here. He didn't even try to stand. Let it come to him. He sat and waited.

As he looked up, the old motor home appeared out of the trees. It lumbered slowly across the block-wide clearing and disappeared again. Yardley didn't even have enough energy to pick up his radio and call anyone. He was beginning to feel like a hare to the motor home's tortoise.

Screw it! Where was that damn Humvee?

Gunther's leg was throbbing. Yardley had looked at it closely. Clean wound. No major muscles or tendons. Just a clean hole in and out. Two Band-Aids and some Scotch would do the job.

He put pads over the wounds and wrapped an ace bandage around it. There was still a job to be done. Gunther's period of convalescence was already over.

The deep, unseen voice of a big V-8 rumbled out of the forest, moving fast. Yardley smiled. Finally! He grabbed his MP5 and a bag full of magazines. The crew could carry the rest. He turned towards the road just as the Willys flashed into sight. He barely had time to recognize it when it was gone. A trail of dust lingered in the air.

"Dammit!"

He crawled into the chopper and sat down. The air was cooling off and the sweet smell of the coming dusk floated in one side of the chopper and out the other. A deer appeared at the edge of the clearing, nibbling the fresh grass. It took one look at the Hughes and darted back into the trees.

Yardley was too irritated to appreciate his surroundings. He had barely begun to feel sorry for himself, when the Humvee roared into the clearing. It slid to a halt when someone spotted the helicopter and turned sharp right. It looked like a beetle as it bumped and thumped across the uneven ground towards them.

About time! The motor home was a few minutes ahead and barely moving. They would catch them easily.

The RV had no sooner pulled up beside the wounded Stinson, when the Willys roared into the clearing. It slid to a halt just past the RV. Maggie and Roberta leaped out. Maggie ran up to Sam, for an instant mistaking oil for blood.

"Sam!" Concerned furrows creased her face. She touched the liquid on his head. She rubbed her fingers together, identifying it.

"Oh!" Her face relaxed. "You're a mess, you know."

Longfeather was walking around the Stinson counting holes. The last time he'd performed that duty was as a crew chief on one of Tipton's Phantoms. The mission had been over Hanoi. This time, he counted nearly twice as many holes.

Frederick had just fallen out of the motor home behind Yee when Jack Tipton had the two of them by their collars like a pair of unruly puppies.

"Just what in the hell is going on," Tipton alternately glared at each old man. "Why are these guys after you? As far as that goes, why are they after us?"

Frederick was silent and Charley Yee was in the process of

muttering something about going to see his gods, when Maggie suddenly remembered.

"We have to get out of here! Right now!" She blurted. "That brown four by four isn't far behind us and the helicopter came down only about four miles back."

Longfeather had already emptied the litter bay of the Stinson and piled everything into the Willys.

"Let's go! Come on, let's go!" Sam began urgently herding everyone back into their vehicles like a tour guide for a lagging bunch of tourists.

Charley Yee only smiled and abruptly sat down cross-legged in the dry grass next to the motor home.

"Charley not go. Charley not worried!" He had regained his typically serene look.

Maggie squatted down facing him. She put a gentle hand on a shoulder. "Charley there are some really bad men after us, and we can't stop here."

"Charley go to his gods." He stood and began walking.

"Charley, where are you going!" Sam was trying not to get irritated, but he also kept checking up the path to see what other surprises the afternoon had in store for them.

"To my gods." He seemed certain of his destination.

Out of patience, Sam had just picked Charley up and tossed him in the motor home when all hell broke loose.

"Try not to hit Frederick or the old Indian. They know where Cobalt Blue is hidden. Kill everyone else!" Anderson yelled from inside of the Humvee as it raced down the narrow path. The motor home, Willys and airplane were all dead ahead.

"Fire!" he yelled.

The light machine-gun mounted on the roof mount barked. Empty casings and belt links rattled cross the vehicle's roof before whipping past in the wind.

"Oh, my God!" Maggie screamed.

"Go! Go! Go!" Sam shouted as he yanked the duffel bag and both rifles out of the open back of the Willys.

Dirt erupted all around them and the nasty snap of bullets passing close filled the air. A sound like hail on a tin roof erupted as the gunner found the range of the motor home.

Instantly, a yellow ball of flame mushroomed up around the

back of the motor home as a tracer bullet ripped through the propane tank. It billowed up like angry, black-edged whipped cream.

"Maggie wait! Wait!" Sam yelled into the open back of the Willys.

He and Longfeather sprinted the few yards back to the RV. Charley Yee had already stumbled out of the side door, with the Fredericks close behind. Sam again tossed Charley Yee over his shoulder and ran. Longfeather did the same with Mrs. Frederick. Frank was doing his best to keep up.

A line of bullet holes magically appeared in the side of the Willys even as Tipton tossed his burden in the back. Longfeather stuffed the hysterically-screaming old woman in the side door. Her husband scrambled frantically in the other side.

"Maggie! Go!" Gravel and dirt peppered his legs as Maggie's foot nailed the pedal to the floor.

Tipton had grabbed the rifle case and duffel bag, preparing to run into the trees, when he saw Longfeather standing against the front of the motor home. The Humvee was barely visible through the flames and smoke. It was less than fifty yards behind the burning hulk and closing fast. The gunner kept his finger on the trigger. Dirt erupted at Tipton's feet. The telltale streaks of tracers seemed everywhere.

In the fraction of a second before he dropped to the ground, Tipton saw Longfeather finish thumbing a stripper clip of five rounds into the old bolt action.

The big Indian shot his head around the edge of the burning motor home. A quick look. Then back under cover. He'd located his target. He stepped out into full view. Threw the rifle to his shoulder. Fired a single round. Stepped back behind the motor home. It was as precise as a choreographed dance step.

Tipton heard the distinctive boom of the thirty-ought-six amidst the chaos surrounding him. Then Longfeather was running towards him, using the motor home as cover. Longfeather knew he'd done his job without waiting to see the effect.

The effect of that single one-sixty-eight grain slug punching a clean hole through the Humvee's windshield and through the driver's face was spectacular. The vehicle was traveling fast when it slammed head-on into the back of the flaming motor home.

Sam watched just long enough to see the doors of the still-rocking Humvee pop open and men start tumbling out. For a moment they'd forgotten their prey and were worried about their own survival.

"All right, Sergeant York, let's get the hell out of here!" Tipton yelled at his friend.

Longfeather didn't need urging. The duffel bag was already strapped to his back. The two of them ran down the trail after the Willys.

A single submachine gun fired at them from the carnage behind. Too far away and ineffectual, it nonetheless told them the enemy was still out there.

Longfeather and Tipton had both forgotten the Indian in the cowboy hat. If they had been looking back as they ran, they would have seen Kwan Yamuchi drop out of the RV's driver's door. He had his rifle slung over one shoulder and duffel bag over the other. In a matter of seconds he disappeared into the trees. He glanced back. The burning RV was between him and the Humvee. Yardley couldn't see him. Crouched low, Yamuchi raced into the trees and disappeared.

"Who'd we lose?" Richard Yardley was looking around. It was like something out of his youth, when so many jungle firefights had gone wrong.

Oily smoke boiled up where the Humvee and the motor home had welded themselves together. The aluminum skin of the RV was already blistered and melting. It dribbled inside as flaming, molten drops. Heat threatened to blister one side of Yardley's face while mountain air cooled the other side.

Gunther limped up. "Only the driver is dead. One of the new guys has a broken arm. The machine gun and all the M-16s are lost in the fire."

Yardley counted silently. That left nine men, including the helicopter pilot and those who had arrived with the other chopper from Flagstaff. All were frantically yanking supplies out of the crumpled Humvee. The front half was in flames. The driver was still strapped in his flaming seat and the sickening smell of roast pork filled the air. Yardley hadn't smelled that for several decades.

Anderson's freshly starched, white dress shirt and neat black windbreaker were smudged with smoke and blood. In a daze, he absentmindedly flicked a piece of gray brain matter off his shoulder. He had been in the passenger seat when Longfeather's bullet exploded the driver's head. His face had a pale, green pallor and his eyes weren't fully focused.

"Hey Anderson," Yardley yelled over at him while laughing, "Welcome back to field ops."

The Washington bureaucrat stared at him but appeared not to hear.

Tipton had been prepared for a long run to catch the Willys but was brought up short when the path curved and he broke out into a clearing. The Willys sat on the other side.

The old vehicle was parked where the path ran into a jumble of rocks. Past the rocks there was nothing but clear afternoon air. It was the edge of the Mogollon Rim. The Willys was empty and one of the rear doors stood open. Tipton glanced in and slammed the door as he passed.

Tipton and Longfeather both scrambled through the rocks and looked down. They were standing on the edge of a narrow canyon which cut into the face of the rim like an ax into the edge of a clean board. Wide at its mouth, where it opened out on the rim, the canyon tapered slowly until the walls met where a low mountain took over.

A narrow, barely visible path snaked down the canyon wall under his feet. No one was in sight.

"Maggie!" Tipton's voice echoed off the bare stone walls. For the most part the walls were smooth and slightly overhung, as if the canyon had at one time been a gigantic cavern and the roof had caved in. Where they weren't smooth, the walls were so steep the only vegetation was the occasional stubborn juniper rooted in a crack.

"We're down here!" Maggie's voice echoed back up at him. It was impossible to pinpoint the source. With Longfeather watching the path behind, Sam hung out over the edge trying to find the girls and their charges.

"Where are you?" The echoes were surprisingly clear..

"Here!" Came a feathery answer. Sam was still looking down, when the boom of Longfeather's Springfield nearly knocked him off the cliff. The canyon's acoustics amplified the normally deafening roar many times over.

Longfeather's voice rang out. "Hey, Tipton. If you have a minute, I could sure use a hand!"

Sam had guessed as much.

Longfeather's position in the rocks gave a good view of the path and the entire clearing. As Tipton dropped next to him and pulled the old single shot out of its case, he saw the situation immediately. They had a wide, "C" shaped clear area in front of them, with their position at the gap. The forest rimmed the clearing right down to their position.

"We can keep them from coming right at us," Tipton said, "but sooner or later, they're going flank us through the forest." Longfeather nodded silently. Tipton glanced both ways up the rim. No obvious high ground. This was as good as it was going to get.

"Let's try to keep them pinned down on the other side," he said.

Longfeather looked over, "I make it almost exactly two hundred yards."

Sam squinted in the late afternoon sun and turned the vernier on the old rifle's sight slightly. He was ready.

He yanked a small nylon bag out of the duffel. The clink of metallic cartridges sounded as he sat it at his elbow. He'd been meaning to have Maggie make him a cartridge belt for the rifle. Maybe later. If there was a later.

He rolled his flying jacket up, placing it in a crack between two rocks. He laid the heavy rifle barrel on it and squinted through the slot.

Longfeather's first shot had warned them off. They now knew they were up against a high-power weapon.

"Hey, ..." Tipton said, "So far we haven't heard anything but submachine guns. You don't suppose that's all they have, do you?"

"Don't forget the machine gun!" he replied.

"Yeah, providing they got it off the Humvee before it got toasted."

"Well, we're about to find out." There was motion at the edges of the clearing. A submachine gun rattled in short bursts. Bullets knocked divots out of rocks all around them. There was no focus to the hits. The gun didn't have enough long-range accuracy for that.

"There, just to the right," Sam said. "I've got him."

Sam pushed a round into the breech and thumbed the big hammer back. The set trigger clicked. It was ready. The lightest touch would set it off.

    He found his target. The man thought he had adequate cover. Crouching low behind a rock, he didn't know the afternoon sun made his face glow. Easy target. It was too far away to see the eyes. Longfeather was right. That made it two hundred yards. Facial features were visible at one-hundred yards, the face only at two-hundred, but the face blended into the body at three hundred yards. It was an infallible measure.

    Sam Tipton took a deep breath. Let half of it out. He touched the trigger. The heavy rifle slammed into his shoulder. He barely heard the noise as it built and rebuilt off the cliffs. Rolling thunder. He wondered if Charley's gods heard it.

    The face disappeared.

    "Hit!" Longfeather announced.

    "Thank you, Ivan," Sam Tipton whispered quietly.

    Richard Yardley was down to eight.

"Shit!" Gunther yelled from the other side of the path. He didn't have to tell Yardley what had just happened. Yardley had seen the man's head vanish in a crimson spray. He was one of the replacements from Flagstaff.

    Yardley glanced over at Anderson. He was sitting, back to a rock, staring with glassy eyes at what was left of the downed gunman. More gray flecks were sprinkled over Anderson's jacket and in his hair. This was definitely becoming a hard day at the office for the bureaucrat.

    Crouching down, Yardley made silent signals with his hands. Gunther understood immediately. He huddled with his men. The orders were simple. Stay down. Stay out of sight. Work around the clearing and out-flank the two shooters. Gunther and Yardley both knew this would take time. But the cover made it safe. The shooters' position was indefensible from flank attacks. Yardley had to assume Tipton knew that as well as he did. He was probably figuring a way out of his situation right that moment.

"Okay, who goes first?" Longfeather asked. Both had seen heads bobbing as the team on the other side split up. It was time to retreat to a more defensible position, but someone had to mount a rear guard.

    "Toss for it?" Longfeather grinned.

    "Stuff it! I don't trust you. Besides, I lost the last one so you owe me." As he spoke, Tipton was inserting cartridges between each of the fingers of his left hand. That made them instantly accessible. In a machine-gun world, single-shot shooters had to work every advantage.

Longfeather knew the look. No use arguing. He reached for the orange duffel.

"Hold it a sec," Tipton said, as he reached into the bag. His hand returned with three fresh Browning magazines and a small coil of heavy fishing line leader. He ejected the empty magazine from the Browning into the bag and slammed a new one in place. The extras went in the other back pocket.

Holding up the automatic he smiled at Longfeather, "Just in case."

"Yeah, right! Hang in there, brother!" Longfeather stuck his hand up, palm open. Tipton grabbed it. Their eyes locked for a second, both wore grim smiles. Then Longfeather was gone. His boots made scraping sounds as he hurried down the path. The screeching of a hawk overhead was the only other sound.

As the hawk looked down, it could see men creeping through the woods on either side of a single, long-haired man holding an ancient rifle.

Tipton had something he had to do. But he needed time and they had to think he was still a threat. He looked between the rocks at the clearing. No obvious target.

Hoping there were only submachine guns on the other side, he stood up for a second, then dropped to his knees. Immediately, small caliber submachine guns rattled away. Bullets peppered the rocks and he dropped to the ground. But, he'd seen the muzzle flashes. He knew their approximate positions.

Make them think he was interested.

He sighted in on one of the positions and touched the trigger. Boom! The sound was still echoing when he slammed a new round in place and touched the trigger again. Boom! Both positions knew Tipton had them zeroed in. They'd either be finding deeper holes or keeping their heads down for a few seconds.

Sam pulled his jacket back on, stuffed the bag of cartridges into a pocket and started down the path, rifle in one hand, coil of fishing leader in the other. He couldn't wait until the flankers showed up. That wouldn't give him enough time.

One end of the heavy, clear plastic fishing leader was wrapped around a stout Juniper at ankle height. The other was tied around a short piece of twig and wedged behind a boulder on the other side of the path. It was hardly a path, more like a vague place to put your feet between rocks. It was barely as wide as his boots. He wondered how Maggie had possibly been able to get the Fredericks down it. The old couple must have had his and hers heart attacks.

Sam looked off the edge to the canyon below. His stomach tightened and a familiar weak feeling attacked his knees, giving them the consistency of guacamole.. He glanced at the nearly invisible fishing leader. Maybe it would work, maybe it wouldn't. He and Longfeather usually used the line to trap jackrabbits, when out camping. Maybe this would trap a human.

He continued to scramble down the path.

He did not look down.

Fifty-four

Fear of heights can be such a bitch! Tipton molded himself to the up-side rocks, doing his best imitation of moss. It was through sheer willpower, he kept going.

When the path leveled out about halfway down the walls, the path split. The left fork followed a narrow, flat shelf protruding out of the canyon wall. The shelf was clearly visible all the way around the canyon.

The other fork left the shelf and worked its way down to the floor of the canyon. Ancient hands had hacked small footholds in the stone. He hadn't been the first in the canyon. The sounds of a happy brook burbled up from below and broke the silence. Aspen and sycamore formed a soft canopy reaching nearly up to the shelf where he was standing. It was a tranquil oasis in a land already filled with tranquility. The Anasazi had chosen well.

At that moment, however, Sam wasn't feeling very tranquil.

"Sam!" Did he imagine his name being whispered by the canyon breeze?

"Over here!" A movement caught his eye.

Longfeather had magically appeared on the shelf at the end of the canyon. He was standing next a rock slide which had broken free from a wide overhang.

The canyon walls above where he stood were water worn, smooth and tan-colored. The rock slide looked as if part of the overhang had let go and crashed down.

Sam glanced down at the trees and when he looked back up, Longfeather was gone again. Then he re-appeared.

When Sam drew close, he saw that there was a small cave opening, a jagged space between fallen rocks. It was barely large enough to let two people through and was nearly invisible behind two small junipers. He squeezed inside, immediately turning to look back up the trail. So far nothing. For the time being, they were safe. He eyed the area outside the cave. Even if they were found, it would take a flame thrower to get them out of their hole. As soon as he had that thought he regretted it. Humvees, machine guns, several helicopters! These guys didn't appear to be working on a budget.

The light reached inside just far enough for Sam to see May Frederick crumpled on the floor weeping quietly. She looked up as he entered. Her eyes were red and questioning. Frank Frederick and Charley Yee were barely visible in the soft glow of a kerosene lantern towards the back of the cave. Maggie and Roberta stood in the half-light watching Sam with expectant looks on their faces.

Why, Tipton wondered, was he always the one they looked at when the obvious question was once again, "What Now?"

He looked around. Counting noses.

"Hey!" He yelled over at Longfeather who was already exploring. "Where's the other guy? The Indian in the hat?"

"Dunno!" Longfeather re-appeared from the dark. "When the RV was nailed, Frederick said he grabbed his rifle and bag and bailed out. That's the last anyone saw of him."

Tipton shrugged. Hitchhiking always had its dangers but this was ridiculous. He couldn't blame the guy for disappearing to let the white people kill each other.

"Let's barricade the entrance and set up a defensive perimeter," Tipton said.

The two men wrestled large rocks to the entrance, piling them up in a wall slightly more than head high. It reached less than half way to the top of the opening. They left two small openings, one higher than the other, on opposite sides of the wall.

"I'll take the right one!" Tipton said as he poked his rifle through, checking the field of fire. Longfeather would be aiming the other direction, covering the field Sam wasn't.

Listening intently, Tipton heard nothing. The canyon was so quiet, it would be difficult for men to move without disturbing the peace. They apparently hadn't discovered he had left the rim.

The duffel bag produced a worn pair of binoculars and he leaned against the rock wall to study the situation outside. It was a good-news, bad-news situation. The bad news was the bad guys up on the canyon wall would have clear shots at the cave entrance from practically anywhere. The good news was they'd have a helluva hard time getting down to the cave.

Tipton trained the glasses on the path. It was in plain view all the way up. First man down was a dead man. To storm the cave, they would have to find another way down. Rappel off the cliffs? Maybe. Sam scanned the cliff walls. He'd hate to be dangling on a rope in plain view of a guy who had just thumped one of their men on the melon from two-hundred yards. Gentlemen, we need another volunteer.

Of course, it wouldn't be necessary to storm the cave. The Pitacho Irregulars weren't going anywhere. The bad guys could just sit and wait. Fly in provisions and wait. Time was definitely not on the side of the good guys.

"Girls?" Tipton said, "Do me a favor and keep a watch out here? I need to look around."

Maggie stepped forward and rested the Winchester carbine in one of the openings.

Sam headed for the light of the kerosene lantern at the back of the cave. The afternoon's light faded to nothing the further he got from the entrance until darkness was complete. It compressed the yellow light from Charley's lantern into a tight ball. Little or no light reached the high cavern ceiling.

He looked around. Longfeather was elsewhere exploring their stronghold. The glow from his flashlight was the only clue to his whereabouts. Sam knew he was one unhappy Indian. Joseph Longfeather felt the same way about caves that Sam Tipton felt about high places. Apaches weren't meant to be in tight, dark spaces.

Frederick was in near ecstasy as he slowly circled a metal case which sat on a homemade altar. The flickering, yellow light encouraged a dull metallic gleam to escape from under a heavy layer of dust. Charley Yee was on his knees chanting quietly. Frederick looked ready to kiss the object any minute himself.

A chest-high effigy stood to the left of the altar. With some imagination, it could be seen as a man. It was a man but it wasn't. It was a typical Charley Yee sculpture…a wildly disturbed kachina. Everything out of proportion and non-Indian.

This man-like image had big eyes, closed as if sleeping. Oversized head, out of proportion with the spindly, pot-bellied body. Although layered with dust, it looked as if Charley had made it of leather. Crude stitching ran up its middle and around the head above the eyes. Was this one of Charley's gods? The old Indian certainly had a vivid imagination. And a weird idea of what a deity looked like.

A long, crudely-fashioned wooden shipping crate stood against the cave wall on the other side of the altar. The top lay beside it. Inside lay a long, dust-caked metal cylinder the size of a soft water tank. Some sort of pressure cylinder? A big one. Nearly shoulder high. Perhaps nitrogen? Or oxygen? Another desert treasure had found a home with Charley Yee. The old Indian was at least as much a scrounger as Sam was. Sam, however, hadn't made it a religion. Or had he?

Focusing his attention on the dull silver cube on the altar, Tipton felt his hair stand on end. Nothing about it looked familiar. Nothing except the fluorescent circle of triangles on its front. The universal symbol for radiation. Tipton was about to ask Charley where in the hell he got the object, when Longfeather called. His voice was quiet and ominous. It floated out of the dark on the other side of the cavern barely above a whisper.

"Sam...I think you'd better come look at this!"

Sam's flashlight painted a path ahead. The floor of the cave was smooth and nearly level, but littered with fractured rocks and boulders. The slide which had sealed the cave had been violent.

It was difficult to gauge distance in the dark, but Longfeather appeared to be on the other side of an area nearly the size of a football field. It was a huge cavern! Periodically flicking his light upward he saw stalactites hanging from the ceiling. Sam recognized the signs. The cave was all that remained of a much larger cavern. Once it had been buried deep in the earth. Stalactites don't form that close to the surface. They need slowly seeping ground water to form. These were dry. Dead. They had stopped growing millenniums ago.

His flashlight picked up reflections on the floor. Silver reflections. Something returned light at his feet and he kicked it. Torn, wrinkled aluminum!

Longfeather's light was a short distance ahead.

"Sam?" Longfeather's voice was close.

"Yeah. I'm right here!"

Sam spoke as he stepped around a corner and shined his light in Longfeather's direction.

"Ho...l...y Shit!" Tipton's light flashed rapidly back and forth. Reflections were everywhere. It couldn't be!

He cursed the narrow beam of the flashlight. It whittled away at the darkness only a sliver at a time. He wanted to flick a wall switch and flood the scene with a billion watts of incandescent understanding, but he focused the light in one spot and walked forward. He had to place his hand on it. He had to feel it. Otherwise he wasn't going to believe it.

The aluminum was cool. And surprisingly undamaged. The airplane's nose, where it protruded under the stalactite, was still smooth and rounded. It didn't look as if it had been moving very fast when it rammed its nose under the hanging piece of stone.

Moving his light up, Tipton could see the aircraft had been moving fast enough, however. Shattered glass and wrinkled metal was all that remained of the pilot's windshield. Sam shined a light into the cockpit. From where he stood, he could see nothing but dust and stone.

Longfeather's light glowed through the dusty windscreen on the co-pilot's side. He was inside, moving forward.

Sam flailed at the darkness with his flashlight. Frustrated! As it swept the incredible scene, it was like examining a large painting through a soda straw. He had to keep remembering the last tiny piece of the puzzle as the flashlight revealed the next. And the next.

The airplane lay on its belly, impaled by the stalactite. It was obviously a Twin Beech, a military C-45, light twin-engine transport. Both outboard wing panels were missing. Jagged metal stubs showed the amputations had been traumatic. One engine was twisted nearly off the airplane, its main case split open. The engine lay like an eviscerated robot, its life blood pooling in various fractured cavities. The gentle aroma of motor oil barely tainted the still air. It mixed with the sweet smell of cool, clean stone and gave texture to the darkness.

A propeller lay like a dead spider, blades curled in on themselves like stiff, withered limbs.

Joseph Longfeather broke the silence. He spoke from inside the fuselage, his voice sounding hollow, "Check this out!"

The fuselage was nearly intact and the darkness inside the open door was even blacker than that in the rest of the cavern. The door was twisted. It had been forcefully levered open a long time ago. Probably while Charley Yee was still a strong, young man.

Had he been searching for his gods?

Sam ducked inside and his flashlight revealed a vacant, dust-covered interior. Only the pair of seats against the cockpit bulkhead were installed.

Longfeather was leaning through the narrow cockpit door. Hearing Sam approach, he moved aside.

"Take a look." Longfeather was not smiling.

A small, gold oak leaf caught Sam's flashlight. The pilot had been a major. Sam's eyes flowed down the tattered, dusty sleeve. It reached toward throttles that commanded nothing. They were pushed forward against the stops. Bone white reflections showed where a hand had once been wrapped around them. Over the years, disintegrating fingers had slowly settled between the knobbed levers until the collection of bones was no longer a hand. Just a fragmented puzzle which would never be reassembled. Its last move had been to save the airplane. Full power hadn't been enough.

The copilot's half of the cockpit was complete. Ready to fly again. That could not be said of the pilot's side.

Sam slid into the copilot's seat.

His light moved slowly, his eyes examining every detail. The windshield and instrument glass threw distracting reflections at odd angles. As he moved the light, the reflections moved. He steadied his light under the instrument panel on what was left of the pilot's feet. The brown shoes on the rudder pedals gave him a crude time frame. Officially, the Air Force had gone to black shoes in late 1947. They were brown before that.

His light stopped in the middle of the sunken chest. A name tag said "J. Williams." The deceased now had a name.

The deceased, however, had no head. Where there should have been a gleaming skull was hard, yellowish stone. Behind the tip of the stalactite Tipton could make out scattered white fragments. A few patches of black hair. When it happened, it hadn't been pretty!

Death had come in an instant. Major J. Williams hadn't even completed his last thought.

Neither Tipton nor Longfeather said a word until standing back outside the fuselage. Longfeather shut his light off and Tipton pointed his down to keep the glare to a minimum.

"Looks like Charley's gods came airmail," Sam said quietly.

Longfeather took a long time to answer. Tipton couldn't see his face in the dark. "I wonder if he saw the cave coming?" His words were quiet. His mind was somewhere else.

Both pilots couldn't help but imagine the last moments. That was part of being a pilot. You always put yourself in the other's place. Would you have done anything differently? Could you have saved the plane?

"I wonder where he was headed?" Tipton played the light on the crumpled fuselage looking for clues. Numbers and insignias were the key to the universal military code. Everything military was identified.

The light played across a wrinkled white star. There were no red and white bars on either side. Another time clue. Red bars would have dated it after September, 1947. Sam liked military trivia. It stuck in his head whether he wanted it to or not. That's one reason the block letters between the star and the tail caused him to hesitate.

At first Sam was amused. It was a whimsical coincidence. Then he suddenly snapped his head in the direction of Charley Yee and Frank Frederick. Their light was barely visible across the cavern. He remembered all of Charley's stories about his gods arriving from the heavens. He remembered his vivid descriptions of roaring gods with fierce breaths.

Then, Sam Tipton remembered what stood on either side of the altar.

The effigy stood on one side, the long metal cylinder on the other. It couldn't be!

His light played on the fuselage again. Even after a half century in the dry air, the letters were barely faded. He read them again and looked back in Charley Yee's direction. His hand went out and grabbed Longfeather's arm to get his attention. He didn't have to.

"I've got it," Longfeather's tone was one of disbelief.

The second line of print on the side of the fuselage identified the location of the air base which had been missing an airplane for half a century.

Pieces of a historical puzzle fell into place in Sam Tipton's mind. That Air Force base had been missing some very important cargo in addition to losing an airplane. Questions answered. Questions raised.

The identifying stenciling on the side of the long-dead airplane said "Roswell Army Air Field, Roswell, New Mexico."

Fifty-five

The blond Austrian stooped down and picked up a spent shell casing from among the rocks on the canyon edge. He recognized it and frowned. 7.62 Russian. Curious!

"They are gone," he shouted to the others.

Yardley was first up. He scanned the canyon in both directions as he walked through the rocks. "They couldn't have gotten past us." He spoke to no one in particular. His eyes continued searching. There was no place to hide, so where had they gone? He examined the canyon edge and saw it. A small path, nothing more than a narrow stripe of worn dirt, threading its way between the rocks and down.

"Binoculars!" A pair of olive-drab, rubber-coated binoculars with huge objective lenses was thrust into his waiting hand. He could count the blades of grass on the far wall, if he so desired. He rapidly swept the walls and the bottom of the canyon. Where were they? He saw nothing. They had to be hiding in the trees against the bottom of the wall at his feet. It was the only blind spot in the canyon. His eyes rapidly swept the perimeter of the box canyon.

"Gunther, take three men and circle around to the other side. We need to be able to see both walls."

Without a word the Austrian signaled two men. Ignoring his painful leg, the muscular mercenary jogged back the direction they had come for a second and returned with a black, fiberglass golf case over his shoulders.

"I take this to the other side." With that he was gone, hidden by the rocks and trees which fringed the canyon. The two others followed single file.

"Anderson," Yardley said glancing around for the Washington bureaucrat. He spotted him leaning against a rock. Even though the air was cool, sweat glistened on Anderson's forehead and he was breathing hard. He was out of shape and being over a mile above sea level made it worse. He was speaking into a sat-phone. Yardley was too far away to hear what he said. Whatever it was, it wasn't making him happy. Probably calling his boss.

Yardley thought back to Foster Ward, now Mr. Secretary, Anderson's boss and this project's benefactor. He'd never liked the guy. Actually, it wasn't so much that he didn't like the person, he just didn't like the type. Lots of words and attitude. Very judgmental. Self-aggrandizement but no self-involvement. He would have liked to have seen Ward here out on the canyon rim. Ex-Marine or not. Anderson had tossed his lunch once already. Seeing the second guy's head explode all over him had done the trick. Ward wouldn't have fared any better. The thought pissed Yardley off. Here they were fifty miles from nowhere, chasing a crazed Indian, a drunk ex-agent and a man they thought they had killed once already. And for what? So the goddamned bureaucrat, Ward, could live like a king when he retired? Ward should have been in on this one. He needed to earn his retirement.

Yardley swung his glasses in the direction Gunther's party had gone. He caught glimpses of them where the trees thinned to scrub oak at the canyon's edge. Then the binoculars began wandering through the trees on the canyon's floor.

"Sam Tipton, where are you?" Yardley whispered to himself, as he scrutinized the canyon.

Kwan had his own binoculars to his eyes. They were trained on Richard Yardley. Periodically, he'd check on the Austrian's progress. Satisfied he knew where everyone was, he went back to working on the rifle in his lap. The telescopic sight slid smoothly into its machined grooves. A small, leather-bound tool kit appeared in his hands. Besides opening locks, the pouch had the necessary Allen wrenches for tightening the scope in position.

He glanced up again to make certain no one had moved. He already knew what Richard Yardley didn't know. He'd been in position on the edge when Sam Tipton slowly shuffled down the narrow path. He'd seen him disappear into an unseen opening in the end of the canyon. An excellent defensive position. But no way out.

A few yards to his right, he could clearly see the charred remains of a campfire. It was on the very tip of a rock point sticking out into the clear afternoon air. Charley Yee had left many signs behind indicating the precarious perch on the Mogollon Rim was his. His signature triangles were edged deeply into nearby rocks. The campfire remains sat in the intersection of three triangles, where their tips met. It looked as if Charley had been coming there for many, many years. Perhaps his entire life.

Kwan Yamuchi removed his sunglasses, carefully polished them with a clean handkerchief, and settled back to wait for the next move.

"Let's go get some answers!" Sam said. He flashed his light around the crumpled fuselage one more time and walked carefully around the jagged wing stub. He drew as straight a line as the rocks would allow back to where Charley Yee and Frank Frederick were still huddled together.

"Frederick! Charley!" Sam's voice echoed off the walls. He hadn't meant to make it so loud, but he wanted answers. He was trapped in a cave with men outside waiting to kill him and he still didn't know why.

Both old men looked up, their surprise showing. Frederick had dusted off the shining cube. It now looked to be made of brushed stainless steel. A hinged panel broke the smooth expanse of one side. The radiation warning sign looked even more ominous, how that it was clean.

"Okay, Frederick, you first!" Sam stood nose-to-nose with the ex-agent. He noticed the old man looked energized. Almost excited. Strange, considering all he'd been through and the situation they were in. His wife definitely showed the strain. She had collapsed against a boulder, completely spent. She was no longer weeping.

"Just what is this Cobalt Blue thing and what the hell does it have to do with me?"

Frank Frederick tried to look defiant, but failed. His eyes flashed over to the stainless steel rectangle. He said nothing.

"There are some very determined people out there with guns and I want to know why!" Sam fought the urge to grab the old man by the shoulders and shake him. "We stand a very good chance of getting ourselves killed and I think you know why.

"Is this Cobalt Blue?" Sam pointed at the rectangle. His eyes were stabbing at Frederick.

The old man hesitated. Then dropped his head and nodded. His body slumped in resignation.

"What is it?" Sam looked at the unit carefully, but had no idea at all what it could be. All he knew was that he wasn't happy being around something he couldn't identify which bore a radiation warning symbol.

"It's a trigger," Frederick said quietly. His eyes lost focus, as a lifetime of yesterdays floated to the surface of his thoughts.

"What kind of a trigger? If it came in on that airplane back there," Sam jerked his thumb in the direction of J. William's final resting place, "it's been here a long time. It has to be really old technology. What makes it worth all the commotion outside?"

"Well," began Frederick in the drawn-out tone that says a long story is just beginning, "it's not exactly just a trigger. It's a lot more than that.

"Back in 'forty-seven, I was a fresh young Agent-In-Charge at Los Alamos nuclear labs."

He sat down on a low boulder. What energy he had was gone. He was once again a tired, old man.

"I was assigned to run the security detail for Cobalt Blue, because it was going to be transported to Utah and destroyed."

"Why destroy it?" Sam asked. He was sitting opposite Frederick. Longfeather and Roberta hovered over the two, listening. "And, if its not just a trigger, what is it?"

Frederick spoke without looking at them.

"This was just at the time they were going from atomic to hydrogen bombs and they weren't sure what kind of triggers they needed, so they built some test units. This was one of those units.

"To be sure they worked, they built the proof-of-concept units with a small, thermo-nuclear charge attached so it actually would explode. So...." Frederick hesitated and looked over at Sam, "I guess this actually is a bomb, but a very small one."

Longfeather piped up, "Just exactly how small, is small?"

"About a tenth the size of the one used at Hiroshima," Frederick answered.

"Damn!" Whispered Longfeather. "That's still a pretty big bang."

Tipton nodded, "That's a lot more than a nuclear firecracker, but what makes it so important to the guys outside? For this amount of effort, they could just as easily grab a more powerful warhead from some ex-soviet missile site."

"For one thing," Frederick continued, "this is a very simple device. It's all mechanical. They made it that way on purpose. One of the technicians showed me all they had to do was slip a normal forty-millimeter anti-aircraft shell in it, set the timer and it would go off. The shell is stored in there." He pointed at a long rectangular compartment screwed to one side of the cube, ruining its otherwise perfect symmetry.

"But that's not why everyone wants it." Frederick continued. Longfeather couldn't contain himself, "Who is everyone?"

Sam held up a finger, "We'll get to that in a minute.

"So, what makes this thing so popular?"

Frederick shifted position, trying to get more comfortable, "The reason it was going to be destroyed rather than used, is because it's cased in cobalt. When they first built it, they didn't realize how dangerous cobalt was to use in a bomb casing."

Sam was ahead of him and looked up at Longfeather who had questions written all over him. Tipton explained, "The isotopes of cobalt have incredibly long half lives. Wherever this thing was detonated, an area a couple miles square, or bigger, would be so radioactive it couldn't be entered for something like ten thousand years. It would, for all purposes, cease to exist.

"Do you remember how General MacArthur wanted to eliminate the Chinese threat during Korea by dropping a string of cobalt bombs around China? There would have been a barrier two hundred miles wide they couldn't cross for thousands of years. He and Truman really got into a pissing contest over it! That's one reason MacArthur was canned."

Turning back to Frederick, Tipton said, "How did it end up in a C-45 stuffed in a cave in Arizona with a very dead major named Williams?"

"Williams?" The name obviously tripped a long forgotten memory, "John Williams?"

Tipton nodded.

"I'm not surprised," Frederick said. "I don't know how it wound up here, but Williams and the trigger disappeared the night it was supposed to be transferred. He was in charge of the military side of the detail."

Frederick lost what little color he had, as he said, "I was relieved of my post and one of the largest, and most secretive, searches in FBI history took place. It simply vanished without a clue. Now I see why."

"So how did those guys out there find out about this thing?" Tipton asked. "As far as that goes. How did you find it?"

"I saw the box at Charley's," Frederick replied, "I then made a couple of phone calls to Washington trying to sell it. I told them I had Cobalt Blue. That was a mistake. I know that now."

Frederick seemed to age before Sam's eyes.

Then, his eyes flashed and suddenly re-focused on Sam, "If you can help me get this out of here. I'll give each of you," he looked at Longfeather and Sam individually, "a million dollars."

Longfeather started laughing. "A million bucks? How?"

"I have a buyer. A Japanese mercenary who was going to pay me three million dollars for it." He conveniently forgot the exact amount negotiated. "I'll give you two million."

"A terrorist would have a field day with something like this!" Sam said. "He could put in the trunk of a Toyota, park it in front of the White House, and 'bam! You couldn't cross the Fourteenth Street bridge for another ten thousand years."

"It could be used anywhere. The Panama Canal. Or Norfolk seaport. Or NORAD HQ." Longfeather intoned. "Or that pesky neighbor down the street with the dog that always dumps on your front yard. Lots of convenient uses."

"We'll pass on the two million. In fact, right now," Sam started, "I'd personally guarantee you two million, in exchange for a way out of this mess."

He looked over at the girls still playing watchdogs at the entrance. Maggie had the binoculars to her eyes.

Longfeather laughed, "I don't know, Sam. A million bucks would let us paint the Stinson!"

"And then there is this thing." Sam Tipton stood and walked over to the effigy next to the altar. He leaned over and played the flashlight on it, while dusting it off. Under the dust, the covering had a smooth, worn texture like that on a well-used basketball. He couldn't decide whether it was leather or some sort of synthetic. He looked for seams. Other than the crude stitching up the belly and around the head, there were none.

"Charley! Did you make this?" Tipton asked.

The old Indian had been drifting somewhere out on the edges of the ozone layer when Sam brought him back to Earth. "What? Make what?"

Sam pointed at the effigy.

Longfeather interrupted before Charley could answer.

"Sam, look at this!" Longfeather was over at the long wooden crate leaning against the wall. He had dusted off the top end of the long metal cylinder inside. A small amber light on top the cylinder could be seen to be slowly flashing. He dusted further and a narrow, flush-mounted viewing port or window, surfaced.

He pointed at the cylinder and asked Charley, "Where did this come from?"

"It came the same as my Gods." Charley Yee pointed back towards the aircraft wreckage as he answered.

Longfeather looked at Sam and said, "Okay, so we've got Cobalt Blue and two crates in the airplane when it took off. One crate with this cylinder in it and the other with this dummy."

As he spoke, Longfeather leaned over shining his light in what appeared to be an inspection port.

At first he jumped, then he cupped his hand around the window to better direct the light, and let out a long low whistle. "I don't believe...!"

He was interrupted by Maggie's insistent voice breaking the silence. She spoke without taking her eyes from the binoculars she had trained on the path down the canyon wall.

"Boys, it looks like we have company."

Fifty-six

Richard Yardley had gotten his report from Gunther on the other side. He couldn't see anyone in the bottom of the canyon. The trees were too thick.

They were going to have to go down.

He spoke into his radio, "Okay, we're going to send a patrol down. Cover them."

He nodded at two aggressive-looking young men. The taller of the two had introduced himself as Dane something or other. Yardley had already forgotten his last name. He remembered the first name only because "Dane" fit him so well. He was mid-twenties with short blond hair and pale blue eyes. Lean and muscular with a distinct Nordic look. He'd washed out of SEAL training and had an eager out-to-prove-something look about him. That made Yardley a little nervous.

Yardley's team had forsaken any effort at the desert-casual look. They now wore black nylon combat vests hung with magazine pouches, knives, flashlights and smooth, baseball-sized grenades. Yardley had donned a similar vest. This was combat, not intelligence work. The time to go from covert to overt action had come.

Each of the two men glanced quickly over the edge. Seeing it clear, Dane stepped quickly and lightly onto the path. He moved like a well-trained karate boxer—quick and decisive. No wasted motion. His partner joined him as soon as they were twenty feet apart.

They handled the treacherous path more quickly and easily than any who had gone before. They were in their athletic prime. They were trained for this kind of work. A lot of taxpayers' money had gone into making them good at what they did, and the same taxpayers would have taken their money back had they known these two had gone over to the other side.

The black-suited men looked incongruous shuffling down the narrow, dusty path, framed by yellow-tan canyon walls and stunted juniper. Alien warriors out of place. Out of time. The path belonged to moccasins and buckskin, not nylon and jungle boots. Their eyes clicked back and forth, watching their surroundings through the sights of their submachine guns. They were seeing everything. They knew other eyes, Gunther's men on the other side and Yardley behind them, were watching. Being point on patrol was always exciting. Dane welcomed the rush. Both were young. They didn't know any better.

Yardley glanced over the edge, Anderson at his elbow. He looked across the canyon at Gunther and his two men. Where ever Tipton was, he wasn't getting out.

Sam Tipton looked over at Longfeather. "Well, do we try to stop them at the edge?"

Longfeather was squinting as he studied the scene outside his shooting slot.

"Yeah. We don't know if they know where we are, but they'll figure it out sooner or later. If we can keep them out of the canyon, they can't get in range with their pop guns."

Tipton watched the two figures on the top end of the path. "One thing is certain, if they get down here, we can't stop a rush with single-shot rifles."

Tipton took his jacket off and again rolled it up. He stuffed it into the narrow slot they had left when building the wall. The old rifle laid on it, he squinted against the sun. It was setting quickly and they were looking almost directly into another gorgeous Arizona sunset. If it hadn't been such a desperate situation, he would have admired the way the sunset had bronzed the entire inside of the canyon.

He sensed, rather than saw, Longfeather take up a similar position in the other slot. Maggie stood on a rock, her head barely above the rock wall, binoculars to her eyes. She was constantly scanning the edges of the canyon and the path. Flashes on the left wall caught her eye. She focused. A blond man ducked into the brush. At least one other was with him.

"I see at least two on the left wall almost directly across from where the path starts on the other side," Maggie reported. "I caught glimpses of two, maybe three others at the top of the path behind the two coming down. All of them are wearing the same black jackets as the guys you're looking at."

She re-focused on the two coming down the path. They were a third of the way down and moving quickly, but carefully. The front one wore a black baseball cap. The other had close-cropped brown hair. Both had stubby submachine guns in their hands.

"You have those two on the path?" she asked.

"Yep!" Sam spoke without taking his eyes off the rifle sights. The fishing line trap was at about three-hundred yards. That's where he set his sights.

Even as they came into his pre-determined range, he saw the lead figure stoop down.

He pushed the trigger forward and felt it click.

Ivan's rifle was ready to speak.

The trap might have worked with lesser-trained troops. Part of the taxpayers' money, however, had gone into training these men to look for mines and booby traps. The young man named Dane caught the faintest glimmer across the path at ankle level.

Instantly a clinched fist flashed in the air. His partner stopped immediately and dropped into a crouch. His MP5 was up on his shoulder and ready to fire.

The blonde youth carefully looked around rocks at both ends of the fishing leader and laughed. No explosives. No booby trap. It was simply meant to trip them.

Very amateurish.

A knife was whipped out of a chest sheath and he bent down. The knife flashed through the fishing line as if it didn't exist. Standing up, he reached across his chest to slip the knife back into its sheath. He was looking the length of the canyon as he did. He couldn't know he was looking directly at Sam Tipton at the exact instant Tipton touched the trigger on Ivan's long rifle. The young mercenary named Dane something or other saw the flash. If it is true, you see the bullet with your name on it, then he also saw the slug coming. But only for a fraction of a second.

He probably never felt the bullet slice cleanly through his right wrist as he reached across his chest, the knife still in his hand. The slug didn't slow until it slammed into a hand grenade fastened to his vest.

"Oh, God!" Maggie whispered. She had been looking directly at the black-suited figure when the grenade went off. Sam heard her words before the short "krump" of the grenade worked its way down the canyon.

Even as she watched, the second figure, the one with short brown hair, was flung backwards from the force of the explosion. Maggie couldn't see the hundreds of slashes and tears throughout his young body. The tiny fragments of tightly-wrapped wire inside the grenade had done their job. Both figures toppled off the path, bouncing repeatedly off the canyon walls.

Neither uttered a sound on the way down.

The sounds of their bodies crashing through the trees below briefly broke the silence.

"**Yardley! Did you** see that?" Gunther's incredulous voice crackled in Yardley's radio. "Do they have some sort of rocket launcher?"

Yardley didn't immediately answer. Seeing one of his men literally cut in half by an explosion had caught him by surprise.

"Where'd that come from?" He finally replied.

"I don't know...wait!" Gunther interrupted himself.

"One of my guys says he saw a muzzle flash down at the bottom of the rock slide at the end of the canyon."

Yardley crept to the edge and focused on the rock slide.

At first he saw nothing, then one of Gunther's men stood up, unknowingly making himself a target. This would give Yardley something to look at.

"**On the left, just** past the tall pine on the edge," Maggie said quietly from behind the binoculars.

Sam saw the figure standing behind some scrub brush. He must have thought he was invisible. No face. Three-hundred yards. He touched the trigger and the rifle jumped.

He looked up at Maggie. She had her fingers in her ears. She had learned on the first shot.

Gunther jerked his head around as one of his men grunted. He was still falling, blood pumping from his chest, when the booming voice of Ivan's rifle rumbled out of the canyon. The man was dead before the noise that killed him arrived.

Yardley's voice exploded out of the radio. "I see 'em!" He sounded excited. "Give your man a bonus! He was right. Just to the left of the rock slide at the bottom. Right about where those two little trees are."

"Save your bonus money," Gunther replied caustically, "Tipton just killed my man." He was exasperated. Not because a man died but because that put them another man short. Tipton was definitely whittling down the odds. What frustrated the

Austrian even more was that it was of no use to shoot back. Their submachine guns fired nine millemeter pistol rounds. They didn't have the range. And they had lost their M-16's and machine gun when the Humvee burned. But, they weren't completely out of long-range weapons.

He scrambled through the brush to the black, fiberglass golf club case, tripped both latches and threw it open.

The dying sun was absorbed by the dull finish on a shoulder rocket launcher. Designed to kill tanks, it was just as effective at killing people. It nestled in the foam as if it was a custom-made driver and the three projectiles next to it were putters.

"Let's go!" he called to his remaining men. One of them he had trained himself. Gunther motioned at the launcher and the man picked it up. Without saying a word, he pulled caps off both ends and began setting the sight. Gunther slid the projectile in the back of the tube, fastening the two fine guidance wires to contacts on the back of the launcher.

The wires guided the missile to the exact spot where the green crosshairs of the laser sight lay.

Gunther spoke into the radio, "It will go next to the entrance so we don't harm your precious Cobalt Blue, it's in there."

The gunner crept up to the edge where he could barely see over. The laser sight rendered the canyon in eerie shades of green, a brilliant neon green cross cut through the middle of the scene. The cross was centered on one of the junipers shielding the cave entrance when he squeezed the trigger.

The gunner with the rocket launcher didn't make it to the canyon edge unobserved. Maggie happened to have her binoculars on that part of the canyon rim, when he quickly came up into a kneeling position and shouldered the launcher.

"I think they have a bazooka or something," she said.

Tipton didn't take a second to react.

"Everyone away from the entrance! Now!" He shouted.

Maggie didn't have time to absorb the words before Sam was dragging her around the corner. He forced her against the cave wall, wrapping his arms around her and putting his body between her and the entrance.

The rocket was absolutely silent while inbound.

The juniper tree on which the laser designator had rested saved some lives that evening. Twisted and gnarled, it had taken root in some loose soil at the base of a rock slab which William's abrupt arrival in the Twin Beech had knocked out of the overhang. Gunther hadn't realized the slab was there. Neither did the gunner.

The missile hit exactly where the laser told it to. It flashed through the small evergreen and exploded against the slab. A foot to the left and it would have gone right into the edge of the cave.

Dust and debris erupted through the partially-blocked cave entrance. The air became a choking mixture of burned explosive and pulverized rock. The primary background noise was an acute ringing in the ears and May Frederick screaming hysterically.

"J!" Tipton's voice rang out, "Check everyone. I'm going to get the shooter before he can reload!"

"Sam! No!" Maggie's cry was wasted. Sam Tipton was already scrambling over the stack of rocks, nearly invisible in the dust.

Tipton was counting on the dust to keep him invisible, but it also stopped him from shooting. They couldn't see in. He couldn't see out. So he crawled out from under the cloud.

He lay against the edge of the rock slide staring at the spot where Maggie had seen the launcher. Then he saw movement. By squinting, he could make out several men moving in the brush right at the edge.

Sights lined up, he touched the trigger.

The rocket was already in the launcher and the gunner was settling the laser on the cloud of dust. As soon as it cleared just enough to see the entrance more clearly, he'd fire another rocket.

Gunther's hands were moving quickly, attaching the guidance leads. He was crouched at the back of the launcher when the gunner suddenly stood bolt upright, as if spring loaded. Before Gunther could reach out and grab him, he teetered briefly on the edge and fell. The launcher was grasped in a death grip. The sound of a rifle shot rolled over him.

That was when Gunther noticed the blood splashed on his own hands and sleeves. The gunner's.

Damn that Sam Tipton!

"Yardley!" He screamed into his radio. "That sonuvabitch just killed Jacobs and the launcher went over the edge with him! Fuck!"

Secretary Foster Ward's words rang in Yardley's ears, "Never underestimate Sam Tipton." Yardley didn't even reach for a weapon as he watched Tipton scrambling back over the pile of rocks at the cave's entrance. He smiled grimly. He had to hand it to Tipton. He was good and getting better, but he wasn't winning. Not by a long shot.

"Get back over here. I've got an idea," he said quietly into the radio.

He focused his binoculars at the other side and saw the Austrian's blond hair being turned gold by the setting sun as he rushed through the sparse woods at the canyon's edge. He noted Gunther was staying a safe distance from the canyon edge.

The sun was barely visible by the time Gunther made it back to Yardley's position. Night had already come to much of the canyon below. Keeping one man on the edge with night-vision goggles to watch the cave, Yardley sat down with the rest.

"Okay, here's what we're going to do," He shifted his eyes from face to face. "Gunther, once it's gotten completely dark, you're going to rappel over the edge directly above the cave. They won't be able to see you coming and you should be able to creep up right alongside the entrance. Then you toss this inside and wait."

As he spoke, he handed Gunther a square, hard-plastic package half the size, but roughly the same shape, as a brief case. On the outside a white stenciled placard identified it as "Explosive-Concussion."

"I'm tired of fucking with this guy," Yardley said. "The rest of us will go over the edge the second the charge goes off and we'll storm the cave and finish off whoever is left."

"When we had them stopped back there before they burned our helicopter, Frederick said they were going to pick-up Cobalt Blue," Yardley said, "so, we can assume this is where they've been hiding it."

"But what about Cobalt Blue?" Anderson protested weakly.

"The charge won't hurt it because it generates a concussion wave but very little shrapnel," Yardley answered, "It'll flatten the shit out of anyone in the cave and kill those close to it, but it won't hurt the assembly."

Gunther looked around in the dark as he stood on the cliff over the cave. His night-vision goggles turned the landscape into an exotic painting. The nylon rope attached to his rappelling harness stood out a brilliant green, straight line to a sturdy pine tree a dozen yards away. He checked the safety knot at the end of the line which would stop him short if something failed.

Equipment check: satchel charge. MP5 submachine gun. Ten magazines in hip pouches. Sig-Sauer automatic in shoulder holster. Two grenades.

He was ready.

"Yardley, I'm getting ready to go. Everyone set?"

Voices checked in on the radio from around the canyon.

"One!"

"Two!"

"Three!"

"Four!"

Gunther grinned. He didn't hear Anderson's voice. He wasn't surprised. Anderson didn't look like the type who would enjoy rappelling into a canyon in the dark, even though the goggles turned the dark into day. That's what made this all so easy. It was night only to those in the cave.

As he backed up to the edge his body teetered out in space, held only by the taut rope. He glanced at the horizon behind him. All that was left of the day were horizontal stripes of orange and yellow running together with purple highlights. He turned and looked down his rope towards the pine tree.

Suddenly, he could no longer see the tree. His view was blocked by a dark figure in a cowboy hat, who wasn't an arm's length away. Gunther hadn't heard a thing. He saw the figure's arm flash forward.

"What was that?" A clattering sound resounded through the silent canyon. Metal on rock. Then silence. It was right outside the cave entrance. Tipton raced up to Longfeather, who had been standing guard at the entrance. Maggie was with him. He listened intently. Total silence. It was so quiet he could have heard a man breathing fifty feet away.

"Maggie! The flashlight. Just flash it," Tipton said.

She held the light over the rocks, punched the button and released it.

For an instant, they were looking directly into the blue eyes of a blond young man wearing a black vest. But something was wrong. The face was upside down.

Pistol in hand, Tipton scaled the wall. Hand covering the lens, he flashed the light again. It was as he thought.

"Longfeather! Your knife!"

Tipton stood up on the wall, swung the knife where he thought the rope would be and jumped down. The sound of his landing was absorbed in the sound of an inert body hitting the ground. Head first.

Maggie stood at the entrance watching through the slots. This time a submachine gun was in her hands. A pair of night-vision goggles was clamped over her head. Sam had joked she looked like a weird welder-woman from outer space. She hadn't found it funny.

Sam, Longfeather and Roberta kneeled around the body of the young man. He lay on his back staring at the ceiling. Sam ran a hand over his eyes to close them and wrapped his fingers around the knife sticking out of the black vest. He pulled.

He held the knife up in the light. Roberta turned her head. "Fairbairn-Sykes dagger!" Sam said admiringly. "Perfect upward placement. Dead-centered the heart. Under the sternum. Very professional.

"The big question is, who did it? Someone out there's on our side!" He looked up at Longfeather.

"The Indian in the hat?" Joseph Longfeather ventured. "Frederick mumbled something about an Indian and how he burned their helicopter. I never really took a close look at the guy in the hat. Did you?

Sam shook his head as he ran his hands over the black vest.

"Makes no difference who he is. Besides cutting down the odds, they gave us some goodies." Sam retrieved the pistol and grenades from the vest. He studied one of the grenades, his light making the word "concussion" glow. He pocketed the grenades and tossed the submachine gun magazines to Maggie.

"This also shows us how serious these guys are." He placed an index finger on the satchel charge clipped to the dead Austrian's belt.

"Folks, it looks to me as if we have no choice but to figure a way out of here and right now," Tipton looked at the others as he spoke. "Sooner or later these guys are going to be coming at us with F-15's or flamethrowers. We've been lucky so far. That won't last forever."

He looked up at Longfeather, "You have any ideas? You've done the most exploring."

"Yeah, I think I do." He paused and shined his flashlight up. The beam was clearly visible in the dust-laden air. "Look at that!"

Everyone looked up and Roberta asked, "Look at what?"

"The dust is moving at a pretty good clip towards the entrance," Longfeather answered. "There's a strong current coming from the back of the cave. Something has bothered me since we found the airplane. Everything is covered with dust. If this was a sealed cavern, there wouldn't be nearly that much dust. I think there's an opening in the back we haven't looked for."

Suddenly the radio attached to the body at their feet spoke.

"Gunther! Gunther are you out there? What's happening. We're rigged and ready to rappel."

Sam fought the urge to delivery Gunther's obituary via radio. Sorry, but little Gunther can't come play right now.

"Okay, that tells us what we need to know. They're coming in," Tipton announced. "Let's hope they don't change radio frequencies. We'll be able to eavesdrop. But we need a way out right now. Longfeather, you're going to be pathfinder. Go check it out. The rest of us will try to hold the fort."

"Nice choice of words," Longfeather said. Then he turned and disappeared in the dark.

Tipton relieved Maggie at the wall. Before he put the night-vision goggles on, he watched Maggie sit down next to May Frederick to comfort her. Frank Frederick sat on the other side, a limp arm cradling his wife's shoulders. Charley was ignoring the entire situation and rocked gently on his knees in front of his gods. The last he saw of Joseph Longfeather was his light disappearing at the back of the cavern where the roof met the floor.

Fifty-seven

Joseph Longfeather would freely admit to wishing he were someplace else. On the surface, the night was his friend. He owned the night. Underground, it was a different matter. Each time he thought it couldn't get any darker, it did.

The smooth ceiling pinched down along the back of the cavern. In most places it came clear down to the floor, meeting at a shallow angle. Then, suddenly, his light bounced back off a square object. Then another. And another. He recognized them immediately. Stone structures which conformed to the wall. Small ancient structures. His people had been there many centuries before.

He flashed a light inside one of the vacant, staring windows. The rooms were small, the sloping ceiling of the cave formed the top and back of the rooms. He looked up. No smoke smudges on the ceiling. They were storage areas. Not dwellings. As the ceiling came down, the air seemed to be moving faster. The air was clean and there was no dust from the rocket attack.

He continued walking, searching the far reaches of the cavern. The ceiling gradually came towards the floor, forcing him to walk stooped over. The small stone structures continued to line the walls but got progressively smaller as the ceiling came down. If he had been able to stand, most would have been no higher than his waist.

Then he felt gravity change direction. The cave floor was sloping gradually down hill. The ceiling stayed parallel to the floor. At one point his boots slipped on the hard stone and he put out a hand to break his fall. The stone was dry and cool.

He could hear his own heart pounding.

Then his light picked out small, straight marks in the floor. Hand chiseled steps. He hadn't been the first to slip.

Then he sensed a change. The air smelled different. It felt different. The roof disappeared upwards into the darkness. Speckles of light overhead caught his attention.

Stars. He was looking at the night sky!

In another few steps, the walls on either side became rough, carefully stacked stone block. He passed a square hole and shined a light inside. A sizable living chamber. Collapsed ceiling timbers laying through the room reflected his light. He swung the light back and forth, walking as quickly as the littered ground would allow. Everywhere he looked on either side were stone dwellings nestled against the rapidly-rising wall. Several yards beyond, his light no longer reflected off a floor. It disappeared into nothingness. He was standing on the edge of a cliff. A half-moon broke from behind a cloud revealing another canyon nearly identical to the one he had left behind.

He took a deep breath of fresh night air and turned around. He began to run. How far was it? A hundred yards? Two hundred? It was too far. Those he'd left behind were running out of time.

"Check in!" The voice on the radio was quiet but demanding. Someone was very much in charge. Sam thought he recognized the voice of the phony geologist from Roberta's. He kept the volume turned down as he stared into the dark. The team checked in.

"One."
"Two."
"Three."
"Four."

The words from the radio were quick. Terse. Very professional.

"Gunther?" The leader's query was short. He knew something was wrong.

"Team, go on my signal. Plan two."

They were coming down. Tipton scanned the canyon rim. He could see nothing. Most likely they'd be coming over the rim closest to the cave, where he couldn't see them.

The moon skipped in and out of a broken cloud layer, alternately throwing silver light and dark shadows. The goggles Sam wore built that light into a mid-day sun. The canyon could hide nothing from Sam Tipton that night. But the attackers were seeing the canyon the same as Sam. The advantage the goggles gave him was surprise. Not vision. They thought he was blind. So, he'd play blind. Until the last second. Where was Longfeather? It seemed he had been gone for an hour. Tipton inched his sleeve up to glance at his watch. The hands leaped out at him, a luminescent green. It had been less than five minutes.

The radio spoke, "Go."

The canyon was so quiet, Sam could hear nylon line quietly singing as it raced through caribiner rings on rappelling harnesses. He counted each pair of boots as they tried unsuccessfully to touch down quietly. A landing butterfly could have been heard in the silence. The sound of Maggie pulling the hammer back on the Winchester next to him took on the sound level of a sledgehammer. The entire canyon was holding its breath as it watched the black-suited figures closing in on the narrow cavern.

"Back, back. Everyone get away from the entrance," Tipton spoke as quietly as possible. He looked around and watched as Roberta herded the Fredericks deeper into the cave. The old man had his arm around his wife. Roberta was prodding Charley Yee. He didn't want to leave.

"Sam!" Maggie tugged at his sleeve. She was pointing back into the cave.

A new light had appeared and was coming their way. It was Longfeather.

Sam whispered to her, "Go see if he's found a way out."

She hesitated, looking out into the canyon. She didn't want to leave Sam.

"Go!" Tipton's voice was harder than usual.

She turned and walked quickly towards Longfeather's light.

Sam clicked the safety off the submachine gun and felt for the magazines in his belt. The two figures he'd seen come over the edge had been joined by others who had landed out of sight. They wouldn't need the radio to communicate. He had been cut out of the loop. Now all he could do was react.

He studied them carefully as they fanned out, creeping slowly towards the cave.

Sam heard the command drift quietly out of the silence, "Now!"

He saw a green phantom make a quick movement. Almost immediately, something metallic clanked on the floor behind him. He jerked his head around. He didn't need the night-vision goggles to spot it. The tiny smoke trail contained minute sparks clearly marking its position as it rolled around on the floor.

"Grenade!" Sam's shout broke the black glass of silence into sharp edged pieces. No place to hide.

Sam took two long steps and scooped up the small metal globe like a shortstop. He had begun counting to himself the instant he saw the airborne sparks. The internal fuse would take five seconds to reach the powder charge. At least one, possibly two, were gone by the time the explosive package was delivered.

"One, one-thousand…"

He got his hand on the lethal baseball.

"Two, one-thousand…."

His arm was still back winding up.

"Three, one-thousand…" The words left his mouth as he continued the follow through on the high, hard throw. Center field to home plate. Anything less wouldn't help.

Four one-thousand was just forming on his lips when the fierce light of the explosion blossomed through the canyon followed by a deafening noise, much louder than the sharp "krump" of a normal grenade. Sam's eardrums protested as the pressure wave hit them. Concussion grenade, he was thinking. They were trying not to destroy Cobalt Blue.

That grenade hadn't reached the ground before it went off and he knew what was coming next. He started running as fast as he dared towards where the other lights were gathered.

The next grenade wouldn't be thrown until the best pitchers in the bad guy's line-up had counted to three one-thousand. There would be no throwing it back. He had to be gone by the time it arrived.

"Sam!" Longfeather was walking quickly towards him. He started to talk, but Tipton cut him off.

"Concussion grenades inbound!" The words had barely left his mouth when two metallic clanks close together resounded from the entrance of the cave.

As if on command, the two men dropped to the ground in unison, their hands over their ears.

Instantly, two closely-spaced explosions filled the cavern. The flash strobed into every crevice and the pressure threatened to take their breath away. Then all that remained was the harsh smell of explosive and ringing ears.

Neither spoke as the two broke into a run in the direction Longfeather had come from.

"J," Tipton started speaking as they ran. This time it was Longfeather's turn to interrupt.

"There's an exit into another canyon on the other side. The others are halfway there by now."

The sound of a submachine gun echoed through the cavern. Sam looked back. He couldn't see the entrance because of a bend in the cave wall. The bad guys weren't shooting at them. They were just hosing down the area in case the grenades had missed anything.

Tipton's last thought as he stooped into a crab-like shuffle through the low cave, was about those they'd left behind. He wondered how Charley Yee's gods had fared.

The grenades had barely gone off before Yardley was against the cliff next to the cave entrance. He reached over the stack of rocks barricading the entrance holding his MP5 in one hand. He held the trigger down, his hand sweeping back and forth until until it was empty. Nine-millimeter bullets ricocheted endlessly around in the front part of the cave.

Two men dove over the wall into the cave while empty brass cases were still clinking against the rocks. Yardley slammed a fresh magazine into his weapon, slapped the bolt back and scrambled after them.

The cave was dark. And quiet. Their night-vision goggles saw the veil of dust but nothing else. All three stayed with their backs to the wall. Waiting. Listening.

The green cloud in their vision moved rapidly out the entrance. In less then a minute, they could see the inside of the cave as far as the moonlight from the entrance would let them. There was no light anywhere in the cave. If there had been, their goggles would have built it into bonfire intensity. The far reaches were black. And quiet as death.

Then Yardley saw a subtle light. Tiny. Then it was gone. Then back again. Something flashing rhythmically on the far wall. Something mechanical. A bomb? He took a chance and flashed his light briefly in that direction. The blinking light was on top of a long cylinder in a wooden crate against the wall.

There were no sounds. No movement. The cave appeared empty. Yardley wasn't willing to make that assumption. He signaled at the other two. They separated, each going deeper into the cave against diverging walls. If there were others, they would find them.

Minutes passed. Finally, his radio spoke.
"One! Clear!"
"Two! Clear, but there's an old airplane crash over here." A

flash of light identified his position.

"Everyone in!" Yardley barked into the radio. Instantly, the remaining black-vested figures scrambled over the rocks. The last one turned and stationed himself at the entrance, submachine gun at the ready.

Yardley switched on his flashlight, removing his goggles as he did. The others did the same.

"Get a light going in here," Yardley barked.

In seconds a powerful battery lantern was throwing long shadows against the high walls.

One of the shadows was almost perfectly square. Yardley walked in its direction. The lantern light gave the silver of the rectangular case a dull yellow cast. The triangles on its side vibrated in the light, they were so fluorescent.

Yardley knew instantly he was looking at what they had come for. Cobalt Blue! They had it!

"You!" He grabbed a black vest. "Get back up and bring Anderson down. Tell him we hit pay dirt, but don't let him fall off that damn trail. Put these on him." Yardley thrust night-vision goggles into his hands.

Yardley had done a quick inspection of Cobalt Blue's silver case and was just walking over to the cylinder with the flashing amber light when one of his men rushed up.

"I went over that airplane with a fine-tooth comb, boss. It's an old Air Force C-45 and not as damaged as you'd expect. What's left of the pilot is still in it."

Yardley thought for a minute, "Any identifying unit markings on the aircraft?" He expected the reply to be Los Alamos. Or White Sands. He did not expect he answer he got.

"Yessir, Roswell Army Air Field, Roswell, New Mexico."

Yardley was surprised and he thought back to the records he'd read on Cobalt Blue. He remembered the year the records said it had disappeared. July, nineteen-forty-seven.

Roswell, New Mexico! Damn, Yardley thought. Nineteen-forty-seven was a big year in Roswell's past, as well. Probably the biggest year it would ever have. It was still making headlines a half-century later. He started fitting historical facts together and his mind conjured up images. Images too fantastic to be believed.

Yardley's eyes followed the young soldier's arm down to where it rested on the short, vaguely man-shaped statue. Yardley looked at the sculpture closer. Then he squatted down and played his light on it. He touched it. Unusual covering. He looked at his own fingertips as they came away from the dusty skin. He didn't know what he expected to see, but it felt strange.

He played his light on the stitching which zig-zagged up its belly. He'd seen the pattern before. Mortuary stitching. Heavy thread. Wide stitch pattern not unlike that on a baseball. Also used in closing autopsies. His mind made some more historical connections. Outlandish connections.

His head snapped around, his eyes homing in on the small amber light atop the cylinder leaning against the back wall of the cave. It answered by not changing its slow, rhythmic beat. It wasn't flashing so much as it would build in intensity, then drop back until nearly invisible, only to build again. He noticed it was only slightly out of sync with his own breathing. He looked at the statue again. Or what he had thought was a statue. More connections were made. He was breathing quickly. The altitude? Or the excitement of what he was thinking?

Standing, he stepped quickly to the cylinder in the crate. Someone had already brushed much of the dust away from the top. Using the forearm of his jacket, he wiped a flush-mounted, dark glass or plastic panel clean. He squatted again, putting his light against the panel. Much of the light bounced back, making it impossible to see past the glare. He cupped his hand around the lens, capturing the light so it all went inside.

He placed his own eyes against the glass.

At first he saw nothing. Then...

"Shit!" He blurted, as he involuntarily jumped, falling backward into a sitting position.

He stared at the cylinder.

"Yardley, what're you doing?"

Yardley looked around, his eyes slow to focus. Anderson was standing over him. The lantern behind formed a dust-halo completely around Anderson's outline.

"Yardley!" Anderson repeated.

For a second Yardley didn't respond. Then he blinked and a wide, incredulous smile split his face.

"Get on the phone to Ward! Right now! Tell him to screw Cobalt Blue! We've just hit the jackpot of the century. Maybe of all time!" Yardley's voice got increasingly excited as he spoke.

"Call him, dammit! You absolutely won't believe what I've

just seen!" He scrambled to his feet and yanked the phone out of Anderson's hand, which still trembled. The phone glistened with sweat. The bureaucrat had not enjoyed his night-time stroll into the canyon.

Yardley looked at the phone. The "out-of-service" light flashed back at him.

"Dammit! Oh...wait...! It has to be the cave. It won't let the phone see the satellite. Let's go." He walked quickly towards the entrance Anderson in a breathless ambling jog next to him.

As he walked, Yardley slowly shook his head from side to side while quietly repeating, "Damn! Damn! Damn! Damn...!"

Breaking rhythm for a second, Yardley barked at one of his men, "Get the others and carry that stuff out of here!" He pointed at the general area of the altar. "And be damn careful!"

Longfeather and Sam Tipton caught up with the others just after they'd made it into the cliff dwellings. The moon cast eerie shadows, making the old stone buildings appear young, their infirmities hidden in shadow.

The moon also outlined Frank Frederick where he leaned against a wall, coughing. His inhaler was in his mouth, his wife at his side.

Tipton put the submachine gun in Longfeather's hand, "Watch the tunnel. I'll check on the others."

The answer was a quiet grunt.

Maggie appeared out of the shadows. Her arms flashed out and locked around Sam's chest. Her hair still smelled of strawberries. Dusty strawberries, Tipton noted.

She said nothing. Just squeezed.

"I'm okay," Sam finally said. He felt her head against his chest.

"What about the others," he asked.

Maggie finally let go and stepped back.

She said, "They're okay. The Fredericks are really tired and I doubt if Mrs. Frederick will ever cry again, she used up so many tears."

She looked around, silently counting noses, "Where's Charley?"

"I don't know!" Sam said, suddenly alarmed.

"Oh, no!" Maggie exclaimed. "I haven't seen him since we got here."

"Damn, that crazy...He probably went back after 'his gods'!" Sam was not pleased.

He turned and started past Joseph Longfeather, then stopped. "Get them out of here. I'll be back in a minute. I have to go find Charley." He paused long enough to take the machine pistol from Longfeather's hand and was gone.

Longfeather called quietly after him, "Keep a hand on the left wall."

The distance back seemed shorter. His left hand skipped lightly down the cool stone wall. No light. No reason to let the bad guys know where he was. Pure black. But the floor was smooth. He slipped only once.

Charley had made this trip the same way. By instinct. But then, maybe Charley had known this connecting cave was there all along. This was, after all, where his gods lived.

He slowed his pace. The dull glow of lights around a corner warned him. He stopped and listened. Voices. They were in the cave. Probably looking for him and the others. Or congratulating themselves on their finds. Now they didn't need Charley Yee or Frank Frederick. Did they need Sam Tipton, he wondered?

He moved slowly to the edge of the last corner. Yardley and his men were just out of sight.

Crouched down, he inched his eyes around the corner.

"Dammit, Charley!" He breathed the words silently.

The cluster of lights in the distance clearly outlined a frail old Indian, as he walked directly into the midst of some very excited men with guns.

fifty-eight

"**Leave my** gods alone!"

The shout came out of the dark. It was loud and unexpected. Yardley stopped climbing up the rocks and turned around. Charley Yee appeared at the edge of the yellow dome of illumination as if a withered visage from a peyote dream.

"Leave my gods alone!" Charley Yee's voice was quiet, but strong. Much of his age had disappeared to be replaced by determination. He was upset. Two men in black had grabbed his gods. They showed no respect and no understanding.

A black vest sprinted up to Charley's side. A pistol instantly pressed against a wrinkled temple. Young eyes, hard eyes, turned to Yardley, silently asking the question. His finger tightened on the trigger in anticipation.

"No!" Yardley said from his perch on top the rock wall. He surprised himself. Maybe he did have limits after all. "But we don't want him following us, either. Just belt him."

Instantly, the pistol whipped around catching Charley Yee on the side of the head with a muted thump. The old Indian didn't make a sound. He landed in a limp heap, as if his clothes were empty. A scarecrow without his wooden backbone.

Blood flowed slowly from a gash by his left eye. The eye wasn't closed. Neither eye was closed. As he lay on the floor, Charley Yee stared angrily at the young men hoisting his gods onto their shoulders as if they were moving furniture.

Sam Tipton winced when the pistol made its mark on his friend. He crouched behind a rock pointing his weapon at the small group. But he didn't press the trigger. He couldn't. The submachine gun would spray bullets all over the place and Charley was right in the middle of them. So was Cobalt Blue. What would happen if several bullets hit it? Probably nothing. But what about radiation? He didn't know.

The group collected Charley's gods; a crate containing a long cylinder, a statue, a shining cube. Charley lay on the ground not moving.

The last black-vested figure carried the lantern to the

entrance. As he climbed over the rock wall, darkness gradually returned to the cavern. The last thing Tipton saw of the cylinder was the flashing amber light.

As the cylinder neared the entrance and sky opened above it, the small light on its top, a beacon, flashed faster and faster. Signals which had been mute for half a century found a new voice. Signals which had been frustrated by hundreds of feet of rock were now free to travel millions of miles unimpeded. Somewhere a receiver was listening.

Then a piercing, pain-filled scream filled the cavern to its deepest recesses. It was Charley Yee.

"Don't...take...my...gods!" The words were an anguished collection of drawn-out syllables, each launched from the absolute depths of an old man's pain.

"Dooon't take my goooodds!"

The moonlight revealed the scarecrow as he scrambled over the rock wall.

Charley Yee was out of sight and through the entrance, even as Sam Tipton sprinted towards him.

A fresh wind whipped through the entrance, hitting Sam in the face. For a brief instant it smelled of rain. A storm?

Then he felt it. A gentle pulsing pressure. His ear drums sensed it, even though there was no sound. They were being stretched. And they tingled. Then the rumble of thunder. But he didn't hear it. He felt it.

Tipton jumped in surprise and squinted his eyes as a bright, neon-blue light shimmered through the entrance. It was so bright, blue-black shadows danced on the cave walls and Tipton put his hand up to shield his eyes.

Sam's skin tingled and he raced towards the entrance, towards the source of the light. The hair on his hands and forearms stood up. The air was electric. He could feel it. He could smell it. He scrambled over the rocks just as the light was fading. Darkness slammed back down on the cave. It was as if nothing had happened. But, something had happened. Only he didn't know what. He had crested the rock wall an instant before the light disappeared and he saw the rock shelf in front of the cave bathed in a dense column of intense neon blue. For that brief instant, the light rose out of sight into the black night sky. There was no fire. No noise. Then, there was nothing. Where there should have been a half dozen men with a distraught old man in pursuit, there was nothing.

Sam dropped his hands to his sides. The sudden darkness caused momentary vertigo. He felt light-headed and dizzy. He sat down, resting his head in his hands.

Whatever had happened had taken only a few seconds. Several heartbeats out of the millions that make up a lifetime. Sam knew he'd remember those heartbeats till the day he died.

Sam Tipton sat bolt upright. What had happened to Charley? The sudden quiet was as tangible as the darkness. The canyon night sounds were those of an owl. Nothing more. Where was Charley?

There was only the sweet, artificially clean smell of ozone. Hands searched the cavern floor for night-vision goggles. Putting them on, he raised his head slowly over the rocks to look out. The ozone smell was stronger.

The sky was absolutely clear. Blacker than black. Stars the brightest he had ever seen. The moon painted the canyon in shades of black and silver. Nothing in-between. The tops of trees below were silver feathers floating on a sea of black.

There was no one in sight.

Where was Charley Yee? He listened intently. Where were the men in black?

Sam Tipton pointed his weapon. His eyes flicked left and right. Looking. Listening. There was nothing. Linear shadows littered the ground only a few paces outside the entrance. He recognized them. The moon accentuated Cobalt Blue's silver sheen where it sat on the smooth rock shelf. It was surrounded by a random collection of weapons of all types. Pistols, submachine guns, ammunition, knives were scattered haphazardly around. Wherever Yardley and his men had gone, they had taken no weapons with them.

In the midst of the weapons was the long crate from inside the cave. It was empty and the cylinder which it had held was missing. There was no sign of the effigy. Sam was beginning to doubt it was simply an effigy.

Tipton looked up at the sky and thought about the wrecked airplane in the back of the cave. He was beginning to understand. Maybe Charley wasn't crazy after all.

What Sam could not see was a solitary figure in a cowboy hat on the canyon rim directly over his head. It sat against a tree staring into the silver-black void of the canyon. Kwan Yamuchi was softly smiling. He had just seen his own vision. Charley Yee had been right all along and Kwan had just seen his gods.

He tilted his head back and focused on the night sky. An almost unseen pinpoint of neon blue was rapidly growing smaller directly overhead. It was all that was left of the intense column of light which, for a few seconds, had sliced through the darkness and knifed into the canyon turning it daylight bright. Then it had disappeared into the heavens taking everything within its circle with it. The Roswell cargo, Yardley and his crew, and Charley Yee, the Mogollon religious man, had gone with the light.

Kwan smiled at the singular knowledge which only he and Charley Yee possessed: Humankind was not alone.

Sam Tipton's voice echoed up from below calling the old Indian's name. Kwan knew there would be no answer. He looked at the heavens again and smiled. Charley Yee had finally gone with his gods.

Fifty-nine

As a tired group of survivors stumbled out of the canyon and boarded the Willys, Maggie leaned hard against Sam's chest. He held her tightly and spoke. His voice was soft and sounded as if he didn't want to believe what he was about to confide in her.
"Do you understand what's happened here?" He said quietly. "We stepped into the middle of something far bigger than that nuclear trigger they're calling Cobalt Blue. Far, far bigger. And I think I know what it is."
He looked over at Longfeather, barely visible in the dark and asked, "What did you see when you looked inside that long cylinder? I heard you almost choke."
Longfeather moved closer so the others wouldn't hear.
"I was hoping you wouldn't ask. Then I wouldn't have to sound like an idiot," he moved still closer. "Sam, please don't think I'm nuts, but I clearly saw a pair of eyes in there. Wide black eyes. And they were looking back at me."
"That's what I figured," Sam replied.
"Here's what I think happened," Sam said, "and even I think it's unbelievable. If anyone has a better explanation, I'm willing to listen."
He took a long breath before starting. "I think the dead pilot, Williams, stole the nuclear trigger, Cobalt Blue, then took an airplane from Roswell Air Force Base strictly as a means of transporting it. He either didn't know or didn't care that the airplane had already been loaded with crates which held what they found at the supposed UFO site at Roswell. Two alien crew members. I think we all touched a dead one. The effigy. I think the other was in that cylinder and the light on the top was a homing beacon. As soon as they took the cylinder out of the cave, some one out 'there,'" Sam jabbed a thumb up at the sky, "saw the beacon and simply took back what was theirs. Charley and those other guys were next to the cylinder and apparently went along for the ride.
"We've spent a lot of years making fun of old Charley," Tipton said, "but, in reality, we were wrong and he was right. His gods did come from the heavens, only he didn't know from where."
Sam looked up at the mantle of stars standing out stark white

against the dark sky, "I only hope, wherever he is, they understand how much they meant to him."

He hugged Maggie tightly and no one spoke for several very long minutes.

It was a long drive back to Pitacho. As the lights of town broke the darkness, the sounds of deep breathing punctuated with an occassional snore filled the back of the Willys. Maggie was leaning heavily against him as he drove and Mrs. Frederick would periodically let out a little whimper. She'd seen the charred remains of their motor home on the way out. At least the repairs to the Stinson would be easy.

Tipton looked at his watch. It was barely ten o'clock, but this had been one of the longest days of his life. It had also been the strangest, by far.

And it wasn't over yet. The rotating red lights on the Sheriff's car and the ambulance in front of Roberta's told him that.

"Where in the hell have you been, Tipton?" Sheriff Wally Rickert said as he greeted the tired-looking entourage, "You missed all the excitement."

"Wanna bet?" quipped Tipton.

As he spoke, the sheriff stepped sideways to let a gurney roll past. A zipped body bag was strapped in place. Another was already in the ambulance.

Roberta's voice cracked as she asked, "Who...?"

"Relax Roberta! Neither were regulars. According to Snuffy, some heavyweights came in and whacked one of their own while he was still taped to a chair. Snuffy got the other one. It left quite a mess. Sorry."

"Incidentally," Rickert said, "I think it would be a good idea if you could convince Snuffy to join us for a trip to the hospital."

Roberta's eyes arched.

"Snuffy caught a nine millimeter in the chest and he won't let us take him in," the sheriff explained.

Roberta instantly wheeled around and stomped into the bar.

Tipton and the rest were already inside and collapsing into chairs.

She reappeared on the sidewalk in less than a minute, pushing an old cowboy in front of her. Stark white bandages were wrapped around his chest under a blood stained shirt.

"But...," Snuffy squealed, "I don't need no damn doctor. I've had lots of practice. I know when somethin' serious's been hit. The bullet went right where one of them others did. Ain't nothing there but hole and scar tissue."

Roberta ignored him as she pushed him to the ambulance. She barked, "Get the hell in or I'm going to kick your ass and revoke your drinking privileges!"

The old cowboy climbed meekly in the back. She handed him his hat and leaned in to kiss him on the forehead before attendants closed the door.

"**Gheez, Tipton. You should've** been here before," said one of the regulars, as Sam settled into a chair, "You just missed Charley Yee!"

"What do you mean? Charley was here?" Sam spit back. The comment had made no sense.

Tipton looked over at Longfeather. It had taken them more than an hour of driving on torturous roads to make it back.

"That's impossible!" Tipton retorted.

Another voice piped up from down the bar, "Nope, he was in here about an hour ago. Maybe longer.

"There was a hellacious storm going on outside. I mean a real barn burner. Wind, blue lightning. The whole works. Kicked up real sudden and in walks old Crazy Charley."

"Yeah, it was wild," said another. "He looked all happy and went around the bar shaking hands like we was all old friends and everything."

"He told us to tell y'all," the speaker indicated Tipton, the Longfeathers and Roberta, "Good-bye. He had tears in his eyes when he said it. Like he really meant it."

Another spoke up from a nearby table, "Yeah, and the weirdest part was he wasn't drunk. He spoke real normal. Roberta, he said he left somethin' for you at his place. Some sort of lucky charm or somethin.'"

"Yep, said goodbye, walked back out into the storm and that was it."

Sam looked over at Longfeather and said quietly, "Come on."

He walked rapidly towards the door and broke into a dead run for Charley Yee's hogan as soon as he hit the sidewalk.

"**I'm not even going** to try to explain this," Sam Tipton said "In fact, I don't think it needs explanation. Not after tonight." He sat on the rocks behind Charley's hogan and stared back towards town. His eyes were focused somewhere far beyond the horizon. Roberta's neon outlined Longfeather as he shuffled around in the dried grass in front of Sam. His flashlight scoured back and forth on the ground. Then the light clicked off and his dark outline came to join Tipton on the rock. Charley's rock.

He was carrying the finely-finished wooden case that had started the entire episode.

"This is all that's left," Longfeather was too tired to transmit the level of disbelief he felt.

"The entire thing is gone. All of it!" Longfeather said. "There's not even a mark in the grass to show it had ever been there! How in the hell do you move a full-sized hogan and not leave a trace?"

Sam's head was bent back, the cool breeze playing over his face. His eyes were closed but he was seeing the heavens in his mind. He didn't bother answering Longfeather. There was no answer.

"What's that?" Longfeather said.

"What's what?" Tipton replied, opening his eyes.

Longfeather got up and walked to the Shrine of the Mogollon sign which still stood in its usual location. He reached up and pulled something shiny down.

He held it out in his palm for Tipton to examine.

It was a silver chain with a heavy, cast-silver amulet marked with a triangular design.

"That's Charley's," Tipton said. "He always wore it around his neck. Said it was his good-luck charm. He was wearing it tonight. Now I guess it's Roberta's"

He went back to staring at the sky. He had no answers and still had work to do.

Sam sat on the square hood of the Willys in front of Roberta's. The noise inside rolled out as a quiet roar forming a backdrop to his telephone calls. The sat-phone was in one hand. His tiny, ragged telephone book in the other.

The phone answered.

Daniel Guy was several notches past incredulous at hearing Tipton's name, much less his voice. He'd thought him dead. How was he doing? Where was he? Could he see him?

Sam listened and answered as fast as he could. He had a mission to run and no time to waste. He hated to call out of the blue in the middle of the night and ask for a favor but that's what this was about.

Daniel Guy was given book and verse on what had happened to Tipton in the preceding twenty-four hours. This included the confessions of a Hispanic gunman concerning the death of his family. Daniel Guy was quiet, both because he was furiously taking notes and because he knew his friend was delving into areas which had to be anchored in pain.

Sam pulled out the scribbled telephone number out of his pocket. Guy added it to his notes. And yes, he thought it coincidental. This wasn't the first time Daniel Guy had been given information about the owner of that phone number. They were already looking at some of his dealings. Tipton wasn't surprised.

As Sam finished he said, "I'm glad to hear you already have him nailed because there isn't any physical evidence for most of what I just told you...why? Just take my word for it, there just isn't."

Sam hadn't bothered telling him all the details. Some of them were simply too unbelievable.

"Oh, yeah, one other thing. Frank Frederick? Yeah, the ex-fibbie. Check around and see if there isn't a reward for finding and returning the Cobalt Blue thing.

"Yeah, Longfeather's flying me to Phoenix right now. I'll be in D.C. tomorrow sometime. Call you from the airport. Do me a favor; get me a toothbrush and a change of clothes, will you? I'm going to be pretty ripe by the time I get there."

Maggie sat on the fender next to Sam. A soft, grimy hand lay on his leg. He leaned over and kissed her gently on the nose.

"Why leave tonight?" she whispered.

Sam Tipton took Maggie Longfeather's face in his hands, cradling it as he would a newborn kitten. He kissed her nose again.

"You're a mess you know. A cute mess, but a mess!" He kissed her again.

"I have some very old, unfinished business that has to be taken care of right now. In the next twenty-four hours!" he said quietly.

"I can't explain a single damn thing that has happened to us today," he said softly, "but I know where at least part of it came from and I'm going to take care of it. Then I'm going to get on with my life."

Maggie Longfeather nodded. The two slipped arms around each other's waist as they went looking for Longfeather.

As Sam Tipton and Joseph Longfeather left Roberta's headed for their airplane, Sam remembered one more call he had to make. Fishing the sat-phone out of a jacket pocket he pushed a nearly forgotten series of numbers.

When the line was answered, he hesitated a few seconds before speaking. A few weeks earlier he couldn't have made the call. His words were warm with emotion, as he said,

"Hi, dad. Yeah, it's me, Sam...me too..."

Sixty

The middle-aged, serious-looking secretary's face was a mixture of surprise and curiosity. Hallowed governmental offices seldom saw the likes of the tall man striding purposefully towards her. His long brown hair was pulled back in a ponytail, his face hidden behind a full beard. A denim shirt was partially covered by a worn leather jacket and dusty cowboy boots protruded from soiled blue jeans. Determined green-brown eyes told her his voice would be equally as determined.

"Is Foster Ward in?" She was right about his voice.

She looked past him at two men in dark suits. They looked to be government issue. She relaxed.

"Yes, Secretary Ward is in," she accentuated the "Secretary" correcting Sam Tipton's lapse of formality. "Do you have an appointment?"

Always the proper secretary.

"I think he'll see us!" Tipton retorted.

"But..." She stopped speaking as Tipton abruptly walked past her towards the tall, dark wood doors which separated a revered member of the President's cabinet from the real world.

She winced as the door slammed open against the wall. She, however, wasn't nearly as surprised as Foster Ward.

"What is the meaning of this!" Ward didn't bother to stand. He preferred instead to use the authority of his position and the imposing nature of his huge desk to protect him. "Who are you men?" He was demanding. On familiar ground.

Sam Tipton didn't give a shit about position or formalities. He leaned across the desk, putting his face close to Ward's.

"Take a good look, Mr. Secretary," he laced the title with sarcasm, "and see if you don't know who I am."

The instant Sam spoke he knew Ward recognized him. A series of emotions flashed through Ward's eyes, ranging from surprise, to fear, then panic.

"That's right, Mr. Secretary, Sam Tipton. Your old Viet Nam flying buddy Sam Tipton. The Sam Tipton who used to be the husband to Marilyn Tipton. And the father of Melissa Tipton."

Sam leaped around the desk and grabbed the prematurely

graying member of the cabinet by the front of his expensive-looking suit. He yanked Ward to his feet and pushed him up against a finely-finished, walnut-paneled wall.

"Yes, Foster, I'm that Sam Tipton!" Tipton snarled.

Ward grabbed both of Sam's hands and tried to break them free. It was a feeble attempt. His eyes flashed over at the two men in dark suits.

"Mr. Secretary, I'm Daniel Guy, FBI," Guy held his identification over Tipton's shoulder where Ward could see it. "I have some questions to ask you, but I can see that you're busy. We'll return in a few minutes."

Sam interrupted the conversation by slamming Ward against the wall. The second agent retreated and quietly closed the doors to the office, leaving Daniel Guy inside.

Tipton slammed Ward against the wall again and hissed words into his face, "You killed my family!" The words were slow, mechanically-spaced and so cold and sharp they could have drawn blood on their own. Sam's teeth were clenched in rage. "And you sold out your country!"

Ward saw his own death in Tipton's eyes.

"Mr. Secretary," Daniel Guy began, "I'm sorry to interrupt, but before I leave, is there anything you'd care to tell me about some of your business dealings?"

Sam slammed the bureaucrat against the wall again. One hand curled around his throat. Ward's naturally pale face had lost what color it had. Shades of pink arrived. Then a hint of blue. His eyes looked down over puckered cheeks at the FBI agent and he nodded.

"Sir, do I understand you are willing to speak with me freely and under no governmental coercion?" Agent Guy said.

Sam slammed Ward against the wall again. A picture fell off onto the floor. The glass shattered. His hand tightened on a bureaucratic windpipe.

Mr. Secretary nodded again. Vigorously.

Daniel Guy stepped up and placed a gentle hand on Sam Tipton's shoulder. It was trembling.

"Excuse me, Mr. Secretary, is this gentleman bothering you?" Guy asked the Secretary of Commerce, who was also trembling.

The FBI agent looked at Sam Tipton, "Sir, would you please leave Secretary Ward alone?"

Sam let go and stepped back.

The esteemed member of the cabinet slumped down, barely able to stand.

Again addressing Tipton, Daniel Guy said, "Sir, would you like to apologize to Secretary Ward for this intrusion?"

"Yes, I think I would," Tipton replied. "Mr. Secretary, I'm sorry."

As Tipton spoke, his right hand flashed forward with a decade of pain, bad dreams and humiliation packed behind it. That decade caught Secretary of Commerce Foster Ward squarely in the nose.

Ward slid slowly down the wall, his eyes staring at nothing. Blood ran freely down his face. Secretary Ward's nose was twisted at an unnatural angle.

"Oh, Mr. Secretary," Daniel intoned, "You appear to have fallen and hurt yourself. Here, use my handkerchief."

He carelessly tossed the handkerchief into the barely conscious soon-to-be-ex-bureaucrat's face where he lay at the base of the wall.

Sam Tipton stood at the door, his hand on the heavy brass door handle and addressed his old friend, "I have something I have to do. Then I think it's time you took a vacation. How about a road trip?"

Guy grinned and nodded. Ward groaned.

"Oh shut up, asshole." Guy snapped down at him.

Tipton was gone when he looked up.

The lobby of the office building was typical Washington, D.C. Impossibly high ceilings, polished marble, lots of glass, security personnel, and telephones.

As Sam stepped out of the elevators on the way out, he located the long collection of telephone books in their polished stainless steel rack. His finger ran down the yellow page listings. When he found what he wanted he put a check mark next to it and wrote down the number. The check mark was next to "Van der Graff Funeral Home."

"You know," Daniel Guy said, "it's not easy finding a good country music station in beltway territory."

He had to speak louder than normal to be heard over the country tune rocking out of the radio and the wind blowing in both open windows. At seventy miles an hour the countryside on both sides of Interstate 40 whipped past. The early morning smelled clean and fresh. He looked over at Sam Tipton behind the wheel. Sam caught his glance.

"You did a helluva job taking care of the Blazer. I owe you." Tipton ceremoniously patted the dash.

"Hey," Guy replied, "I knew you'd be back. And I knew you'd be pissed if I didn't take care of your truck."

Daniel Guy smiled and looked out at Kentucky as it slid past. It felt good to be outside the beltway. Out in the real world. He glanced into the back seat where a small box was carefully held in place by the seat belts. A melancholy feeling briefly touched his thoughts. This cross country drive had been a long time coming.

"This is it, partner, this is home," Sam grinned as he herded the Blazer around the last turn into his valley.

Daniel Guy didn't say a word. His head was on a swivel, taking in everything as quickly as possible. It had been a terrific trip. He was loving it.

Sam pulled up in front of the tin sheds behind the mine and immediately pushed one of them open. The sunlight of late afternoon ringed the fresh bullet holes in the Stinson's cowling with gold, as it came into view.

Good, Longfeather had gotten the old airplane fixed.

"Daniel," Tipton began, as he reached into the back of the Blazer for the small box, "I have to do this alone."

Daniel Guy understood and started to climb into the Blazer.

"Hey, while I'm up, why don't you make yourself at home." Sam pointed into the big building.

"Clear!" His eyes swept the area around the prop. In seconds the engine was running and in another minute the patchwork airplane was off the ground. Daniel guy shaded his eyes and watched for a second before stepping inside. This ceremony was for no one's eyes but Sam Tipton's.

The sun was barely two-fingers above the horizon. It was Sam "Cowboy" Tipton's favorite time of day. The sunlight flowed almost parallel to the ground, throwing long black shadows. The rock cliffs above the valley and the old mill stood out as bronze sculptures.

Sam hoped Ivan was watching. He knew he was.

He kept the wheels just barely out of the pines above the valley, circling around to the closed end. The sun shone directly down the nose as he eased the airplane down into the valley.

His free hand twisted the top off the bronze urn in his lap. He reached out the window with it in his hand and turned it over. As he did, he said, "Welcome home you guys. I told you I'd come back for you."

The sun transformed the gray dust of two beloved souls into a golden powder which drifted gently down to become one with the valley.

The Tiptons were once again together.

Daniel Guy was in the kitchen, trying to decide which was the refrigerator when Sam Tipton burst in the door and dashed up the wide stairs to his rustic bedroom.

"Gimme forty-five minutes," he said on the way past. "I have some cleaning up to do then we're heading into town."

Roberta's juke box was painting the atmosphere with a slow country tune and the mid-week crowd was sparse. Subdued. The music fit the mood. Maggie Longfeather was leaning over the bar talking to Roberta, a half-finished beer between them, her back to the small crowd.

Roberta looked over Maggie's shoulder and a subtle smile flickered across her face.

"Care to dance?" A gentle hand touched Maggie Longfeather's shoulder from behind.

She turned to look up into familiar green-brown eyes set into a smooth-skinned face. The jaw line was well defined and a broad smile set off dimples on either side, accentuating the playful fire in the eyes. The brown hair was carefully trimmed just clear of the dark blue shirt collar where it showed above a tan, western-cut corduroy jacket. The hair swept gently back over the ears with a touch of gray in the short sideburns.

Both women mouthed exactly the same words at exactly the same time, "Oh, my God! Sam!"

Both scanned him up and down. They couldn't help but notice the softly shined boots at the bottom of new jeans. The last time they'd seen those boots they were in a plastic bag during the move from the adobe.

"Well?" Sam Tipton repeated, "Do you want to dance or not? I don't do this very often."

Maggie slid off the stool and into his arms in a single, fluid motion. She felt herself melting deeper into his chest with each step. The two of them shared the feeling of floating. Of no longer touching the floor. They moved as though one brain was commanding both bodies.

Daniel Guy and Longfeather sat next to Snuffy at the end of the bar. All were beaming. And all saw and recognized an older gentleman as he stepped onto the dance floor.

"Mind if I cut in?" The gentleman asked.

Sam looked around, soft surprise in his eyes. He recognized the voice before he turned. He stepped back to offer Maggie, but found himself wrapping his arms around the tall, thin, gray-haired gentleman with the handlebar mustache.

He was so choked up, he couldn't say a word.

Finally, the older man said, "Sam, you always get things screwed up. You were that way as a kid too," He stepped back and smiled warmly, "I want to dance with Maggie. Not you."

"Damn, it's good to see you," Sam said.

"You too." One old arm was around Maggie preparing to dance. He hesitated. Another arm went out around Sam's neck pulling him close, "Welcome home, son. God, I've missed you!"

Then Samuel Tipton, Sr. stepped out on the dance floor and proceeded to show his son how it was supposed to be done.

Sixty-one

Ted Fowler was so excited he allowed his BMW to bump harshly into the curb in front of Roberta's. He usually tiptoed into parking spots. But, he'd been looking forward to this night for weeks. He started to vault from the car, but hesitated to grab forgotten papers off the front seat.

Shuffling them into order as he walked quickly into Roberta's, he couldn't suppress his grin. This would teach the bitch. And Tipton too. He'd gotten them both. He was so pleased with himself he was humming, as he walked.

Roberta saw him coming. She didn't like the look on his face. When Ted Fowler smiled, someone was in trouble.

Fowler pushed his way past the old guy dancing with the Longfeather girl and dashed up to the bar.

"Okay, bitch! You're outta here." He'd actually stood in front of a mirror practicing that particularly eloquent line. The auction was that afternoon, which meant the bar was now his. He'd been in Flagstaff all day, but had called to make certain the property was on the list. As the only bidder, he was automatically the owner. Roberta was finished.

"Don't call me that, you little shit!" she shot back.

"Talk nice to me, Roberta. I own this place now." Fowler was positively glowing. He lowered his voice, "Yeah, if you're nice to me, maybe I'll let you stay in business. Maybe. It depends on how good you are at doin' me."

Sam Tipton heard the commotion and stepped next to Fowler at the bar. He noticed the toupee was crooked, as usual.

"What the hell are you doing, Fowler? Leave her alone!" He put a hand on Fowler's shoulder, who brushed it away with a slap. He looked at Tipton with a practiced sneer on his lips. He'd been looking forward to this moment, too.

"Well, well! If it isn't the town drunk all dressed up and ready to go to church. It'll be a shame to see that nice jacket in the gutter where you usually wind up.

"Incidentally, Tipton, it's moving day again," Fowler shook the papers in Sam's face.

"I just bought that worthless mine out from under you."

Fowler's voice was rising in pitch. His face glistened with moisture as the excitement put his adrenal glands on high. "Don't you just love it!" Fowler was practically screaming. He put his face right into Tipton's and sneered, "Gotcha!"

Tipton frowned, shook his head and sat down on a bar stool. He hesitated for a second then stood again and grabbed Fowler by the shirt, "You know what, you miserable little geek? I don't care if I wind up in jail for this. I'm going to break your scrawny little neck."

"Sam, hold it!"

Eddie "Mad Dog" Mandell appeared out of the dark from a corner table and waddled towards the two. Sam put Fowler back on the floor.

Mandell moved up to the bar and said, "Fowler, you really should pay a little more attention to business. Like going to auctions, for instance. You shouldn't take anything for granted."

With that, Mandell slapped a folded piece of paper on the bar. "Roberta, this is for you. You now owe me free beer for the rest of my life."

Roberta had a puzzled look on her face, "What the hell is that, Mandell?"

"That, my dear is the deed to this property."

Roberta's mouth fell open.

Another piece of paper was slapped on the bar.

"And that, Sam Tipton, is the deed to your shit-hole in the mountain. You can pay me back out of your patent royalties."

It was hard to tell who was more surprised, Tipton or Fowler. Sam let go of Fowler's shirt and turned to Mandell. The words were confusing and he was having trouble sorting them out.

"You mean to tell me you bought the mine?" Tipton said.

"Yep and it cost me plenty. About the price of two sets of tires for my Caddy," Mandell laughed.

"And what patent royalties?" Sam asked.

"Well, partner, and we can be partners, if you want. Do you remember giving my guy, Larry Crandall, that computerized gizmo for his lathe? Well, the machine rep that calls on us, loved it. I saw his reaction and said to myself, 'Eddie, there may be some money here,' so I patented it in your name. The rep came back to us and they want a bunch of 'em. Looks like you may have a business going."

Sam grinned awkwardly, "I don't know what to say"

"Say 'Thank you, Eddie' and 'Yes, I'll let you finance me for a piece of the action.'"

Sam nodded numbly. So many things. So fast. Maggie squeezed his arm. She was jumping up and down.

"Now, just a goddamn minute," Fowler had finally found his voice and the words sputtered out. "I bid for those properties and was the only bidder, how..."

"Well, my friend, it seems your people-skills really suck, which worked to my advantage in more ways than one." Mandell hesitated and looked back at his table, "I'd like to introduce my date and recent companion."

Deputy Assessor Stephanie Goodlin stood and walked towards them, a triumphant smile on her face.

Turning to Roberta, Mandell said, "You know, you can throw Fowler out of here if you want. Or we'll do it for you."

"Not just yet," said Deputy Assessor Goodlin. She walked up to Fowler, her right arm whipping forward. The slap was so hard, it jarred the toupee loose. Seeing that, she grabbed it and held it over her head.

"This is for every woman you've ever demeaned," even enraged she lacked the proper nasty words. Her left hand slapped him again, putting a matching palm print on the other side of his pasty face.

Fowler reeled back for a second then lurched for the toupee. Too late.

Sam Tipton snatched it and leaped up on the bar. "Roberta!" he shouted.

She saw where he was headed and tossed the staple gun up to him. In a flourish, Sam spun around and stapled the toupee alongside the other two on a beam over the bar.

As he looked down, Longfeather and a biker had Fowler by his arms and legs. They were headed out the door with him at a brisk trot. The sound of a body landing on the hood of a car rang throughout the bar. Everyone cheered.

Sam Tipton stood on the bar and looked down. All he saw were friends looking up at him. And smiling faces. And family. Most of all he saw a future. He felt joy welling up in him and his clenched fist shot into the air. "Yeeess!"

THE END

Epilogue

The moon had traveled most of the way across the night sky, chasing shadows from one side of the canyon to the other. Kwan Yamuchi sat in the shadows of the cliff dwellings. He could feel the presence of the Anasazi, the ancient ones. He drew a deep breath and felt the West invade his lungs. It had already invaded his mind. And heart.

He threw his bedroll out where he could lay and watch the moon playing with the small brook below.

His telephone vibrated in his pocket. Before anything could be said on the other end, he quietly said, "Hold all my calls. No...indefinitely."

He turned it off and dropped it in his duffel bag.

He leaned back and closed his eyes. An owl hooted and Kwan Yamuchi fell asleep in his new home.

The night-nurse poked her head into the room. He was talking again. A lot of the older guys in the veterans hospital talked at night.

"Colonel Johnson, is that you talking again? You know it's time for bed."

Watery old eyes looked back, their lids sagging. A stray wisp of hair hung down between them. The grin was gray but cheerful. He laughed.

"You know something nurse?" The voice was raspy but strong. "Nobody will ever know. But I know. The weather balloon story the next morning? That was pure bullshit!"

The nurse nodded agreement and moved to tuck him in. His eyes followed her. The voice continued. It became insistent. He wanted her to understand.

"We had 'em. Two of 'em! Took 'em right out of the crashed ship. Tiny little buggers! Opened one up. Really weird inside!"

He coughed and she stroked his few remaining hairs back into place.

"Then the damn airplane disappeared! Can you believe that?" His body went rigid and he tried to rise on an elbow. He looked at her with big eyes.

"Somebody stole the goddamn airplane!"

He laid back, his eyes tracking the nurse as she left the room. Colonel Ralph Johnson, United States Air Force, Retired, was still talking when she reached back in and shut the lights off.

"No one will ever know. But I know..."

Author's Historical Note

The events at Rosell actually went public at 0830 hrs, July 8th, 1947, when Lieutenant Walt Haut stepped in front of a frantic group of reporters gathered at Roswell Army Air Field, then designated as Area 51 and home of the 509th Bomb Group, the world's only operational nuclear bombing unit. At the direction of his superiors, he had written a press release which, in part, said, "...we have in our possession a flying saucer. It crashed north of Roswell and we've shipped it all to General Ramey, Eighth Air Force at Fort Worth...."

The next morning Brigadier General Ramey's weather forecaster, Warrant Officer Irving Newton told another group of excited reporters that what they had erroneously reported the night before as a crashed space ship was actually nothing more than a weather balloon. He said that contrary to comments by the rancher who found the wreckage, there were no alien bodies.

The controversies have raged since. As with all such conspiracy theories, there will never be an adequate explanation for the Air Force's seeming change of face. Cobalt Blue offers but one possibility: The Air Force denied the existence of their find because it was stolen from under their noses.

My personal view is that only Charley Yee actually knows the truth.

Budd Davisson
Phoenix, Arizona
10 June, 2000